Studies in the Psychosocial

Series Editors
Stephen Frosh, Department of Psychosocial Studies,
Birkbeck, University of London, London, UK
Peter Redman, Faculty of Arts and Social Sciences,
The Open University, Milton Keynes, UK
Wendy Hollway, Faculty of Arts and Social Sciences,
The Open University, Milton Keynes, UK

Studies in the Psychosocial seeks to investigate the ways in which psychic and social processes demand to be understood as always implicated in each other, as mutually constitutive, co-produced, or abstracted levels of a single dialectical process. As such it can be understood as an interdisciplinary field in search of transdisciplinary objects of knowledge. Studies in the Psychosocial is also distinguished by its emphasis on affect, the irrational and unconscious processes, often, but not necessarily, understood psychoanalytically. Studies in the Psychosocial aims to foster the development of this field by publishing high quality and innovative monographs and edited collections. The series welcomes submissions from a range of theoretical perspectives and disciplinary orientations, including sociology, social and critical psychology, political science, postcolonial studies, feminist studies, queer studies, management and organization studies, cultural and media studies and psychoanalysis. However, in keeping with the inter- or transdisciplinary character of psychosocial analysis, books in the series will generally pass beyond their points of origin to generate concepts, understandings and forms of investigation that are distinctively psychosocial in character.

Series Peer Review Policy:

Proposals for books in this series are single-blind peer reviewed by experts in the field as well as by the Series Editors. All manuscripts will be reviewed and approved by the Series Editors before they are accepted for publication.

More information about this series at
http://www.palgrave.com/gp/series/14464

Nigel Williams

Mapping Social Memory

A Psychotherapeutic Psychosocial Approach

palgrave
macmillan

Nigel Williams
University of the West of England
Bristol, UK

ISSN 2662-2629   ISSN 2662-2637 (electronic)
Studies in the Psychosocial
ISBN 978-3-030-66156-4   ISBN 978-3-030-66157-1 (eBook)
https://doi.org/10.1007/978-3-030-66157-1

© The Editor(s) (if applicable) and The Author(s), under exclusive license to Springer Nature Switzerland AG 2021
This work is subject to copyright. All rights are solely and exclusively licensed by the Publisher, whether the whole or part of the material is concerned, specifically the rights of translation, reprinting, reuse of illustrations, recitation, broadcasting, reproduction on microfilms or in any other physical way, and transmission or information storage and retrieval, electronic adaptation, computer software, or by similar or dissimilar methodology now known or hereafter developed.
The use of general descriptive names, registered names, trademarks, service marks, etc. in this publication does not imply, even in the absence of a specific statement, that such names are exempt from the relevant protective laws and regulations and therefore free for general use.
The publisher, the authors and the editors are safe to assume that the advice and information in this book are believed to be true and accurate at the date of publication. Neither the publisher nor the authors or the editors give a warranty, expressed or implied, with respect to the material contained herein or for any errors or omissions that may have been made. The publisher remains neutral with regard to jurisdictional claims in published maps and institutional affiliations.

Cover image: 'World's End' © Nigel Williams

This Palgrave Macmillan imprint is published by the registered company Springer Nature Switzerland AG
The registered company address is: Gewerbestrasse 11, 6330 Cham, Switzerland

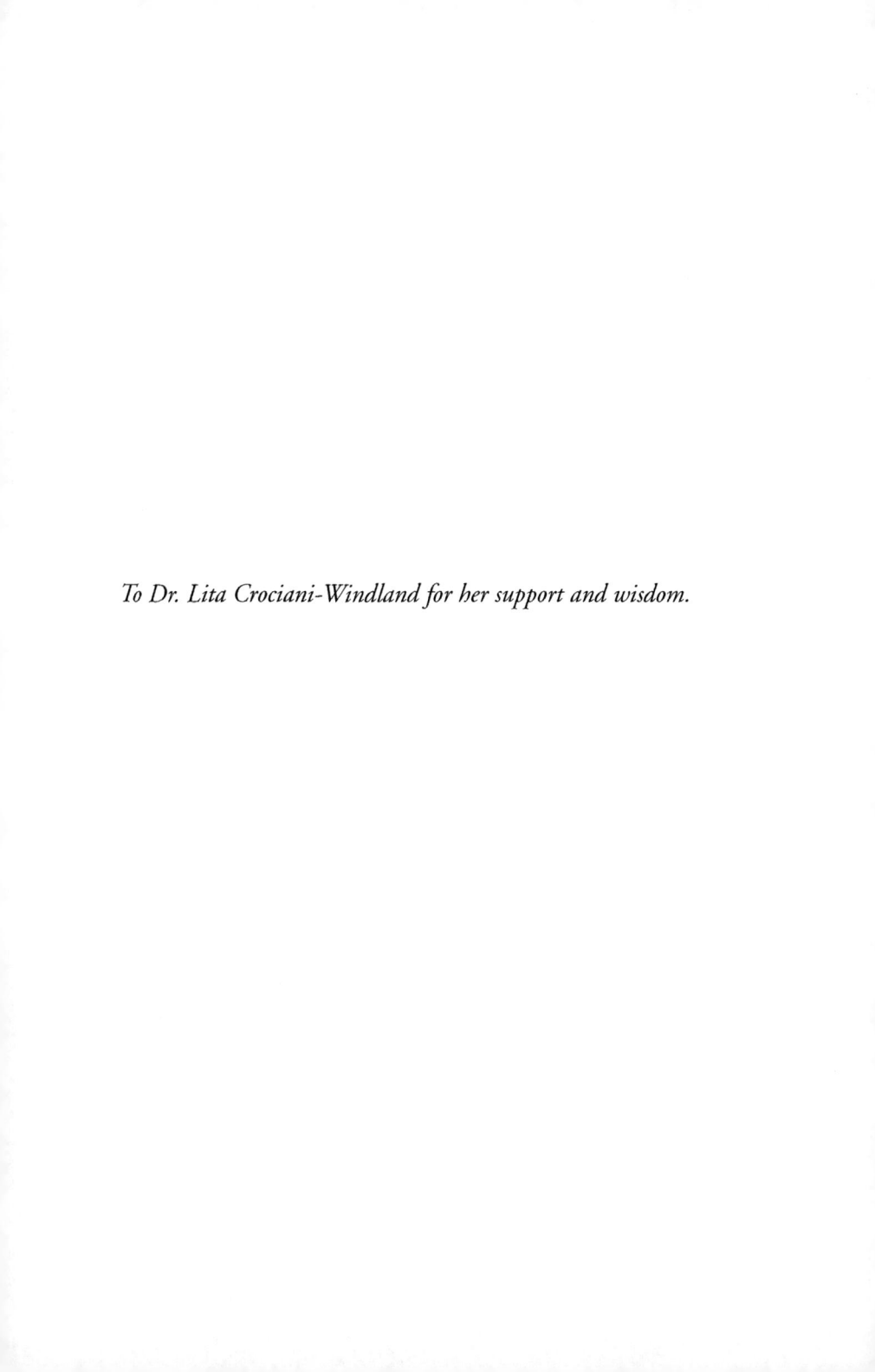

To Dr. Lita Crociani-Windland for her support and wisdom.

Foreword

In a talk given in Vienna in 2020 to commemorate the anniversary of Freud's death, Jacqueline Rose reflected on how Freud was shaped by living through the global pandemic of 1918, two world wars, and the necessary losses these events entailed for his family. Commenting on Freud's internal struggles, Rose states that she "became acutely aware of the way the disasters of history penetrate and are repudiated by the mind" (2020, np). She goes on to note that psychoanalysis begins with "a mind in flight", because of the inherent ability of the human mind to take the measure of its own pain, and she offers rich illustrations from Freud's own writings of the difficulties Freud had experienced in holding on to a capacity for thought as political disasters loomed and inconsolable personal losses weighed him down. Rose traces a trajectory in Freud's writing from valorizing self-preservation and mastery as core elements of his theory of psychoanalysis to acknowledging the power of the repetition compulsion and the apparent human capacity for destruction embodied in the death instinct. Drawing on Freud's paper "A phylogenetic fantasy," suppressed by Freud but finally published in 1985, Rose notes how far

Freud shifted from *science* to *feeling* in acknowledging the phylogenetic and genealogical origins of contemporary psychic suffering:

> What passes through the generations, then, deep within the psyche of the people, is anxiety. Anxiety in response to an imperilled world, but also as a reaction to the tyranny of the powers that come to meet it. This is what children usher down through the generations: 'the children bring along the anxiousness of the beginning of the Ice Age.' The child is repeating the history of the species, offering Freud support in his belief in phylogenetic transmission—the 'preponderance of the phylogenetic disposition over all other factors'. An emphasis which, he also insists, does not eliminate the question of acquisition: 'It only moves it into still earlier prehistory.' What this strange unpublished meditation allows us to infer is that the concept of phylogenesis is his way of acknowledging the parlous state of mankind: want, poverty affliction and trouble, the catastrophes of history, the burden of the past. Modern-day psychoanalysis talks of 'transgenerational haunting', the unconscious passage of historical trauma from one generation to the next. We bring our ancestors trailing behind us, which means that, while we may die our own death, we also die on behalf of others who were there before us. Once more way ahead of his time, Freud has taken this reality, which is now clinically recognised, and injected it into the bloodstream of humankind. (Rose, 2020, np)

Acknowledging the death instinct entails, as Rose notes, coming to terms with the darker aspects of our own being and accepting that the forces of darkness that underlie colonialism, genocide, fascism, ecocide, and other forms of mass violence, are rooted in each one of us. Can a society possibly heal from the consequences of slavery, for example, without owning historical patterns of colonial conquest by ancestors as well as acknowledging the white supremacist hatred within white people, and within the institutions and systems in which white people seek comfort and belonging? (O'Loughlin, 2020). What are the consequences if we avert our eyes? By failing to subvert the colonial gaze are we not paving the way for a repetition?

The *feeling* versus *science* struggle manifests in psychohistorical research and memory studies as the polarity between socially-based psychoanalytic and critical inquiry on the one hand, and positivist forms of anthropology and history on the other. This tension is readily evident in one of my own areas of inquiry. Born in Ireland, I have an interest in Irish history, and particularly in the psychological sequelae of chosen traumas (cf. Volkan, 2001) such as Ireland's Great Famine. The term "Famine" is highly contested as Britain exported large quantities of livestock and grain during the period, suggesting either genocidal intent or, at best, a Malthusian indifference to the lives of its colonized subjects. In a recent paper I summarized the state of Famine scholarship this way:

> The potato was the almost exclusive diet of the poorest segments of the population. From 1845 to at least 1850 Ireland suffered successive catastrophic failures of the potato crop because during those years climatic conditions were ideal for repeated outbreaks of blight caused by what was identified forty years later to be the fungus **phytophthora infestans**. There had been prior crop failures and scattered famines during the previous century, but a cascade of failures, beginning in 1845, led to mass starvation among the poorest segments of the population. Approximately one million people died of starvation and famine related diseases including typhus and cholera, under the most appalling conditions. Many more fled the country in the steerage compartments of often perilously inadequate sailing ships, sometimes referred to as coffin ships. Following 150 years of silence by the government of Ireland, a period in which only desultory attempts were made at commemoration, this famine finally became a speakable trauma in the mid-1990s. Irish historians, too, had been silent. Cecil Woodham-Smith's (1962) bestselling book *The Great Hunger*, written by a scholar outside the academic establishment, was derided by Irish historians. Woodham-Smith broke two taboos: She documented in painful detail the emotional toll of the Famine and she laid considerable responsibility at the door of Sir Charles Trevelyan, the British civil servant ultimately responsible for Famine relief. This counternarrative threatened a comfortable status quo of denial and studied silence within both the Irish government and the academy (Kinealy, 2006). Official commemoration of the Famine and critical scholarship on that national catastrophe were not to emerge until the mid-1990s in Ireland. It appears that a culture of silence, censure, and negation reigned in official Ireland. This left little room for interiority, emotional soothing, reckoning with losses, or any recognition of the ways in which linkages between current personal and national suffering and genealogical and ancestral

lineages of the kind discussed earlier might have facilitated mourning. (O'Loughlin, in press)

As new scholarship has emerged, influenced by cultural anthropology, psychoanalysis, psychosocial studies, and feminist and postcolonial studies, the ensuing interest in feelings and psychological remnants has produced a burgeoning of new ways of thinking about memory, memorialization, and cultural and transgenerational transmission of trauma in Irish Famine studies. In my own work, for example, I embrace folklore, poetry, and music, as well as oral history and autobiographical introspection as legitimate forms of evidence that can illuminate the psycho-historical record. Particularly relevant to the Irish context is the issue of language loss. For a variety of complex reasons, including the cultural genocide associated with colonization, the Irish language came close to annihilation. Reckoning with the massive cultural severance this entailed—what de Fréine (1978) called *The Great Silence*—Irish poet Nuala Ní Dhomhnaill speaks eloquently to the need to come to terms with this buried past: "Famine and the trauma of colonisations is something that we are finally coming to terms with. It is as if we are waking up from a state of zombification, of a waking death where we had no emotional memory of who it was that we were or what it was that happened to us" (1993, p. 69). Speaking of a visit to Ireland's National Famine Museum, she summarized the lack thus:

> Is it any wonder, therefore, that I leave the museum somewhat dissatisfied, as I always am when faced with memories of that time, by a sense of overwhelming and unconscionable loss? Unconscionable, because of what has been lost to consciousness, not just the tunes, and the songs and the poetry, but because the memory that they were all in Irish—and that they are part of a reality which was not English—has been erased so totally from our minds. This seems to be part of the Famine trauma which is still not acknowledged by the post-colonial Irish reality. This collective memory-loss, this convenient amnesia is still one of the most deeply-etched results of the Famine. (1993, p. 72)

Despite these eloquent pleas it is disheartening that Irish historians such as Foster (2004) and Ó'Gráda (2001), and cultural historians of the

Famine such as Mark-Fitzgerald (2013) are skeptical that psychoanalysis or trauma theory can inform historical studies, with Foster going so far as to dismiss any study of melancholic residue or transgenerational transmission as psychobabble.

How then are people who have been estranged from their genealogical, linguistic, and mythic origins, people whose autobiographic consciousness has been erased, to regain a foothold in history? Davoine and Gaudillière (2004) speak of bringing back the voices of the dead, of acknowledging the spectral *revenants* of which Derrida (2006) speaks. Similarly, Abraham and Torok are clear on the need to investigate the phantomic presences at the root of ancestrally and genealogically inherited suffering:

> The concept of the phantoms moves the focus of psychoanalytic inquiry beyond the individual being analyzed because it postulates that some people unwittingly inherit the secret psychic substance of their ancestor's lives… redraw[ing] the boundaries of psychopathology and extend[ing] the realm of possibilities for its cure by suggesting the existence within an individual of a collective psychology comprised of several generations. So that the analyst must listen to the voices of one generation in the unconscious of another. (1994, p. 166)

In his Nobel Prize acceptance speech, Derek Walcott (1992) reminds us of the beauty and possibility of such genealogical work. Speaking of the polyglot culture of his native Antilles, and the pain stitched into its history, he outlines the reparative possibilities thus:

> Break a vase, and the love that reassembles the fragments is stronger than the love which took its symmetry for granted when it was whole. The glue that fits the pieces is the sealing of its original shape. It is such a love that reassembles our African and Asiatic fragments, the cracked heirlooms whose restoration shows its white scars. This gathering of broken pieces is the care and pain of the Antilles, and if the pieces are disparate, ill-fitting, they contain more pain than their original sculpture, those icons and sacred vessels taken for granted in their ancestral places. Antillean art is thus restoration of our shattered histories, our shards of vocabulary, our

archipelago becoming a synonym for pieces broken off from the original continent. (1992, np)

Nigel Williams' erudite book is a meditation on memory that is consistent with the spirit of Walcott's vision. Nigel's ambition is to account for the sociohistorical origins of subjectivity. He explores the kinds of subject formation that emerge from migrations, displacements, language loss, severance of social linkages, and the "unhappy internment" of family, community, and national traumas. His literature review is comprehensive and evocative and seeks to reach for an articulation of a mourning and a reclamation of spirits that obviates melancholia and leads to generativity and subjective possibility. In addition to exploring relevant literature across a wide range of disciplines, Nigel incorporates narratives from a diverse array of conversational partners so that this work is grounded in the hopes, lives, and hauntings of living people—a process that Nigel refers to as research in action. While grounded in a vision of reconciliation and dialogue, Nigel's work does not shy away from the difficult political questions of decolonization and of how societies may become hardened in a Kleinian paranoid-schizoid manner where dialog is foreclosed and where possibilities for affiliation, mutual understanding, mentalization of past traumas, and reparation are purposely occluded.

Nigel is a psychotherapist. In addition to speaking to the social implications for communities, societies, and nations he takes us into the consulting room and explores in detail the complex issue of engaging psychotherapy patients with the ghosts of their pasts. Preoccupied not only with the question of where generational suffering goes, Nigel seeks to articulate a therapy which allows such demetaphorized affect and what Garon (2004) calls *skeletons in the closet* to be reclaimed, named, and metabolized. Drawing on the language of hauntology Nigel understands that ghosts must be invited in and he offers an eloquent discourse on the critical role of attuned listening and the importance for therapists who are to become cultural and ancestral interlocutors of developing a refined autobiographic consciousness.

As I write these words, the entire world is in the grip of a pandemic the management of which has been characterized by necropolitical callousness, managerial ineptness, and a striking opportunism by too many world leaders. It will create another traumatic residue for our world to absorb. Will this, too, become an unspeakable tragedy—one in which older people, people of limited means, and people who have already been deprived of opportunity because of their racial or ethnic origins, become further burdened with unnamable suffering? Nigel's book, written in an engaging critical voice, and drawing on a lifetime of attuned, humble listening is a reminder that our world might be otherwise, and that we should struggle hard to fight for an ethic of care and a true psychology of reminisces and a reclamation of lore that will allow people to embrace their pasts and hence live their lives more freely.

Professor Michael O'Loughlin
Ruth S. Ammon School of Education
Derner School of Psychology, College
of Education & Health Sciences
Adelphi University
New York, USA

References

Abraham, N. and Torok, M. (1994) *The Shell and the Kernel.* N.T. Rand (Ed. and Trans.). Chicago and London: University of Chicago Press.
Davoine, F. and Gaudillière, J.-M. (2004) *History Beyond Trauma: Whereof One Cannot Speak, Thereof One Cannot Stay Silent.* S. Fairfield (Trans.). New York: Other Press.
Derrida, J. (2006) *Specters of Marx.* London: Routledge.
Foster, R.F. (2004) *The Irish Story: Telling Stories and Making It Up in Ireland.* Oxford: Oxford University Press.
Garon, J. (2004) Skeletons in the closet. *International Forum of Psychoanalysis.* 13, pp. 84–92.
Kinealy C. (2006) *This Great Calamity. The Irish Famine 1845–52.* 2nd ed. Dublin: Gill and MacMillan.
Mark-Fitzgerald, E. (2013) *Commemorating the Irish Famine: Memory and the Monument.* Liverpool: University of Liverpool Press.
Ní Dhomhnaill, N. (1997) A ghostly Alhambra. In: Hayden, T. (Ed.) *Irish Hunger: Personal Reflections on the Legacy of The Famine.* Niwot, CO: Roberts Rinehart Publishers.

Ó'Gráda C. (2001) Famine, trauma and memory. *Bealoideas: Journal of the Folklore of Ireland Society.* 69, pp. 121–143.

O'Loughlin (2020) Whiteness and the psychoanalytic imagination. *Contemporary Psychoanalysis.* 56 (2–3), pp. 353–374.

O'Loughlin, M. (In press) Cultural ruptures and their consequences for mental health across generations: The case of Ireland. In: Lambrecht, I. and Lavis, A. (Eds.) *Culture and Psychosis.* New York and London: Routledge.

Rose, J. (2020, November 19) To die one's own death: Jacqueline Rose on Freud and his daughter. *London Review of Books.* 42 (22). [https://www.lrb.co.uk/the-paper/v42/n22/jacqueline-rose/to-die-one-s-own-death\.

Volkan, V. (2001) Transgenerational transmissions and chosen traumas: An aspect of large-group identity. *Group Analysis.* 34 (1), pp. 79–97.

Walcott, D. (1992). *The Antilles: Fragments of Epic Memory. The Nobel Lecture.* New York: Farrar, Strauss & Giroux.

Preface

The personal inspiration for this book is to do with my own interest in ancestry. I have researched both sides of my family and through this exploration have had several surprising and unexpected meetings with living relatives, my ancestors and descendants of some of their friends. I mention friends because I am not deeply enamoured with the idea of bloodlines. I'm as happy with a lateral movement through the records which has allowed me to meet people who were descended from friends of my grandfather or my great-great-grandmother for example. In this sense I am curious: I want living history, not a done-and-dusted family tree. Ancestry, like life, is messy.

Meeting people from the past is rarely a neutral experience. I have been moved to tears by some of the things my ancestors went through and did to themselves and others. I found that I met them through what they had done, decisions and actions taken for better or worse. I have often wondered why I continued with my quest. Looking back now, I realise that a series of attachments had formed inside me to people I had never met. I felt compelled to get to know them better. Sometimes they seemed to speak to me, particularly throughout the tedious process of record-based research. I made some odd and intuitive leaps. Looking at the conclusion of this book, I'd now say that I had learned to use my sociological imagination. In doing so I felt 'increased', as if there were more of me than when I started studying ancestry.

My professional life has been in psychotherapy. I offer this detail as a caveat and for context. As a psychodynamic psychotherapist I am interested in the past in the present, and this book is in step with my working model. I have an interest in loss, mourning and creativity—these themes are staples in the psychodynamic tradition. I was less familiar with haunting (a key theme in this book) and tended to think about the more troubled side of human psychic life—psychosis, dissociation, trauma, abuse—in very personal terms, or not influenced by any wider a circle than the family of the individual involved. As a therapist I know that without a grasp of the details of people's lives and experiences, no real work is possible. Writing this book has stretched and sometimes redefined this latter assumption, for which I am grateful.

My experience of engaging with my ancestors has brought a sense of increase. I recognise some of my own strengths and weaknesses and some familial and less familiar traits and talents. I know more people than I knew before; my network is deeper and wider. This book and its central argument is a product of this expanded viewpoint and the key idea of intergenerational companionship comes out of it. The idea is not new, but it does come out of my experience and the experiences of people I have talked to during the research.

Are some of the ideas wild and unrealistic? I hope so! I am, after all, an idealistic and political animal. Many of my ancestors and their friends were too, and on occasion it got them into big trouble!

There is a slightly self-conscious concept in psychosocial research called 'wild analysis' where, because of the subjective methodology, data may be constructed in a self-fulfilling way or over interpreted. Psychotherapy is vulnerable to similar problems, and supervision is the usual control. In relation to research it is broadly the same; collegial oversight sometimes passes by the technical name of 'triangulation of data'. In the psychosocial tradition, this is typically done in Balint groups (Salinsky, 2013) to maximise the peer collaborative components and the all-important element of 'free association' alongside the routine discipline of hypothesis formation.

Talking of free association, that staple of psychodynamic therapeutic practice, the capacity to use one's imagination in the presence of another is a very useful way of exploring what is happening with people in many other settings. More recently it has become evident to me that it is very useful when thinking about things as well, such as buildings or technical systems. To someone artistically or poetically trained, this will be no surprise. Since Keats, we have had a term for it: 'negative capability'. Since the Surrealist movement, we have been able to see it and experiment with imaginatively informed inquiry.

Memory is a deeply contested subject both in ordinary life and in the sciences. In writing this book I have picked out the theoretical and research strands that in my view make the most sense when thinking about the multigenerational transmission of memory. In Chapter 1, I introduce a narrative on memory and how it works, weaving a story as well as defining some key ideas. These ideas are discussed in more depth in Chapter 2. I alternate between narrative and exposition throughout the book: it is a way of writing that I hope will help readers, whether academics, therapists or students, find the book accessible.

This book is at root an invitation to imagine, to enter a social and psychological trance about our ancestors and forebears. It is a book about social memory, remembering and forgetting. It also anticipates a future in which thinking about several generations at once might be more commonplace for our social cohesion and survival.

Any wild analysis or overly free interpretations in this book are entirely my own. On a more technical note, in a book with a subject matter as complex and wide ranging as this one, there will be gaps and contradictions. Like the generations themselves, it is a work in a progress.

Since a research project sits behind the book, I would like to acknowledge separately the enthusiasm and interest that those who have taken part in the study have shown. Without their participation, this survey would have been much reduced and the ideas less grounded in social and psychological reality.

Bristol, UK
July 2020

Nigel Williams

Reference

Salinsky, J. (2013) *Balint Groups and the Balint Method*. Available from: https://balint.co.uk/about/the-balint-method/ [Accessed 10 September 2020].

Acknowledgments

Dr. Jane Woodend for her untiring work on data analysis over several years.
Dr. Phoebe Beedell for her help with the literature review.
Susannah Sallé for her editorial oversight.
Sophie Savage for her editorial assistance.
Dr. Kieran McCartan for his support of the research at the University of the West of England.
Liz Frost, Miltos Hadjiosif, Tim Hockridge, Liz Maliphant, Marianne Pawloff, Jem Thomas and Paul Zeal for their feedback and comments.

Organisations

The Association for Psychoanalysis Culture and Society, USA, for providing a space in its conferences for valuable exchanges and connections with like-minded colleagues.
Group "O", UK, a UWE alumni group, for peer support over many years.

Contents

1	Introduction	1
2	Imagining the Generations: Introduction to the Nature of Multigenerational Memory	11
3	Mapping the Generations: Survey of the Literature on Multigenerational Memory	41
4	Reconceptualising Loss and Reaching for Creativity	81
5	Haunting	97
6	Images of Nature in Multigenerational Memory	117
7	Therapeutic Implications of Working with Multigenerational Memory	125
8	The Psychosocial and the Transgenerational	151
9	Conclusion	173
Index		195

About the Author

Nigel Williams has been a psychotherapist for forty years. He initially trained as a social scientist and in the last sixteen years has worked at the University of the West of England, helping to train psychologists and counsellors in psychodynamic approaches to therapy and psychosocial approaches to research. He is co-editor with Anne-Marie Cummins of *Further Researching Beneath the Surface* (Routledge, 2018) and his focus on ancestry is reflected his writing about migration and diaspora.

List of Figures

Fig. 2.1	A typology for multigenerational relationships	15
Fig. 2.2	A typology of memory processes	33
Fig. 7.1	A typology of multigenerational memory: Intergenerational emphasis	141
Fig. 8.1	A psychosocial map of the overlapping dynamic fields in which the generations operate	160
Fig. 8.2	Typology of multigenerational memory: Transgenerational emphasis	168

1

Introduction

It is important for us to account for our origins. We do this through reference to kinship or friendship or a mixture of both. We like to be able to talk about what and who formed us, our closeness to or distance from social events we or our ancestors lived through. For some, bloodlines are important; others are drawn to finding a sense of continuity in community, people and place.

The term 'generations' suggests something further: that creative generative processes occur over time, such that we progress or even evolve. While this idea of the generations can give a reassuring sense of social and personal development, they are as much about discontinuity, attenuation and rupture with the past. But the idea of generations doesn't necessarily suggest progression or regression; it can also refer to continuity. For non-Western cultures, the generations can be seen as human links in a web of life or a cycle of time. The idea of progress, like the idea of childhood, is culturally and historically relative and has itself only been around for a very short time. In their construction of family genealogies, many people find disturbing and upsetting details and stories. Whole societies suffer similar problems and constantly swing between self-idealisation and denigration in their dialogue with their national identity. Just like

© The Author(s), under exclusive license to Springer Nature
Switzerland AG 2021
N. Williams, *Mapping Social Memory*, Studies in the Psychosocial,
https://doi.org/10.1007/978-3-030-66157-1_1

individuals, some societies are good at remembering while others are good at forgetting.

A closer definition of terms can help make clear what the issues and problems are. The current interest in ancestry in Western society is tied up in a wider search for identity. It is quite individualistic, despite often revealing the part one's ancestors may have played in social events. It can also bring a newly discovered sense of belonging to places, times and communities that have passed. In short, it always involves experiencing and thinking about some sort of loss, but in these losses can be found new beginnings, and pointers to the future.

In the research that informs this book, I have been curious about memory, and consequently many of the findings have been about what is remembered and what is forgotten and what that in turn means for personal and social continuity. The way in which people remember has changed radically in less than one generation due to the Internet and data algorithms. These comments were written at the time of the COVID-19 global pandemic. From a pre-printing press past, we might draw on the playground game of *Ring a Ring of Roses*, a warning to children of coughs and sneezes but also a cautionary reminder of the catastrophic effects on a community in which 'we all fall down'. Much memory that is carried between the generations is more story- and game-like than family and social record data might indicate.

Do we know more about our past and how this might relate to our present and future *because* there is so much more information 'out there'? I think not. Through the Internet and social media, we are developing an extended sense of self and community but at the same time withdrawing from the affective conditions that bind people together: the shared problems of looking after others, and working at problems of survival and flourishing. It's a paradox. The Internet is too young yet to know whether it ushers in a new, more socially distanced way of being, or if the social bonds of attachment and a society based on them will prevail. We probably face a future in which a mixture of the two aid and abet our survival as a species.

The capacity for the generations to remember and learn from each other ebbs and flows. This two-way learning can get interrupted by trauma, social dislocation and different access to social and economic resources. Sometimes it turns out that a hidden web of connections helped a person or a whole people through a difficult time. Multigenerational memory always operates somewhere on the continuum between the visible and the invisible. Sometimes remembering is very tangible; sometimes it works in more unexpected ways. Our capacity for survival and flourishing is predicated on it. Yet to think about it properly as a social process we must redefine what memory and remembering are and how they work. That is the subject of this book.

Synopsis

In Chapter 2, I think about how social memory works and the ways in which memory can be thought of as existing beyond the individual. I talk about First Nation people's ideas and practices around memory and how this diverges from Western ideas about the generations, time, progress and development. I begin a definition of the difference between intergenerational and transgenerational memory. This is central to clarifying the issue about how individuals and societies are more or less integrated/disintegrated in certain periods of time. The social sciences background to understanding memory and the generations is introduced which gives an initial working model of how we might think about social memory and its vicissitudes. I identify four dimensions that group types of explanation: those emphasising the longer-term processes in culture, and those focused on the shorter term in families and groups, linking particularly to attachment theory. These time-based explanations are intersected by theory and research concerning the physical transmission of memory and trauma on the one hand, and social transmission on the other. The forms of explanation here are in genetics, molecular biology and epigenetics while the latter are to do with group processes, social contagion and the subject areas of sociology, psychology and psychosocial studies. The chapter builds on some extended case studies drawn from psychotherapy practice that show how the intimate and personal level of crisis and problem-solving leads us out of our sense of self as unitary into a sense of self as multiple and troubled by times longer past that that of our own lives. The case studies also show how intergenerational memory and trauma are complicated by transgenerational issues of ethnic and cultural identity which limit how much an individual can resolve and work with problems, without there being change at a social and cultural level. The focus here is on war trauma and migration.

The book introduces and outlines the main findings of a psychosocial research project on which it is based. I identify a cycle of memory which moves through a number of zones, each of which raises familiar issues about remembering and forgetting. The first phase of the cycle I call 'reconceptualising loss': the capacity to think about and work with loss in individuals' families and groups. It is more intergenerational and concerns our ever-changing ability to mourn losses of all kinds. Alongside it is the capacity to reach for creativity and, by implication, for solutions to problems. Just over 50% of the data in the research underpins this theme. The second major theme, that of hauntings, is an area of memory and experience that is more ambiguous yet very influential. The data in this area showed that much traumatic memory haunts and troubles us and that we struggle to make sense of it. Hauntings typically take longer to work through, and the role of the third generation witness is identified as a key factor in hauntings being looped back into the process of reconceptualising loss or the experience going out of personal memory, where it is either lost or makes its way into transgenerational or cultural memory. Hauntings are often associated with the loss or breaking of social links, and much of the reparative work by the third generation is in daring to reconstruct these lost connections: it can be painful and conflictual. The role of nature also emerged as a strong but less dominant theme in the findings. Nature was a way for respondents to talk about much longer passages of time and geographical spaces that they felt were part of their or their ancestors' identity. Nature also allowed people to talk about social ecology and forms of generational awareness convergent with some First Nation people's ideas and traditions about the unborn generations and a sense of social responsibility extending in time before and beyond the everyday self. To illustrate the research findings, the chapter contains an extended narrative example of a migrant family group living through three generations. It was these findings that led me to put forward the idea of a multigenerational self—an extended self beyond that of the unitary individual—which I elaborate throughout the book.

Chapter 3 provides a survey of the existing science and social science literature to help define and clarify this multidimensional view of memory and experience beyond the individual. The research is thereby situated in an academic background that is wide-ranging and interdisciplinary. Consequently, I discuss both the epigenetic and social transmission of trauma alongside key discourses from sociology, psychology and psychosocial studies on memory, post-memory and haunting. I explore the social unconscious, individual psychoanalytic contributions alongside recent developments in social dreaming, migration studies and sociology of the generations. In so doing, I attempt to create a series of intellectual connections across fields of study that are typically disparate or contained in professional silos. I offer these connections as the beginning of a map of resources to help understand multigenerational experiences.

The next three chapters discuss the research findings in detail and are largely based on data derived from participants' experience of multigenerational issues and memory. I explore the tensions between creativity and shutting down against a backdrop of the ways in which people prepare for and deal with losses of different kinds. The experience of migration and preceding war and famine emerge as issues that disturb and challenge people and their descendants. Chapter 5's theme of haunting tries to more clearly define what the processes are at work by closely observing examples drawn from diverse experiences. Hauntings are seen both as varieties of traumatic memory but also related to experience that is closer to the body, social action and objects. In this sense, they form a deeper background to the experience of being in time. They provide some of the ground for the idea of an extended self and the concept of the 'many in the one' which we find so difficult in the West. Chapter 6 on nature falls more clearly into the area of transgenerational memory but contains many intimate stories about how people's relationship with nature is transformational and allows a thinking about the self in longer spans of time. These findings are closer to the First Nations' view of the generations as operating in much longer cycles, with an emphasis on a past-to-future movement of which the individual is a part. The role and power of place and different landscapes resonate with journeys of migration and diaspora.

Chapter 7 discusses the findings in relation to the practice of psychotherapy and focuses on how professional work-based generations emerge and are the site for creativity or its attenuation. I discuss the role of the training institute along with leave-takings and relationships between younger and older practitioners. There are implications for training and for the practice of working with multigenerational memory, incorporating assessments, the practice of supervision and the ways in which training both inhibits and promotes awareness of multigenerational issues. I develop the idea of intergenerational companionship alongside that of generational mentalisation. Psychotherapy methods such as reverie, free association and storytelling could perhaps provide new ways of working with memory and experience beyond the individual. While I offer a map and working model of intergenerational memory specific to psychotherapy, the limits of this model usher in the themes of the next chapter which are specifically social and transgenerational.

Chapter 8 focuses on the psychosocial approach to the generations and multigenerational memory. In it, I document how more personal family-based intergenerational memories can turn into transgenerational ones. I discuss the interrelationship of social fields; transitional phenomena show that social fields exist both in time and in space, and this can help us understand and come to grips with social hauntings across the generations. I offer another map that shows how intergenerational memory can turn in transgenerational memory and illuminate this by looking in the data at the power of 'hidden migrations' and other historical diasporas such as slavery and enforced migration and genocide. I explore the idea of research as social intervention and the way in which psychosocial perspectives can give rise to new ways of working with multigenerational issues using large group meetings and new forms of social matrices such as social dreaming.

In Chapter 9, I discuss the dangers of haunted relationships between peoples and nations. I return to the themes of identities and groups and think about how the generations can be more or less connected through intergenerational mentalisation in different periods of time and in different cultures. I develop the idea of the Sociological Imagination as a way of holding a psychosocial focus on problems that can only be understood if approached with 'binocular' vision. The role of witnessing in social justice is discussed as is the place of memorialisation. The chapter ends with a discussion about developing an 'sensibility for the long term' and the opportunities this brings for attending to delayed mourning, and holding a view that includes a sense of individuals being part of a generational process that at once forms and supports them but bequeaths to them a new role as custodians of the future.

The research which forms the basis for this book was carried out in the period 2013–2018 and involved therapists, academics and members of the public. It also draws on my own more recent thinking about the dynamics and significance of the relationship between the generations. Memory defined in a social and embodied way represents an ever-present potential for understanding current difficulties in surprising and unexpected ways.

A word about sources on which I draw and their ethical issues: I use the ideas and wisdom derived from First Nation people with care, and in full acknowledgement that these people are some of the most oppressed and downtrodden on the planet, whose cultures have been attacked and eroded by centuries of colonial practices of social dislocation and domination. Quoting their culture makes me uncomfortable; they should speak for themselves. Leanne Betasomosake Simpson (2017) is an example. I integrate their concepts in the spirit of the subject matter of the book which calls for developing a cultural sensibility in the West to hearing or rehearing ancestral voices. I also do so in recognition that in our conflict-torn world, those who lived on the land first have some or many of the answers to these problems. I hope this book will help those not prone to listen to these voices to become interested and enquire further.

This leads me onto the subject of migration and diaspora, which formed an important theme in the research for this book. Until relatively recently in human history, migration has been a normal part of the human behavioural repertoire. It is a response to changes in the natural environment. Our capacities to make adaptive journeys and to mix and hybridise are key elements in our capacity to survive and flourish as

Sonia Shah documents in her book on human migration (2020). This has been greatly complicated by the emergence of empires and nation states. In our unequal, crisis-ridden, climatically warming world, we are being challenged to think about migration as the solution to the problem rather than the problem itself. This book outlines not only some of the consequences of migration but also the ways in which the generations may be able to learn from each other about how to navigate social change and conflict. Of the people I interviewed, there was a surprisingly high number of migration experiences embedded in their ancestral stories. This may be a sign that in the West we have tended to bury or denigrate the experience, yet we find it is ubiquitous. I document some of the memory processes that seem to occur between the generations that make remembering fraught.

When thinking about the generations, the subject of population dynamics and patterns comes into play. The current debates about fair and unfair intergenerational economic settlements and what I call 'upside-down societies' are the subject of an article by James Gallagher (2020). Changes in global fertility rates suggest we are looking at some deep-level changes that will also drive migration or cause the most age-imbalanced societies to break down if they cannot change creatively. As with all problems, there are good and bad solutions at hand. As we stand on the edge of the abyss of social and environmental catastrophes, we can choose better futures, but first we must get into the habit of looking. This book suggests some ways we might do that by improving the ways in which the generations communicate with each other, and the allied importance of cultivating a 'sensibility for the long term'. This involves not rewriting histories, but rather writing histories that have not yet been written in a way that rests on the experience of ordinary people and everyday events in longer sweeps of time and geography. Making these voices heard is a challenge and goes against our Western preoccupation with individual identity and consumption. This book also challenges the idea that only the present generation is sovereign. The past has deep subtle and abiding influence; the future and past are ineluctably connected. The 'present moment' is in great need of being expanded and redefined, by several generations in each direction. This book provides some ways of approaching this issue.

Many of our respondents spoke of how they and their ancestors had their identity formed by place and by community, and this forms the other main strand of the book. Attachment to place and to people is fundamental. Generations exist in space and time and have histories and geographies. This sense of attachment to a place that has gone haunts many of our respondents. The processes through which it is recreated are often creative and poignant. Lest anyone think that the idea of the generations is an abstract one, another theme that I document is how care, concern and witnessing also travel through time, and form part of an imperfect but discernible presence of intergenerational care and reciprocity. This needs to be increased if our survival is to be strengthened in the future. With care and concern for others come skills and capacities for which currently there are no qualifications except experience. Much of the background to this book is academic and research-based but at its core are indications of experience of and bearing witness to solving problems (or not) that happen at the human and intimate scale. It is only from these very pressing immediate problems that we get purchase on wider and deeper issues.

The book demonstrates psychosocial approaches, such as those taken by Hollway and Jefferson (2013), Clarke and Hoggett (2009) and Cummins and Williams (2018) involving psychological, psychoanalytic and social understandings. The methods used and described in this book are action-focused, span individual and group experiences and aim to counter one of our main cultural habits, the tendency to personalise issues that are in fact social. In our current period, we are troubled by a problem of narcissistic leaders and short-term management and politics. Developing a sensibility for the longer term in a frame that is focused both on personal and group experiences characterises the approach taken here.

References

Clarke, S. and Hoggett, P. (Eds.) (2009) *Researching Beneath the Surface: Psycho-Social Research Methods in Practice*. London: Karnac.

Cummins, A-M. and Williams, N. (Eds.) (2018) *Further Researching Beneath the Surface (Volume 2): Psycho-Social Research Methods in Practice.* Oxon: Routledge.

Gallagher, J. (2020) Fertility rate: 'Jaw-dropping' global crash in children being born. *BBC News* [online]. 15 July. Available from: https://www.bbc.co.uk/news/health-53409521 [Accessed 10 September 2020].

Hollway, W. and Jefferson, T. (2013) *Doing Qualitative Research Differently: A Psychosocial Approach.* 2nd ed. London: Sage.

Shah, S. (2020) *The Story of Movement on a Changing Planet.* London: Bloomsbury Publishing.

Simpson, L.B. (2017) *As We Have Always Done Indigenous Freedom Through Radical Resistance.* Minneapolis: University of Minnesota Press.

2

Imagining the Generations: Introduction to the Nature of Multigenerational Memory

Social Memory: A Framework

Does memory exist between individuals, inside communities and across generations? Can we meaningfully talk about memory that does not belong to individuals, but rather exists in other ways? I start this exploration by relating some stories that will introduce two of the key concepts that help us to understand social memory. Inter- and transgenerational memory, when taken together but also when carefully distinguished, allow us to better chart the reach, range and significance of multigenerational social memory.

There are some very old memories around. In his book on ice age memories, Patrick Nunn (2018) demonstrates that the Narungga people of southern Australia record in stories the sea-level rise associated with the melt at the end of the last ice age. These stories, consistent across a large region, may refer to an event that occurred more than 11,000 years ago. That is more than 350 generations (I discuss different ways of defining a generation in Chapters 3 and 8).

Here in these ancient stories it is the power of the rising sea that inspires conflict resolution because of the need for cooperation between the earth's rival animal clans after the sea fills the valleys. Some of my findings suggest that nature as the great leveller has an abiding and persistent life in human memory. Later in this book (Chapter 6), I deal with the role of nature in intergenerational memory.

Aborigines in Western Australia seem to remember a time when the Great Barrier Reef did not exist. Stories describe a coastline characterised by a vertical cliff with ancestral creatures swimming in the abyss at its base. This abyssal cliff now sits on the ocean side of the Reef. These stories, if thought of as memories, are 15,000 years old.

These Aboriginal stories are told and remembered in communities that have survived for 50,000 years in the same geographical area, despite recent violent and toxic colonialism. The stories also contain vital information for survival in relation to food, natural resources and other environmental risks like volcanic activity and forest fire. Each story evokes and is a homage to the wisdom of the ancestors and contains advice on how to solve problems. This is an important point to which I will return.

Atkinson (2002, p. 19) points to the importance of indigenous peoples' healing practices and how they can inform contemporary research and social action. She speaks of 'Dadirri'—a listening from the heart and a 'listening to an observing self as well as in relationship with others' illuminating what seems like a form of psychosocial methodology. Peltier (2018) takes the idea further by developing Elder Albert Marshall's (2004) 'Two-Eyed Seeing', or *Etuaptmumk*, as a framework to reconcile the use of Western method and theory with Indigenous knowledge. The indigenous concept of time as linked to the generations is different in important ways to Western models: one generation spans 120 years and encompasses seven levels of a family tree, three of which are as yet unborn. I return to the implications of this in Chapter 3.

I ask whether these ice age memories are being spoken about now because we are entering a similar period of global crisis and change. The memories come from the last big ice melt; we are in the middle of another. These are examples of transgenerational long-term memories. Britain has its own lost world: recent marine archaeological research has revealed 'Britain's Atlantis' (Keys, 2015), the submerged riverbank settlements of Doggerland under the North Sea. Any direct memories within these communities have been lost and yet something does remain in our data on migrants' testimony about the fate and relationship between islands and mainlands (Chapter 6).

By contrast, I found that intergenerational memory directly attributable to and passed down through groups and families has a much shorter range. The memory of the drinking and gambling habits of my male ancestors in Victorian London has lasted three generations. These stories, told from the perspective of the women, are a warning and a commentary on the risks and vicissitudes of migrant life in a foreign land. They also link to one of the key themes in the research: the intergenerational tension between creativity and shutting down, as a Beethoven-playing migrant pianist plays for pints and sinks into alcoholism in East London dockland pubs.

The memories I have spoken of are partly passed down and partly diarised. They are also jointly remembered: the story I just told came up during my research. Somebody contacted me recognising a family name, her great-grandmother—it turned out—having married the younger brother of my great-grandfather. Her great-grandmother kept a diary; I had the stories of gambling outings and binges in my family oral history. Together they made a coherent story.

Through these two examples, that of the Aboriginal people of southern Australia and the shared memory in my own extended family, the first useful working distinction between transgenerational memory and intergenerational memory is brought to light. The first memory, passed down through many generations, contains no personal elements, but rather important and emotionally significant stories of ancestors' and clan animals' responses to flood and risk. It is a story that continues to help guide current behaviour. As such, it is also a guide to the future and contains a warning about the importance of resolving conflict. The second example is a memory that can be traced back to an individual and a migrant group. It has shared aspects, but they are shorter in range (three generations). It also has a moral lesson and a guide to action, and a prescient comment about gender relations and the risks to mental health caused by migration.

This, however, does not begin to convey all the mysteries and debates surrounding social memory. In my research, I have found a clustering of stories and accounts that I have called 'hauntings' and 'unhappy interment'. These relate to memory that disturbs and seemingly has a life of its own. I mention it here because it may represent a combination of inter- and transgenerational components. Somewhat like buried or scattered radioactive material, it appears to have a long half-life. Here we find stories of Irish Americans, focused on the communal politics of running foodbanks to alleviate acute hunger, becoming aware of their own transgenerational trauma of famine and subsequent diaspora in the generation of their great-grandparents (Ramsay, 1997). I ask here whether there is a transgenerational transmission that is at once cultural, unconscious and epigenetic. Some memories seem to work by contagion, picked up from almost nowhere. They have an uncanny character, but the uncanny can extend beyond the life of the individual and into the culture to which their ancestors were attached and by which they were formed.

Research shows that hunger and famine do leave a mark epigenetically (Zimmer, 2018), but does this lead to a propensity to seek reparative acts dissociated, as it were, from the experience of ancestors exposed to extreme famine, poverty and diaspora? Many of my research respondents talk about a journey from not knowing to knowing, involving a process of discovery and revelation.

Another example of the amalgam of inter- and transgenerational memory is a story relating to hauntings and death. I refer to it in detail in my paper on the Anglo-German diaspora (Williams, 2015). This has to do with my grandfather whom I did not know. An anecdote in my family tells of the distress he experienced in his last days, rallying against death for fear of meeting his 'German aunts' who, in his imagination, were coming to get him. While this could have been a psychotic-level experience stirred up in the confusion and stress of dying, it also lived on via my father to myself. I was the first person to ask who these German aunts had been. It turned out they were exactly those people who had had so much to say about the dangers of migration and alcohol! They were actual individuals who had lived on as ghosts in this tale of my grandfather's last days. This is an example of another process that is part of the haunting: the way in which a ghostly story can reveal the existence of an actual ancestor. This is the remnant of actual extended family members who looked after my grandfather as a child during the prolonged illness of his mother. It also contains another disowned memory, that of being profoundly German. For a man who had, during the First World War, committed to an identity of being English, this was indeed a 'return of the repressed'!

Having illustrated through these two stories the potential differences between inter- and transgenerational processes, I will now proffer a more formal working definition that brings in much of the social and biological sciences that are relevant for understanding multigenerational memory. I represent this visually in a typology (see Fig. 2.1).

The vertical axis spanning intergenerational to transgenerational represents time, with the intergenerational end relating to influences that are traceable between families, individuals and groups, and the transgenerational to the transmission of memory across longer periods of time. Although such a distinction is helpful, it is important to hold onto the idea that there is a dynamic continuum between the two. In one way, the inter- to transgenerational continuum is a means of talking about the forms that memory might take over longer passages of time. However, it is also true to say that much of what I present in my research shows how time collapses and the past is more apparent than the present in the experience of some people and groups. I also show how intergenerational memories can be complicated or extended by transgenerational ones, leading to a locking in of trauma such that the conditions

Intergenerational
Shorter term, direct via individuals and families, intergenerational patterns of attachment, traumatic experiences in the parental and grandparental generation

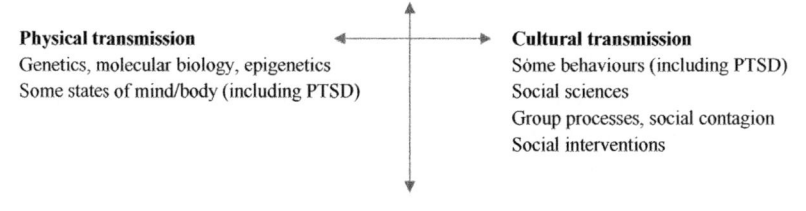

Physical transmission ◄─────► **Cultural transmission**
Genetics, molecular biology, epigenetics
Some states of mind/body (including PTSD)

Some behaviours (including PTSD)
Social sciences
Group processes, social contagion
Social interventions

Transgenerational
Longer term, indirect. Cultural memory, groups and organisations, symbolic systems, ritual, embodied memory

Fig. 2.1 A typology for multigenerational relationships

for remembering and integrating experiences represent a threshold that remains hard or impossible to cross. This is typical of perpetrator–victim dynamics, which have significant and powerful cultural and political components with a much longer life than the individuals involved and indeed go beyond the three-generation boundary of the more personal intergenerational memory. A transgenerational perspective can also help to shed light on long-standing oppressions and injustices. The transatlantic slave trade requires a relatively short memory in transgenerational terms of 15 generations, dropping to five for the last slave boat, the Clotilda, in 1860. Cudjoe Lewis, one of the last survivors, died in 1935 (Bourne et al., 2020).

The horizontal arm of the typology shows how different academic disciplines, different types of memory transmission and different types of intervention can potentially be compared. One of the key contrasts is between biological and physical explanations of memory and that which emphasises the social and cultural. Currently, any cultural- and social-based approach has to deal with the rise of a new understanding of how genetics work.

There is a growing area of memory-based work that is tied at least speculatively to a new branch of genetic science called epigenetics. It is a burgeoning field that has some implications for transmission that may underpin the more familiar process of intergenerational memory in families (i.e. a social–cultural process). The work of Yehuda et al. (2016) is the most well known and asserts a link between the children of Holocaust survivors and the existence of Post-Traumatic Stress Disorder-like symptoms in subsequent generations. The idea is more clearly demonstrated in Isabelle Mansuy's work (Gapp et al., 2014) on mice's sense of smell. Mansuy has been able to isolate an epigenetic transmission of negative conditioning (fear) and a particular smell that was previously a source of pleasure. Mice that liked the smell of blossom but were subsequently given negative conditioning to fear it passed this fear onto the next generation of pups. This seems like a biological early warning system, where a risk associated with a smell is communicated. Mansuy (ibid., 2014) notes that the conditioning 'grows out' over two further generations if the current living conditions do not reinforce the conditioning. She refers to this as 'mouse hotel therapy'. There are many caveats about the application of animal-based studies to humans, and we don't yet know if a study of this kind tells us about human multigenerational transmission.

This leaves us with a question about whether the inheritance of Post-Traumatic Stress Disorder-like symptoms has a 'function'. If non-specific fear and a tendency towards hyperarousal and anxiety are adaptive in situations of high risk and low survival in the parental generation, is this a way of increasing survival in the next? Perhaps it has no function at all but is just a biological process that we are vulnerable to via evolutionary systems developed to respond to predator stress. It does explain why the attempt to reconcile traumas of one generation often seems to fall to the offspring, even that of a third generation, who may be living in more stable social conditions.

It also follows from this that if those stable conditions do not emerge, for instance if a violent diaspora is followed by extended poverty and discrimination, then hyperarousal and its long-term effects on physical and mental health continue and the possibility of regaining psychological equilibrium for an individual or a group becomes less likely. In his pioneering work on social fields, Kurt Lewin (1997) suggests that if one's social field is distorted by racism then it is impossible to assume citizenship without the root causes of racism being removed or effectively countered. This elegant action-based spatial theory could be extended by implication to encompass time, so that the accumulation of past hurts combined with a contemporary situation of victimhood or powerlessness shows how much work would be needed for victims of past atrocities to gain full or meaningful recognition for what has been done to them. It also underlines the point that the conditions for such a change to take place are not only economic, but involve cultural expression, assertion and acceptance.

Another important piece of work on the effects of traumatic events helps to link the idea that traumatic experiences occur and are transmitted through time to the notion of trauma being mediated by social networks, which exist in social space. I discuss this in detail in my Chapter 5 exploration of hauntings and unhappy interment.

Shevlin and McGuigan (2003) used the Revised Impact of Event Scale questionnaire to explore the experience of stress responses in family members of the 13 civil rights marchers who were killed in Derry/Londonderry in 1972. The questionnaire was given to immediate family members, children of the immediate family, and to cousins and second cousins of the immediate family. The results showed that immediate family and their children showed the highest levels of stress responses, with cousins and second cousins showing reducing levels of stress per group. Shevlin and McGuigan (2003) found the stress levels reported by all groups except second cousins were commensurate with stress levels found amongst firefighters and the victims and rescuers of avalanches (four months after the event). Stress levels for immediate family were on a par with those of South African police exposed to violence over the previous year and Vietnam War combat veterans. As Shevlin and McGuigan (2003, p. 431) state, 'the results from this study suggest that the victim's immediate family, their children, and their cousins are experiencing significant psychological distress regarding the events of Bloody Sunday, which occurred 30 years ago. The degree of psychological distress experienced appears to covary with familial distance from the victim'.

Shevlin and McGuigan's (2003) research offers a model for an ongoing longitudinal study of how psychological distress can be mapped through time and across familial distance. It may help us to understand the 'outer edges' of the effects of intergenerational transmission of trauma before transgenerational processes of aggression and non-recognition of the type Lewin (1997) talks about take over. I will return to the issue of social interventions in Chapter 8.

Social and cultural transmission also involves processes that are deeply private and individual. These are common when people feel they are not part of their family or not related to a parent, or do not belong where they live. An example could be someone who is adopted into a family without any paperwork (typical in closed adoptions) (Outerbridge, 2018). Such a scenario can lead to a haunting where the actual parents can only be imagined but where living in the body of someone who is not present is lived out on a daily basis. There may be longings for certain landscapes or a sense of place (Zalme, 2017). Here in these examples it is the social link that is broken. I will return to this issue when I discuss hauntings in Chapter 5.

Memory as an Embodied System

The issues emerging from epigenetics raise a range of difficult and controversial questions. What is memory? What is it for? How does it work? Do you need a brain and central nervous system to have memory? Is memory exclusive to certain animals, or does it exist across the whole animal kingdom? Do plants have memories? For that matter does any complex system have a memory reflected in its structure? Could those systems that are on the boundaries of living and inanimate worlds be included as having changes of state that are built on progressively and therefore may rely for that on 'memory-like' processes?

There is an emerging debate around whether 'life' has been defined too tightly by biologists Bartlett and Wong (2020, p. 1). They assert that

> Lyfe is defined as any system that fulfils all four processes of the living state, namely: dissipation, autocatalysis, homeostasis, and learning. Life is defined as the instance of lyfe that we are familiar with on Earth, one that uses a specific organometallic molecular toolbox to record information about its environment and achieve dynamical order by dissipating certain planetary disequilibria. [...] the four pillars of lyfe offer a novel perspective on the living state that is indifferent to the particular components that might produce it.

It is this type of process I have in mind when thinking about the outer edges of generational memory. In these terms learning does not require consciousness; the idea of cognition is part of an embodied accumulation and memory of experience. These perspectives and the above questions also problematise the brain–body split that can be found in some academic psychology and cognitive neuroscience. To make sense of memory as embodied but less brain-centred helps us to understand some of the experiences this research addresses, namely how far human memory extends and how distributed it can be across space and time. It also gets us closer to how memory beyond the individual can appear to have a life of its own. In his work on the integrative aspects of living organisms, Fritjof Capra (1997) suggests that we lack a language to express the emerging view that all life is connected. The arguments made in this book about multigenerational memory do not rest exclusively on systems theory, but we cannot ignore that systems theory has something important to say about memory. Capra's work has been an attempt to offer a theory of living systems with an inclusive view of 'mind, matter and life' (1997, pp. 95–99) which he calls autopoiesis, or self-making. That creative process of self-making is at the heart of generational relationships which give continuities through time involving bodies, families, groups and cultures.

Self-Making, Extended Cognition, Structural Coupling and Bringing Forth Worlds

Capra's work, inspired by the work of Maturana and Varela (1992), has developed the idea of extended cognition:

> The nervous system of an organism […] interacts with its environment by continually modulating its structure, so that at any given moment, its physical structure is a record of previous structural changes. The nervous system does not process information from the outside world, on the contrary brings forth a world in the process of cognition. (Capra, 1997, p. 267)

Extended cognition is a basic feature of living organisms and memory partakes in this. The generations can be conceptualised as being a part of an extended cognition stretching forward and backward in time and across social and geographical space. I explore this idea further through the data presented in the research section of this book.

The Deleuzian concept of affect as elaborated by Massumi (2002), rather than the more generic use of the word affect in psychoanalysis, is useful here because it specifically points to preverbal, embodied and sensation-based processes (Colman, 2005). The concept of 'affect' is not synonymous with emotion but concerns a pre-personal process of 'becoming' and change, caused by an encounter between bodies. Affect in this formulation is bodily and contagious, able to communicate at a subtle but powerful level, below the surface of consciousness. This helps us to think about how generational relationships can be both continuous and discontinuous across time, certain aspects being transmitted across generations, while others may attenuate or disappear given the right conditions. Affect, particularly that concerned with attachment and danger, can spread very rapidly in a social network, not unlike a virus. Many of the different types of haunting I document in the research (Chapter 5) are affect-based with echoes of bodies, some present and some departed.

I take an embodied perspective to memory, one that emphasises the implicit, procedural and relational aspects where memory is seen as co-produced between people and their environments. Memory itself is performed and made anew with each remembering. In this sense, in contrast to much contemporary neuroscience, I am also interested in aspects of memory that have to do with fluidity rather than structure. This will become clear via the research findings and in this next section on memory and identity.

Memory and Identity

Can we remember beyond our own autobiographical memories? Is the nature of any memory we do have significant beyond the immediate personal context in which it occurred? Usually, these kinds of questions are important only to therapists, or occasionally to a jury trying to ascertain whether a particular memory is 'true'. The false memory debate has made uncomfortable reading for many therapists and contains a powerful cautionary tale for those wishing to state that traumatically acquired childhood memories are 'true'. Holly Watt (2017) talks about Nicole Kluemper's decision to speak out about her experiences of being at the centre of the false memory debate. Contemporary neuroscience suggests that personal biography and memory are so much a part of brain-building that they can't be thought about separately (Dallos, 2006). Memory and identity are inextricably bound together. Yet our memory is also about skill-building, survival and knowing where we are. In psychotherapy, there has been a tendency to see the earliest times as the most significant building blocks for good mental health.

Sue Gerhardt's (2004) *Why Love Matters* charts the profound implications of parenting on brain growth and connectivity from conception onwards. We gain much of our significant capacities for self-soothing and knowing others through this dance of early play and recognition. It is largely preverbal. The related subject of infantile amnesia has given rise to a complex field of research on the nature of early memory (Li et al., 2014). Memory 'traces' continue to affect behaviour long into adult life. Implicit or procedural memory not related to autobiography seems to have the potential to be experienced earlier but isn't consciously stored, so can only be recalled and reinforced by environmental restimulation and reminder. These early memory processes share some of the features of traumatic memory. Traumatic memories are specifically fear-based and can be hidden and trace-like or in full and shocking sight. Some of the hauntings reported in this research have these features of arising when 'triggered'; others have always been known about. The Adverse Childhood Experiences (ACE) framework (Felitti et al., 1998), now widely used for childhood mental health intervention, also foregrounds the power of adverse childhood experiences reverberating through both physical and mental health. Memory arising out of a relationship between bodies can have profound physical and emotional implications deep into the life cycle. This speaks of an intergenerational process characterised by bodies interacting and affecting each other over long periods of time. This leads into the complex problem of the unconscious. Lack of conscious memory has been seen to be connected with repression of early conflicts and this was Freud's primary view. There is less neuroscientific evidence for this, but much for the idea that most of mental life is non-conscious as indicated by the studies above. Solms (2015, p. 143) refers to it as the 'unrepressed unconscious'. Much of this non-conscious life is connected by and built on affect.

Within the generation of psychoanalytic thinkers after Freud, claims made for intergenerational memory rest partly on derivations of Nicolas Abraham and Maria Torok (1994) two analysands of Sándor Ferenczi, who himself had an interest in war trauma.

As Nicolas Rand, Abraham and Torok's translator, speaking of the transgenerational phantom explains:

The concept of the phantom moves beyond the focus of psychoanalytic enquiry beyond the individual being analysed because it postulates that some unwittingly inherit the secret psychic substance of their ancestors lives. The 'phantom' represents a radical reorientation of Freudian and post-Freudian theories of psychopathology, since the symptoms do not spring from the individual's own life experiences but from someone else's psychic conflicts, traumas, or secrets. (Rand, 1994, p. 166)

I return in more detail to the intellectual and research framework of multigenerational memory in Chapter 3. Suffice it to say that the idea of memory stretching beyond the individual and having a life of its own in families and society has haunted many writers. It is a concept that has both common sense appeal (I would not have been able to conduct the research survey without its being part of current culture) but is also controversial and elusive. I hope by the end of this book that the usefulness and scope of the idea of multigenerational memory will be more clearly defined. I return now to the key concepts of inter- and transgenerational memory to flesh them out further.

Intergenerational and Transgenerational Memories in Psychotherapy and Ancestry Research

Some people seem to have experiences that fall outside these familiar psychological and social categories. For example, over the course of several decades of clinical practice I have noticed that a few people's life stories seem to be infused or haunted by troubles or difficulties that, strictly speaking, were not their own. I can now recognise a pattern when thinking about several people with whom I worked psychotherapeutically: each presented with post-retirement depression which didn't shift until they started talking in various ways about their parents' experiences during the First World War (they were children in the early 1920s). They were also typically of the same age as my parents. This multigenerational resonance is important: it seems it is often members of the third generation who feel they have to address the experiences or actions of their ancestors or forebears. Perhaps it is clearer to this third generation that there are consequences to mental health and social identity of not speaking of what came before. It was a puzzle I have become better at noticing: how someone who has led a life without major trauma can have some or all of the main symptoms of post-traumatic stress. It wasn't so much that new memories became available in therapeutic work but rather strong and disturbing affects; extreme grief and rage, connected to imagined experiences of war and suffering, are what emerged in therapy. In some instances, the presence of a contemporary diary or a story from another family member helped to stimulate their imagination. Often these people had been left with almost no clue of what their parents had been through, the social connection between the generations having been broken for this group of post-war children and a consequent failure to imagine what may have come before. This illustrates some of the consequences of war trauma: the loss of social links that break the continuity of memory, and the accompanying complex conscious and unconscious decision by the traumatised generation not to speak.

While there are other experiences like this referred to in the research section of this book, the point I want to touch on here is that something traumatic that had happened to these people's parents could—through therapy—become imaginable so that a new narrative of the self could be woven. We know from current research (Dallos, 2006) that narrative is a key way in which memory is initially organised, and then reorganised through later crisis, change and development. These people had another problem: me, a therapist who thought mainly in biographical and family system terms. I remained a problem for them, like their parents had been, with my sights set firmly on normality and a better future. We both had to change for something new to happen.

Although I did not realise it at the time, several key features of multigenerational memory at work are detectable in these stories. There is something that won't clear up, a wound or a disturbance of some kind; there is the presence of troubling somatic symptoms (often PTSD-like); the one who is trying to help has the wrong approach which deepens the problem of non-recognition. The predicament is counter-intuitive: something is troubling that cannot be imagined, and that something did not actually happen to that individual. It's also a social process. These people represented, as it turned out, a microcosm of a whole generation of the post-First World War children who were surrounded by grief which they didn't understand. They were not unusual; they had losses they couldn't mourn because they were not available in a form that made sense. Furthermore, in the way that post-war children in general often find, they had become a beacon of hope for their parents, something that added further confusion as they never felt what they were meant to feel and so learned to fake it at one level and withdraw at another. In short, they always felt that they were not good enough.

People search for identity through memory and remembering. Groups, families, organisations and nations also engage in significant and complex activities of remembering and forgetting as part of how they manage identity and conflict over time.

Two facets of social memory processes can be characterised, those that are more intergenerational and others more transgenerational. I build on a definition of this distinction by Atkinson (2002) concerning trauma and memory and suggest that with intergenerational transmission, memory is passed down from one generation to the next; with transgenerational memory it is transmitted across several generations. This may seem mysterious, but something familiar to all of us is that we are affected by the families we grew up in, but also by the groups and society to which we belong which themselves have histories. I will build on the situation faced by children of the First World War parents to explain how one form of memory grows out of the other.

This first example from the post-First World War generation of British children who grew up in the 1920s shows an intergenerational process at work. While it is unclear how transmission works, some of the examples I explore begin to shed light on this. Some intergenerational memory confuses and disables: These post-First World War children had a classic warning about the future but were shorn of the essential emotional information that would make it memorable (war memorials on their own do not do this job). To put it in therapeutic terms, they could not digest what had been projected onto them by their parents. This, in my view, is a classically traumatic intergenerational process. It is probably very common. I elaborate on the mechanisms that may be involved when I discuss Abraham and Torok's (1994) work in Chapter 3.

Some of those members of this small group who sought therapy in the 1980s were eventually able to identify that they were troubled by the intergenerational memory of the unspoken trauma of their parents. However, this process of recognition might not have worked for someone of a similar age whose parents had entered the same war but with a different national and ethnic identity. For example, a small but significant number of British soldiers were German or Anglo-German, and German soldiers who had lived in Britain before the war made up another noteworthy group (Williams, 2015). Their war experience is more like that of a civil war: they suffered in a different way because their transgenerational identity robbed them of the capacity to demonise the other in order to kill (although this a basic feature of all war trauma). They found orders difficult to follow, were prone to insubordination and some ended up facing the firing squad. This transmits forward in time a different set of affects: a toxic mixture of anger, rage and shame (worsened in those who received medals for bravery). The consequences for social survival beyond the war for this mixed-identity group were complicated by the need to expunge any of the transgenerational signifiers of belonging to another nation or ethnic group other than the victorious one. Trauma ensues, wrapped up in deep disguise. The first all-British group I have described didn't have this complication; they 'just' had parents who were traumatised by their war experiences. The transgenerational element for these other war survivors is essential to understanding their experience. One could say that for them it has both inter- and transgenerational conflicts within it, which make it harder to imagine and work with. Some intergroup relationships can have deep histories, enmity and fear only a little below the surface. Equally, intercultural love and affinity are also poorly understood sources of creativity as is the part they play in deep social change (Williams, 2015, pp. 134–135). Experiences of migration, intermarriage and friendship loom large here. For the Anglo-Germans in First World War Britain, the loss is of a long-standing imagined community and the straining and sometimes breaking of the bonds of intercultural marriages caused massive strains on identity.

To put this into a more social framework, the British First World War group's experience, once it has been understood, is easier to memorialise; it can be represented as the tragedy of a generation who went to war (culturally, this representation is what has now to some extent happened). For others, the experience of war is still too transgenerationally conflicted to represent. In the aftermath of deep and long-running social conflicts, transgenerational hurts and insults have often never been addressed. This is usually because the issues are still too explosive to approach in the present. It is often the case that a complex transgenerational experience of this kind puts a person or group 'beyond mourning'. This situation makes it more likely that unaddressed hurts are picked up, carried and enacted by the next generation. The Atlantic slave trade and the situation of First Nations people are two of the longest-running examples, but there are others. The current resurgence of unresolved issues in Anglo-Irish politics is another very painful example. The history of diaspora is full of transgenerational memory and trauma. I have some further examples of this in the research. There is also a diasporic experience between each generation made up of the unshared and unshareable experience of living in a different era. Perhaps it is this residue—part of which may be traumatic—that builds up into a transgenerational transmission.

Loss and creativity often sit in a longer time span than individual lives, and in a broader context than personal or group identities, and by implication they also spread out into ethnic and national identities. I see this as a form of social creativity extended through time. I examine the role that individual and social trauma plays in the transmission and blocking of memory, and map the signs and symptoms of this, as well as ways of working with the social dissociation that arises from it.

Finally, I look at whether we can develop a type of long-termism as part of a more ecologically located form of memory, in individuals and within social networks. I call this capacity 'imagining the generations', which involves relocating the individual as an expressive part of wider networks that have autopoietic (self-generating) properties (Capra and Luisi 2014).

I finish the book by focusing on how to mobilise and apply these ideas about the nature of multigenerational relationships, as change requires a careful focus and intent that is related to the type and context of memory involved, as the previous example of post-First World War 'British' children shows.

Introduction to the Research and Findings

From autumn 2008 through to spring 2013, I conducted a series of psychosocial individual and group interviews about multigenerational memory. Fifty-six people drawn from a range of professions and different walks of life took part in the process. I started with counsellors and psychotherapists and then widened my reach to others involved in politics, academia, social care and other professions. Via conferences and professional meetings in the UK and abroad I disseminated some of the findings and proposed an initial sensemaking. These included a sequence of talks in the University of the West of England's *Social Science in the City* programme, as well as presentations to various counselling services, typically offered as continuing professional development for counsellors. After a period of data analysis with the help of co-researcher Jane Woodend, I also ran a short series of 'finishing events', sharing my interim findings with specialist focus groups. This brought us up to spring 2018, when the research formally finished. The pattern of research is classically psychosocial in that it is emergent but also relational, with many respondents giving freely of their time and expertise because it was an area they struggled to understand and felt was important.

The issues surrounding the role of multigenerational relationships and memory are, in my view, particularly topical as the difficulty of making a good economic and social settlement between the generations has become more obvious in the West. This current work has cultural limitations: while the participants had some ethnic diversity amongst them, there is no developing world, southern hemisphere or First Nation perspective here, although I draw on First Nation wisdom on the value of very long-term memory when discussing transgenerational processes and when defining what the generations are.

Many of the participants had migration in their ancestry and a substantial ethnic mixture, but mostly this was within a European or American context. Although the data is rich and the findings significant, another piece of research is clearly needed. There is an element of self-selection: this is not a social survey; it is a survey of people who have felt drawn towards the subject. They are all experts in their own way, usually by virtue of personal and professional experience. My task in these chapters is to convey as accurately and evocatively as I can what they have told us about the nature of multigenerational memory as they understand it. I also suggest what might be the consequences of this interest in multigenerational memory. What do we do that is different, given that knowledge? What are the implications socially, psychologically and culturally?

Finally, a word on interpretation. How did I reduce 126,000 spoken words to a few thousand that at the same time both make sense and express the many themes we encountered? This is of course a problem that qualitative researchers take for granted but it may be a puzzle for the outsider. We have relied on developing thematic coding (Braun and Clarke, 2013) during the course of discussion and feedback between ourselves as researchers as well as through the process of offering interim findings for consultation by focus groups. The first phase resulted in 23 thematic codes and the second involved just five through which I express the major themes. While I have no doubt that a different emphasis is possible, it is a reliable summary. Is it exhaustive? Clearly not, but within the material there is significant repetition; this is a sign in qualitative research that new evidence stopped emerging, in our case about two-thirds of the way through the study. We can assume that not only are we at the self-defining cultural limits of the data, but we may also be at the limits of what is currently understood. Only further work would confirm or reject that. Getting this data into the public domain is important for telling whether there is indeed more or much more to come—either more nuanced arguments and perspectives that were simply not present in the minds of our respondents, or which we missed in our research. I hope that our findings, and those that follow ours, will be relevant not just for the social sciences but for anyone interested in how memory and the generations affects our political and personal identities.

How the Research Themes Emerged

The interviews generated over 100 hours' worth of narrative material from people who came forward to talk about their interest in multigenerational memory. The conversations incorporated extended individual interviews as well as group settings. While the groups tended to have a more discursive style and the individual interviews to be more reflective, I found that the themes that emerged were overall common to each.

In our initial search for themes, I found few obvious connecting threads. My impression was that when people told us about their experiences of working with multigenerational memory, these were diverse and strongly related to each individual's story and professional focus. The data appeared to confirm something I already knew—that a lot of people out there were interested in ancestry, memory and remembering!

There were some initial patterns even so. I noticed that family identity drove many people's search for 'the past', from where something that was incomplete pressed or beckoned. Typically, it might be the power of a partly told story or a notion of mystery contained in a puzzle and sometimes a revelation. Occasionally, it would be a sense of being haunted by something.

The commercial business model of ancestry-research mirrored this, marketising the recovery of 'lost identity' by enabling the tracking of family patterns and relationships. The emergence both of shameful stories and hidden aptitudes seemed to be a significant feature and brought added insight and interest to individuals' lives, as if the elements of shame and revelation made the story more momentous and memorable. This echoes the frequent fascination with unattributable talents and unaccountable shame often encountered in the BBC *Who Do You Think You Are?* TV series. I found a notable number of family stories with experiences of migration embedded within them. This tended to be a detail known to the interviewee, but underdeveloped or covered up. It made me wonder if migration, hidden talents and trauma might be linked in some way.

Another theme that emerged from the description of the activities surrounding genealogy seemed to be a kind of extended mourning. Losses that ancestors had experienced and the sense of loss that surfaced through meeting people whom one had never met before, only to have to let go of them again, appeared to challenge and sometimes alter people's sense of who they were now. I call this process '**reconceptualising loss**'.

Harder to describe and to categorise was a range of other stories from our participants that seemed to link the personal to the political, or to speak to the links between who we think we are (identity) and social action (what we do). I identified two meta-themes in my first run-through of the data: one concerning extended mourning, and the other linked to identity and creativity. Within both these themes, the discussion is underpinned by the idea that recovering 'memory' through genealogy and family or cultural storytelling allows for a deeper and more satisfying explanation to emerge of why I am as I am and why I do what I do. These initial signals in our data led me to do a second trawl, focusing on themes of loss, identity and creativity.

Returning to the qualitative richness of the data was like starting again, and some previously hidden patterns allowed me to get a more nuanced picture that formed the basis for the central arguments put forward in this book. I found that when I broke down the narratives about various kinds of losses, what seemed to happen was that loss was reconceptualised, set in a wider context or framed with a new meaning. I counted no fewer than 55 cases of reworking and making sense of loss in this way. Certain losses were referred to as having the power to **haunt**; that is to affect the present in some way. There were 43 instances of this theme. There was a smaller but significant number of references to the past 'not going away at all' (19 instances), which I refer to as evidence of '**unhappy interment**'.

The theme of identity, the problem of how to be creative and make a contribution or the experience of having that frustrated or shut down showed up in 35 instances. This suggested to me that the themes of reconceptualisation of loss had something to do with the emergence of new identity and that the two were connected in some way. I call this '**reconceptualising loss and reaching for creativity**'.

Standing back and looking at the patterns emerging in the research, one can see the great weight of the problem of mourning, the past in the present, and a lesser but nonetheless significant theme of the vicissitudes of the emergence of new identities and obstructions to creativity.

Additionally, I identified a large and significant group of 25 instances of a link between memory and **identity and the natural world**. These represented an important middle ground, neither past nor present, neither social nor individual, but an area of experience in which the presence of memory and recognition or identity was distinguished or explained in some way through images of or allusions to nature. This allows us to think about the links between ecology and memory.

However, reviewing all the transcripts, I noticed that those stories of past experiences were at their richest when supported by a social context. This seemed very important and I started to think of it as a meta-theme. I call this the '**breaking or loss of the social link**'.

I also noticed a difference between the presentations that tried to speak about or establish the facts (a majority) and those that used imagination to tell a story or provide an explanation. I began to describe this as a capacity or desire to imagine the generations to compensate for what was not known. This seemed to be the emergence of a process I now define as inter- and transgenerational mentalisation, a concept that is elaborated further in the findings and discussion (Chapters 7 and 8).

Summary of Findings

By breaking down the narratives about various kinds of losses, I found that what seemed to be happening was that loss was reconceptualised, by being given a wider context or a new meaning. This chapter therefore gives a rich view of the value and significance of extended mourning, the power of the discovery of past hurts and the reopening of old injustices, and the retelling of stories which are conflictual or laden with shame. In attempting to deal with loss, people tell of the conflict of remaining open to emotional experience or shutting down because of the weight of personal and social pain.

The theme of creativity or the experience of having that frustrated or shut down was very significant. However, some experiences tipped over into a different register emotionally, often linked to extreme or disturbing memories and experiences. Many of these accounts are to do with trauma, shame and secrets. They also involve an important crop of transgenerational stories where the trauma was experienced by a people or a group and may have occurred many generations ago.

People often referred to nature to explain an inter- or transgenerational experience, for instance a 'great river' in which truth or hidden history will out, or a drowning representing a cruel or arbitrary ending. Memory and identity were spoken about in a significant group of responses linking memory and identity to the natural world. These represented a liminal area of experience, neither past nor present, neither social nor individual. One of the values of this category is that it ushers in what might be called an ecological perspective from the generations, and a way of thinking about transgenerational processes.

Remembering and Forgetting in Deep Time: A Typology of Memory

This map or typology of memory processes (see Fig. 2.2) is derived from the research findings and is based on the themes of the data analysis that emerged during the research. Organising them in this way suggests a series of relationships and processes by which individual, group and ethnic memory is lost and found over time.

This map helps to show how the following chapters explore the research findings in detail. It introduces the notion of cycles and patterns in multigenerational memory. However, it is important not to confuse the map with the territory. Here I give a simplified fictional illustration

Creative

Reconceptualising loss **Creativity and shutting down**

Reintegration **The natural world, cycles, complexity and imagination** *Disintegration*

Loss/breaking of the social link **Hauntings and unhappy interment**

Destructive

Fig. 2.2 A typology of memory processes

through the fate of one social ethnic group to indicate how the map functions and might be used as a guide or reference.

Members of a multigenerational ethnic group encounter difficulties which force them to move from a homeland, an upheaval that involves both a journey and the acquisition of a new language. The new arrivals have skills and resources but receive a mixed welcome in their new home country. Much is lost during the journey of migration because of the change of place and culture. This affects different generations of the family in different ways, but all must deal with a social diaspora, despite the fact that no lives have been lost and no one has become destitute.

The social link to home, though strained, is not broken. Nothing overtly traumatic has happened although there is much that can and will go wrong and some members of the family may be more aware of these dangers than others. This may set up tensions between people who would benefit from cooperation. One form this tension may take is between an uncritical acceptance of what the new host society can offer and a more critical appraisal that remembers home as much better than 'where we are now'. The father ignores or underplays the racism he is subjected to; the mother longs for home and misses her aunts. The children have become bilingual and have British friends.

This family works at **reconceptualising loss**; older members hold the culture of the old country while younger members acquire new languages and customs more quickly, acting as translators and go-betweens for their parents and the new culture. They may have English friends; this may extend to partners, although this level of mixing/intermarriage occurs further down the generational line if it happens at all. In trying to come to terms with these losses which can be and often are extreme (losing one's country can be like losing a parent or a child or a close friend), these losses are felt differently by the first and second generations, and this divergent response can produce conflicts.

Skills and capacities to work, trade and provide services come to the fore. In this sense a family or group, while dealing with losses, also **reaches for creativity** in order to better survive. Some family members rise to the top of a national guild yet have no formal education. As the skill becomes a profession they are marginalised and although they continue to provide much-needed services, they feel their creativity is

shutting down. How can they deal with this? What kind of work should the next generation do?

While some losses can be dealt with, others start to haunt: the family have a ritual of going to a big park every Sunday. They don't know why they do it. This is the start of a haunting. It wasn't until Grandad was dying that he was able to say it was just like the fields behind his house back home, but it didn't have 'the Donau River'. The start of a **haunting** is a different kind of memory, the ownership of which is not clear but whose power is subtle and far-reaching. Hauntings of place of this kind also connect us to the **natural world** and invite imagination of what might be as well as what was, in this case for the grandfather and his ancestors. This, it turns out, is an important family memory that opens up a liminal space that helps the third generation deal with some of the things that haunt the family.

It turns out that some first-generation family members have experiences they can't come to terms with. For example, the loss of social links may start to bite: an older sister had chosen to stay behind; she felt too old for the journey. She writes, then her letters stop. It's the last they hear of her. There are changes in the wider social environment. The social mood shifts in the host country: being Silesian never was that great; now it's dangerous. There is a war coming, and the men join up in order to show their loyalty to their new country. They find that they cannot enter a standard regiment but must serve in one that has been repurposed for citizens with dubious and less trustworthy heritage. This shameful experience and the accompanying lack of recognition is so painful that it produces a silence and a range of compensatory stories about military service which are partly or wholly fabricated. Some avoid the draft altogether and are disowned by their former friends and siblings who serve. Families, once close, never talk again. On the memory map, **unhappy interment** of feeling is the partner state to haunting. **Active forgetting** helps shove betrayal and disloyalty into cooler emotions of superiority and authenticity and eventually into something that is not remembered at all, yet traces like social shrapnel live on in the relatives who are seen as dangerous and never visited. In this way, a large social network with all the resiliencies of social solidarity becomes smaller and less effective.

In the second generation, the family is in another phase of multi-generational memory. The ordinary but deep losses of migration are complicated by experiences that haunt. Creativity is harder to find, tears are less available, and the need is to harden up and survive. Individuals who have gone and places that were loved start to be forgotten. Origins and culture begin to be disavowed. **The social link is broken or lost** and it may be actively disowned. Children have become adults and have acculturated more than their parents, yet they are in a halfway place between two cultures, neither fully one nor another. There is an absence of pride and an anxiety to get on, but where and with what? The girls and young women of the second generation lighten their dark olive skin to look more northern European. They want English boyfriends; their mothers have mixed feelings about this.

In the third generation, something different is happening. The recognition and association of being Central European have lessened because the family name has been Anglicised. After the war, the father changed his name, having been chased at gunpoint out of an English village where he was working. Work and social life are still difficult, but much in the host country has changed: difference has become less of an obstacle, and it is more possible to make a contribution that is recognised. The third-generation parents want their children to be in touch with both cultures, not to strain to be something they are not. Even a slight version of the accent which got the father into so much trouble can be 'cool', culturally. The parents also want to set some injustices right and join a campaign for full military recognition of their ancestors' contributions. They find their great aunt's grave in their country of origin. They wonder if they could live there again. They are troubled by how they are seen by others in their country of origin—superior, impossibly successful or traitors. They feel like strangers even though the place feels hauntingly familiar. Now something can shift because the things that haunted have less power and the struggle for survival has eased. Some unhappily interred memories can settle down. The rage and humiliation at a lack of recognition for sacrifices and service have diminished. The ghostly guilt about leaving an ancestor behind has been healed with tears of loss for someone they never knew, as a new headstone is laid next to a big river under a brighter sun.

The social link that was severed by migration has been partly restored, and a new identity has been won, even if it is hard to say what that new identity is. Perhaps this is alleviated by the part these individuals have played in bringing about the social change that gives them a more secure sense of their place in their new society. They know that their social ideas and vivaciousness are recognised, valued and even envied. But it is a one-sided recognition. On the map of memory, they might be moving from

broken social links to **reconceptualising loss** (again) and finding new forms of **creativity**.

Then another shock hits the family as they are caught up in Brexit. Again, they feel they are not wanted by their host country, and some family members face uncertainty. Yet a capacity to fight and face state racism doesn't take them back to square one. They recognise that the society they are living in has lost its way and that they are unwitting victims of a misinformed social policy. They recognise the archaic colonialism coming to the fore in a society that is searching for a new direction. In short, they are better equipped to deal with the ethnic racism than their ancestors were, yet the transgenerational issue of being deeply European returns to haunt both migrant and host nation. At another level, it is as if nothing has changed since this family's ancestors stepped off a boat in Harwich. Hauntings like this recur; they just take different forms.

An **intergenerational** cycle of memory has been completed. Through three generations and with tenacity and resilience, the family has gone through the creative and destructive phases of the whole cycle. It has a new basis for confronting the **transgenerational** conflicts that were there from the beginning and that need addressing again and again. However, the group to which the family belongs has hybridised and, in some ways, has become hidden even to itself. Much of the old identity has been forgotten. But some things remain. There is an abiding feeling about unfairness and injustice. Some of the younger family members identify with some of their black friends' experiences of dislocation and slavery yet can't quite find their voice in solidarity lest it upset the still-fragile sense of acceptance that was such a challenge to acquire by preceding generations. In short, they feel guilty that they were able to change enough to no longer be seen as 'other' and therefore a threat. They have not yet thought fully about the power of white-on-white racism; it still haunts them. Their hard-won identity won't stand still; there are new strains and challenges to deal with as the fourth generation grows to young millennial adulthood. In social identity terms, they are finely tuned to make **destructive** or **creative** contributions to the current political conflicts. Will they be skilful oppressors, siding with the adopted nation state, or outspoken risk-takers and companions to other more recent migrants in upholding civil rights and social change? While this choice is there for any and every citizen, they are peculiarly charged ancestrally to respond.

In the following chapters, I will illustrate in more detail how deeply textured these journeys in memory can be and how many different outcomes are possible, but first I explore the existing literature on multigenerational memory.

References

Abraham, N. and Torok, M. (1994) *The Shell and the Kernel*. Translated from the French by Nicolas T. Rand. Chicago: University of Chicago Press.

Atkinson, J. (2002) *Trauma Trails, Recreating Song Lines: The Transgenerational Effects of Trauma in Indigenous Australia*. North Melbourne: Spinifex Press.

Bartlett, S. and Wong, M.L. (2020) Defining lyfe in the universe: From three privileged functions to four pillars. *Life* [online]. 10 (4), p. 42 [Accessed 16 September 2020].

Bourne, J.K., Jr., Diouf, S. and Brasted, C. (2020) America's last slave ship stole them from home. It couldn't steal their identities. *National Geographic* [online]. 16 January. Available from: https://www.nationalgeographic.com/magazine/2020/02/clotilda-americas-last-slave-ship-stole-them-from-home-it-couldnt-steal-their-identities-feature/ [Accessed 13 September 2020].

Braun, V. and Clark, V. (2013) *Successful Qualitative Research: A Practical Guide for Beginners*. London: Sage.

Capra, F. (1997) *The Web of Life: A New Synthesis of Mind and Matter*. London: Flamingo.

Capra, F. and Luisi, P.L. (2014) *The Systems View of Life: A Unifying Vision*. Cambridge: Cambridge University Press.

Colman, F.J. (2005) Affect. In: Parr, A. (Ed.) *The Deleuze Dictionary*. Edinburgh: Edinburgh University Press, pp. 11–12.

Dallos, R (2006) *Attachment Narrative Therapy Integrating Narrative, Systemic and Attachment Therapies*. Berkshire: Open University Press.

Felitti, V.J., Anda, R.F., Nordenberg, D., Edwards, V., Koss, M.P. and Marks, J.S. (1998) Relationship of childhood abuse and household dysfunction to many of the leading causes of death in adults: The Adverse Childhood Experience (ACE) Study. *American Journal of Preventive Medicine*. 14 (4), pp. 245–258.

Gapp, K., et al. (2014) Implication of Sperm RNAs in Transgenerational Inheritance of the Effects of Early Trauma in Mice. *Nature Neuroscience* [online]. 17 (5), pp. 667–669 [Accessed 22 September 2019].

Gerhardt, S. (2004) *Why Love Matters: How Affection Shapes a Baby's Brain.* East Sussex: Routledge.

Keys, D. (2015) Britain's Atlantis: Scientific study beneath North Sea could revolutionise how we see the past. *The Independent* [online]. 1 September. Available from: https://www.independent.co.uk/news/science/archaeology/britains-atlantis-scientific-study-beneath-north-sea-could-revolutionise-how-we-see-the-past-10480279.html [Accessed 12 September 2020].

Lewin, K. (1997) *Resolving Social Conflicts and Field Theory in Social Science.* Washington: American Psychological Association.

Li, S., Callaghan, B.L. and Richardson, R. (2014) Infantile amnesia: Forgotten but not gone. *Learning and Memory* 21(3), pp. 135–139.

Marshall, E.A. (2004) *Institute for Integrative Science and Health.* Available from: http://www.integrativescience.ca/Principles/TwoEyedSeeing/ [Accessed 12 September 2020].

Massumi, B. (2002) *Parables for the Virtual: Movement, Affect, Sensation.* Durham and London: Duke University Press.

Maturana, H.R and Varela, F.J. (1992) *The Tree of Knowledge: The Biological Roots of Human Understanding.* Boston: Shambhala Publications.

Nunn, P. (2018) *The Edge of Memory: Ancient Stories, Oral Tradition and the Post-Glacial World.* London: Bloomsbury Sigma.

Outerbridge, J. (2018) What they thought then and how they think now: A qualitative exploration of the lived experience of adult adoptees of closed childhood adoptions and their significant relationships. PhD, University of the West of England.

Peltier, C. (2018) An application of two-eyed seeing: Indigenous research methods with participatory action research. *International Journal of Qualitative Methods* [online]. 17 (1) [Accessed 11 September 2020].

Ramsay, C. (1997) The need to feed. In: Hayden, T. (Ed.) *Irish Hunger: Personal Reflections on the Legacy of the Famine.* Dublin: Wolfhound Press, pp. 137–142.

Rand, N. (1994) Back cover. In: Abraham, N. and Torok, M. (Eds.) *The Shell and the Kernel.* Chicago: University of Chicago Press, back cover.

Shevlin, M. and McGuigan, K. (2003) The long-term psychological impact of Bloody Sunday on families of the victims as measured by the Revised Impact of Event Scale. *British Journal of Clinical Psychology* [online]. 42 (4), pp. 427–432 [Accessed 22 September 2019].

Solms, M. (2015) *The Feeling Brain Selected Papers on Neuropsychoanalysis*. London: Karnac.

Watt, H. (2017) 'Some days I think I was molested, others I'm not sure': Inside a case of repressed memory. *The Guardian* [online]. 23 September. Available from: https://www.theguardian.com/science/2017/sep/23/inside-case-of-repressed-memory-nicole-kluemper [Accessed 15 September 2020].

Williams, N. (2015) Anglo-German displacement and diaspora in the early twentieth century: An intergenerational haunting. In: O'Loughlin, M. (Ed.) *The Ethics of Remembering and the Consequences of Forgetting: Essays on Trauma, History and Memory*. Lanham: Rowan & Littlefield, pp. 125–142.

Yehuda, R., Daskalakis, N.P., Bierer, L.M., Bader, H.N., Klengel, T., Holsboer, F. and Binder, E.B. (2016) Holocaust exposure induced intergenerational effects on Fkbp5 methylation. *Biological Psychiatry* [online]. 80 (5), pp. 372–380 [Accessed 22 September 2019].

Zalme, A.M. (2017) *Kurdish Generational Diasporic Identities, Perceptions of 'Home' and 'Sense of Belonging' within Families Among Iraqi Kurds in the UK*. PhD, University of the West of England.

Zimmer, C. (2018) The famine ended 70 years ago, but Dutch genes still bear scars. *The New York Times* [online]. 31 January, p. 5. Available from: https://www.nytimes.com/2018/01/31/science/dutch-famine-genes.html [Accessed 12 September 2020].

3

Mapping the Generations: Survey of the Literature on Multigenerational Memory

Multigenerational Transmission

In much of the contemporary literature, the terms 'intergenerational' and 'transgenerational' have been used interchangeably to refer both to interactions and relationships between living generations of different ages and to wider physiological, psychological, political and cultural affects across past, present and future generations. A degree of ambiguity in the employment of these terms is apparent, for example, where the issue of 'intergenerational equity' might also be classed as 'transgenerational equity' in a discussion about the unequal consumption of finite natural resources by past and present generations to the detriment of future generations (Hartwick, 1977; Solow, 1986). Despite the scope for ambiguity, there are some broadly discernible differences in usage, and Atkinson (2002), considering the traumatic experiences of Aboriginal communities in Australia, provides useful definitions: intergenerational trauma is passed down directly from one generation to the next; transgenerational trauma is transmitted across a number of generations.

It seems that the notion of 'intergenerational transmission' in disciplines such as economics, psychology, sociology and the biological sciences is accepted, and the connections empirically demonstrated, lending weight to the validity of psychosocial and psychocultural studies of inter- and transgenerational effects and affects. Scholarly interest in multigenerational effects and relationships is expressed in a wide diversity of disciplines and applications.

Examples of this academic interest in the 'intergenerational' and 'transgenerational' are found in disciplines and sub-disciplines encompassing molecular and evolutionary biology (Agrawal et al., 1999; Anway et al., 2005; Champagne, 2008) including endocrinology and epigenetics; economics (Hartwick, 1977; Björklund and Jäntti, 1997; Solon, 2002; Dunn and Holtz-Eakin, 2000) including health economics (Williams, 1997); educational and family-based sociology (Amato, 1996; Bengtson and Roberts, 1991; Ehrensaft et al., 2003; Crosnoe et al., 2016) including a sociological 'confrontation' with the Holocaust (Kaufman, 2007); developmental psychology (Bretherton, 1990; Kaitz et al., 2009); and clinical psychology (Shamtoub, 2013).

Adding the qualifier of 'transmission', 'memory' or 'trauma' to these core search terms provides material more relevant to multigenerational memory which appears in interdisciplinary psychoanalytic and cultural studies including representations of traumatic historical events in literature (Goertz, 1998; Crownshaw, 2004), photography (Hirsch, 1999, 2008; Brookfield et al., 2008) and cinema (Portuges, 2003; Lazzara, 2009; Berghahn, 2006).

The term 'intergenerational transmission' is also regularly used in the literature of sociology, economics and psychology with reference to the transmission of economic opportunity (Black et al., 2005), literacy (Bus et al., 2016) and other forms of human capital (Currie and Moretti, 2003) as well as the intergenerational effects of experiences of divorce (Amato, 1996), aggression in marriage (Kalmuss, 1984) and family disruption (McLanahan and Bumpass, 1988).

A Surprise in Genetics

The fashion for exploring family ancestry and genealogy which appears to be an extension of identity politics means that the search term 'ancestry' brings up a wealth of research in molecular biology, with attention focused on uncovering and mapping the taxonomy of DNA, proteins and amino acids (Doolittle, 1981; Peterson and Eernisse, 2001) in animal and plant studies.

In the late 1990s and into the 2000s, the use of these molecular-level technologies seems to have given momentum to research efforts to trace genetic links, or 'genome-wide associations' with human health conditions, for example, in cancer research, using a unique data set of men of Japanese ancestry in Hawaii (Nomura et al., 1985; Severson et al., 1989), diabetes research (Kooner et al., 2011; Mahajan et al., 2014), obesity (Waterland et al., 2008) and autism (Morrow et al., 2008). This genomic research seems to have identified 'ancestry informative marker sets' (Rosenberg et al., 2003; Sykes, 2010) which have been applied to 'population stratification' (Alexander et al., 2009), and efforts to determine (or estimate) the continental origins of human populations. Particular studies have been concerned with American (Kosoy et al., 2009) and Brazilian populations (Alves-Silva et al., 2000), making genetic associations within and between ethnically diverse peoples and 'admixture' populations, and tracing African and native American ancestry (Harding et al., 1997). More recent studies have been concerned with tracing prehistoric human origins (Sankararaman et al., 2014), including addressing the 'contentious' origins of Native American populations (Raghavan et al., 2013). Further molecular/genomic research has sought to discover, and dispute, linkages with psychiatric states (Weber-Stadlbauer et al., 2017; Sanders et al., 2008), all of which raises important questions about the ethical and political implications of such technologies.

Biological scientists have become increasingly interested in transgenerational epigenetic effects since the sequencing of the human genome and continue to investigate the factors that may affect transgenerational transmission of particular diseases. A lot of the work in biological sciences at molecular level and evolutionary scale has concentrated on the transgenerational epigenetic effects of exposure to stress, trauma, famine, radiation and other toxins. Agrawal et al. (1999) were the first to recognise transgenerational effects in plants and animals, noting the development of defensive morphologies in prey animals experimentally exposed to predator stress. This links to the next set of studies about inherited PTSD, which may be a way for one generation that has been threatened with extinction to communicate to the next what that danger is.

Rachel Yehuda et al. (2005, 2008, 2016) and Yehuda and Bierer (2007) stands out from this tranche of literature in her study of the descendants of Holocaust survivors and the connection between the intergenerational biological and molecular effects of exposure to Post-Traumatic Stress Disorder and the intergenerational transmission of trauma. As such, her work might represent a kind of 'missing link' between the empirical biological canon of inter- and transgenerational research and the psychosocial–cultural research on intergenerational memory and transmission of trauma. In a similar vein, the epigenetic effects of the Rwandan genocide have been addressed by Perroud et al. (2014) and biologists Heard and Martienssen (2014) also acknowledge that emotions may be transmitted intergenerationally.

This burgeoning field has some implications for transmission that may underpin the more familiar process of intergenerational memory in families (i.e. a social–cultural process). Yehuda's assertion of a link between the children of Holocaust survivors and the prevalence of PTSD in following generations can be more clearly demonstrated in Mansuy's work (Gapp et al., 2014) on the sense of smell in mice which I discussed in Chapter 2.

While it is unclear how applicable animal studies are to humans, these findings usher in the field of epigenetics as an important underpinning for social memory and the relationships between the generations. They also suggest that therapeutic and social interventions that recognise epigenetic effects may become important in the future and could indicate where an epigenetically transmitted trauma is recognised or is likely to have occurred.

Social Transmission of Trauma: The Shoah and the Contribution of Holocaust Studies

The separate canon of social science literature that addresses the transmission of trauma or uses the notion of 'post-memory' has primarily focused on experiences and memories of the Holocaust/Shoah. Felsen (1998), writing in the *International Handbook of Multigenerational Legacies*, which features other relevant chapters (Auerhahn and Laub, 1998), notes the 'first article' on transmission of Holocaust trauma by Rakoff et al. (1966) and the wealth of literature on this topic that has followed from different perspectives. For example, Fonagy (1999) provides a particularly psychoanalytic case study linking adolescent obsessive-compulsive disorder with Holocaust trauma, while Tschuggnall and Welzer (2002) examine the work of narratives in Holocaust-related memory work.

Other work linking memory and transmission of trauma—incidences of genocide, mass violence, atrocities, extreme oppression and PTSD—are explored in studies of Aboriginal Australian communities (Atkinson, 2001, 2002; Atkinson et al., 2014); human rights violations in Indonesia (McGregor, 2013); Northern Ireland's Bloody Sunday (Shevlin and McGuigan, 2003); Vietnam war and combat experiences (Harkness, 1993; Davidson and Mellor, 2001; Pearrow and Cosgrove, 2009); the experience of Chilean activists (Becker and Díaz, 1998); the Armenian massacres (Karenian et al., 2011); torture victims (Daud et al., 2005); and wartime internment (Nagata and Cheng, 2003).

Colonialism and Migration

Links to the violence of colonialism are made by Marques et al. (1997), with reference to Portuguese experience; they use notions of social sharing and an 'emotional climate' (see also Pennebaker et al., 1997). Colonialism is also implicated in the transmission of trauma within Canadian Aboriginal communities, and in the historic aftermath or post-memory of the Boer War as reviewed by Stanley (Stanley and Dampier, 2005; Stanley and Stanley, 2006). This atrocity-specific literature is often fragmented in disciplinary silos and journals concerned with specific area studies. The geographic focus is intriguingly expanded by an unusual work on *Wounded Cities* (Till, 2012) which links memory work with the ethics of care. As a counterweight to such fragmentation, Schwab (2010) provides a comprehensive account of the 'haunting' legacies of atrocities throughout history, including slavery, forced migration and colonialism. Other examples of work that have reversed the silo effect are those that have used diverse case studies under a thematic heading and with linking essays, for instance O'Loughlin and Charles (2015), O'Loughlin and Barbre (2015), Hamburger (2018), and Hopper and Weinberg (2016).

Although the list of historic and contemporary atrocities above seems wide-ranging, more attention needs to be paid to the absences and gaps: where are the accounts of other traumatically marginalised communities? What of the less-literate indigenous peoples in South America and Oceania, or the Roma of Europe or the Myanmar Rohingya, for example? These gaps are more than just lacunae in the literature; they can be signs of currently developing trauma themselves. The gaps in literature around any diaspora or mass migration become hauntings in time, if the actual events sink below the surface and cease to be witnessed. This is how transgenerational trauma starts. I suggest this happens when it ceases to be inscribed in culture. This is distinct from intergenerational inscription processes which run from parent to child and across communities.

The subject of migration is generally less well addressed, although Apprey (1993) examines the African-American experience and Phipps and Degges-White (2014) explore the experience of young Latin American immigrants. Ali Zalme (2017) gives a very full discussion of the emergence of intergenerational dynamics in his study of Kurdish generational diasporic identities.

The effects of gender on transmission are also less than prominent but are noted in studies of intergenerational transfers of human capital in the modern-day slavery literature (Brewster, 2019). The examination of gender as a factor in trauma transmission has rarely been addressed, with Vogel (1994) and Adelman (1995) being two exceptions.

Healing Practices

Therapeutic and healing processes are discussed by Atkinson (2002), Ralph et al. (2006), Connolly (2011) and Schulberg (1997), the latter writing on the use of art and music in healing, and with reference to the aetiology of transgenerational trauma and resilience by Goodman (Goodman and West-Olatunji, 2008; Goodman, 2013) who explores the experience of counsellors and survivors of Hurricane Katrina. Kleinot (2011) looks at the concept of forgiveness in group analytic processes with Israeli and Palestinian families, as does Adonis (2008), in conjunction with humiliation in post-apartheid South Africa. The complex process of forgiveness in relation to trauma is written about by Muller (2010) in *Trauma and the Avoidant Client*. There is a developing area of literature that involves voicing First Nation peoples' approach to healing and memory. There is a very important development that suggests a model of collaboration between Western science and social science-based research and indigenous methods. The concept of 'two-eyed' research is an example (Peltier, 2018).

Remembering and Forgetting

Regarding memory work and post-memory, Beiner (2008, p. 107) has claimed or anticipated a 'memory boom' and provides a useful commentary on the subject. Post-memory denotes a precarity of 'the generation after experience' where, without direct access to experience x or trauma y, the current generation is vulnerable to having its own stories displaced by those of its ancestors. The processes of forgetting or losing and gaining memory are also discussed (p. 110). The focus on social and cultural amnesia is taken up in a psychodynamic and family systems-based way in this research.

Beiner (2014) also includes a salient discussion of what he calls 'pre-memory'—when memory is shaped by the memory of previous social or cultural events. This is close to the concept of transgenerational memory developed in this book. His concept of vernacular historiography is also a relative of another central idea that comes from this research—that of intergenerational storytelling.

Paul Connerton (1989) discusses the importance of the body in social memory. He describes the ways in which social memory is formed by performance and ritual. This links to some of the research findings that suggest that beyond storytelling, an affective level of memory exists that is implicit and lives in social networks and physical culture rather than individual minds.

While 'intergenerational memory' is most often used in connection with the transmission of trauma, it has also been used to refer to the transmission of knowledge within organisations (Harvey, 2012). Individuals feel themselves to be professionally disabled by the break-up of organisational memory during restructuring. David Armstrong's 'Making present' chapter, in his book *The Organisation in Mind* (2005), documents employees remembering how an organisation can function even if current management no longer knows. Abraham and Torok (1994, p. 253) talk about how the falling out between Freud and Ferenczi affected not only them but a whole generation of analysts. These hidden civil wars within organisations can have significant outcomes in future generations when old battle lines keep re-emerging.

Surveying the literature on post-memory, the number of finds is low compared to other search terms. Hirsch (1997, 2008) and Bataille (1995) appear to be the most cited authors. Hirsch (2008) points out the contradictions of post-memory in regard to elements of continuity and rupture between generations in so far as the younger generation cannot literally share the same experience or memory of trauma. Hirsch also brings attention to two forms or constituents of post-memory: communicative memory, mediated through embodied practices within families and groups, and the culturally institutionalised memory mediated through symbolic systems. This further echoes elements of the distinction I make between inter/transgenerational memory. Sosa (2012, p. 221), writing on theatrical portrayals of the Argentinian dictatorship, claims to challenge Hirsch's notion of post-memory by arguing that 'traumatic pasts are also attires that can be adopted in the context of spectatorship'. This also links to Volkan's (1998) idea of 'chosen trauma', and to Benedict

Anderson's (1983) concept of 'imagined communities' in both of which memory has performative aspects.

In a critique of Hirsch's suggestion that it may not be an either/or scenario between the memory of a prior generation and that of current younger generations, Frosh (2019, p. 13) questions whether 'memory is not such a private thing after all, but is always socially mediated, a cultural affair, or maybe the affective immanence of "memories" that belong to other people is one common experience that deserves the appellation "memory" because it is felt as such it is owned by the subject as if it were her or his'. This points towards the role of affect in memory and memory-like experience and the ways in which we are all vulnerable to identifying with and to some extent internalising experiences which are not our own. Trauma may complicate this, but it is a different process in memory, which I take up later in this chapter.

Complementing the work of Hirsch (2008) and Bataille (1995), Atkinson's research (2001, 2002) on the enduring affects of colonisation and the subjugation of Aboriginal communities in Australia not only provides some clear definitions of terms but spells out, by drawing on Baker (1993), the three-fold and interacting modes of the abuse of power: overt physical violence, covert structural (bureaucratic) violence and 'psycho-social domination' (Baker, 1993, p. 59). She also illuminates what might be considered an indigenous form of psychosocial methodology that is *Dadirri*, which she characterises as both 'listening from the heart' and 'listening to and observing the self as well as, and in relationship with, others' (1993, p. 19). This draws attention to the vital ways in which indigenous peoples who have survived and resisted domination now have the potential to offer cultural leadership. This is echoed in Canadian work with First Nation peoples that describes a 'two-eyed' approach to research involving Western social science methods and traditional medicine wheel practices (Marsh et al. 2015).

Sociology, Memory and the Generations

The length of time a generation might last raise the issue of whether it helps to have a numerical working definition of what a generation is—15 years, 30 years, etc.—defined by biological productivity or professional productivity. This turned out to be important in analysing the data in this research as some participants referred to biological generations while others to professional or work generations. This raises the question of whether the generations are social forces in the same way that social class or migration are and consequently whether there is a sociology of knowledge based on intergenerational relationships. I suggest that if the sociology of knowledge of the generations includes memory, then the tangible generational cycles get longer, towards the three–four generational pattern of 60–120 years. In my own family, I have 'memory' of passed-down recipes for sauerkraut which has come down four generations. By contrast, the last German speaker in my family was two generations ago.

Albert Marshall's (2004) 'Two-Eyed Seeing' or *Etuaptmumk* is an approach to conducting research with indigenous peoples in a mutually respectful way, integrating Western research methods with indigenous knowledge. The concept of time as linked to the generations differs between cultures. One generation for Mi'kmaw people spans 120 years and incorporates seven levels of a family tree, three of which are not yet born. The presence of unborn generations strongly underlines the future focus and the idea of extended social responsibility forward and back in time. Actions are planned with their consequences considered for future generations, with an eye to how they would have been considered by preceding generations. The presence of the three ancestor generations suggests an extended sense of self where individuals occupy only a present moment. The second indigenous eye also connects to the idea of trance, and mediumistic communication, which I take up in Chapters 7 and 8.

Zygmunt Bauman (2000) has established some important social transgenerational accounts of modernity, and while there isn't the scope here to go into his whole sociological canon concerning modernity and its fate, his work on the Lisbon earthquake of 1755 is a very good example of a pivotal inter- and transgenerational event that may have shifted a whole culture towards a mistrust of nature and in favour of its mastery. He maps out the consequences on Enlightenment thought for this seventeenth-century Atlantic seaboard earthquake and tsunami. For Bauman, the whole project of the Enlightenment ignited as a result of this event, because Europeans were terrified of living in a world of inexplicable perils: 'It kicks off the process of secularisation, what Habermas calls the project of modernity. The idea was to tame nature and make it subject to intentional action, hoping that if everything is planned and designed the age of catastrophe will come to an end' (Jeffries, 2005).

However, it is Bauman's interest in utopian/dystopian thinking that is central here. In our struggle to cope with interconnectedness (indeed our current desire to disavow it), we demonise the past and the future. This has implications for the way we regard the generations, dissuading us from thinking about them, and pathologically individualising our experiences. The inability to recognise lost nations, antecedents or alternatives to our own is seen by Norman Davies (2011) as being premised on the Enlightenment arrogance of writers like Voltaire who saw the emergence of individual reason as civilised modernity's *raison d'être*.

The theme of the individual and collective viewpoints for thinking about the generations is taken up by Karl Mannheim (1952). His acute description of generational dynamics as operating in a structural manner similar or equal to social class in importance reminds us of the ever-present transgenerational influence of social forces working through the generations. He also points out that each generation has its own unique character that needs careful documenting and description. It is partly in the interaction of the world view and orientation of succeeding and preceding generations that the sociology of knowledge emerges. In this sense, the generations are an extension of Marx's dictum (1997, preface) that 'Mankind thus inevitably sets itself only such tasks as it is able to solve'. The generations are part of the productive process, some being more creative or revolutionary, others more consolidatory, and yet others conservative, caught up in ideas of backward-looking restoration. However, there is an underlying idea of alienation from creativity that work and the generations represent. In short, from the point of view of the sociology of knowledge, the acknowledgement of the power of multi-generational relationships is as profound as is the acknowledgement of class relationships. Our existential and cognitive horizons are determined by the relationship between generations as they emerge and change over time. This relationship can be highly conflictual, or at other times more collaborative.

The work of Bristow (2016) develops Manheim's ideas further to define more fully what a generation is and what it means to think about relationships between generations. She describes the 'emergence and operation of generational consciousness during times of accelerated social change' (2016, p. 3) and suggests that in order to understand how intergenerational knowledge is transmitted, it must be placed in a social context and in relation to historical events. Her focus on the social tensions and anxieties that build up between the generations is 'to do with the way society's cultural heritage is transmitted to the younger generations, and the particular difficulties that arise from anxieties about norms, values and knowledge of the past' (ibid., p. 13). She tracks this intergenerational dance as weaving between formal education and informal socialisation and emphasises the tension between what Manheim describes as an 'implicit' process of generational renewal and more formal established knowledge. Thus, the relations between the generations are political and in our current era deeply tied up with identity politics.

Continuing the Weberian theme and paralleling Bauman's ideas, C. Wright Mills (2000/1959) suggests that our post-Enlightenment condition to individualise experiences which are in fact social in origin means that we are prone to suffer what we can't imagine. There are numerous experiences that are intergenerational that we have tried to squash inside individual skins. We can suffer another's depression as profoundly as our own. We can easily internalise failures in relationships without knowing the social forces we may be up against. It's the failure of our sociological imagination that traps us in the purely personal or inside the view of our own generation. The application of the idea of cultivating the sociological imagination is vital when thinking about the generations. It is related to but not the same as the psychoanalytic idea of mentalisation that has emerged from attachment theory.

Murray's (2018) work on changes in parenting styles between the generations gives some insight into attachment patterns across time particularly in relation to the role of older siblings as parents. I take up the issue of attachment dynamics and intergenerational memory in Chapter 7.

Kingstone and Broughton (2019) has further conceptualised what a generation is and what part of our current identity it forms. She suggests that the idea of generational identity is tied up with the English Romantic movement and so has as its origin early Victorian thinking and culture. This leads to the suggestion that the generations must in some sense be self-conscious to move beyond being a cohort. She suggests that the generations must have powerful shared experiences to mark them out as a focus for identity. This may be associated with a literature and storytelling expressing the values and identity within that generation.

Karl Manheim's colleague Norbert Elias was influential in the British Group Analytic Movement and promoted the concept of there being a social unconscious. Elias's idea of developing a sensibility of the long term and Manheim's notion about the generations share what Weber would have called an elective affinity. Perhaps the generations are also intellectual and cultural groups in time, carrying the identity and values of their members. I think it likely that we are in the presence of one here; this group of sociologists are a generational/genealogical group, and while it would be diversion here to explore this fully, many of them knew each other in the 1930s. One could ask what was passed on from the Weber brothers to Mannheim and Elias. Ideas are the most obvious currency but more specifically it is the unusual and distinctive holding of a certain capacity to think socially. The idea of Weber's 'verstehen', a form of social understanding and empathy, is central (Tucker, 1965) and an example of a generational signature. I will return to social empathy in Chapter 8.

What follows are views more influenced by psychoanalysis, particularly the intergenerational view of civilisation as expounded by Freud. I present this in a way that is psychosocial, adopting, as Barry Richards (2019, p. 171) suggests, a kind of 'binocular vision, such that some insights from both psychology and the social sciences are held in mind at the same time'. This is particularly important in dealing with the concept of the social unconscious.

The Social Unconscious

Ideas concerning the social unconscious have developed alongside the clinical practice of group analysis in the UK. It has been one of the most productive sites, both clinically and intellectually, for studying the social unconscious.

Tubert-Oklander and Reyna (2014) suggests that the 'social unconscious' denotes two different but interconnected processes. The social context and processes have an impact on and a representation in the unconscious of individuals, and they constitute a motivational force, which is at least as powerful as instinctual drives. Furthermore, there are unconscious dynamics of social processes, which should then be conceived as mental in nature, even if they have no definite subject.

In an extended discussion of the social unconscious, Weinberg (2007, p. 310) offers the following:

> Correspondingly, members of social groups could be said to unconsciously re-live and re-enact in the present emotions related to past events of their society. When regressive conditions occur (such as in times of war or other social dangers) these unconscious fantasies and anxieties might impact the behaviour of society-at-large. It is because phylogenetically and ontogenetically the Social Unconscious precedes the individual consciousness, that a shared unconscious can and does develop among total strangers.

Earl Hopper is perhaps the most prolific champion of the theory of the social unconscious and in 2003 published a book of his selected papers, as well as a three-volume work with Weinberg. However, Kasakoff (1974), Moscovici (1981), Bargh (1997, 2013) and Gigerenzer (2007) are the most frequently cited authors. Brown (2016) holds that the social unconscious is rooted in Foulkes's 1948 *Introduction to Group Analytic Psychotherapy* which brings an important recognition of 'society in psychoanalysis' (Foulkes, 1975, p. 11). Dalal (2001, p. 5) has developed a post-Foulkesian perspective that expands on the social theme and what he calls the 'Radical Foulkes' where the distinction between individual and group is moved beyond. He proposes that the id is deeply acculturated and thus proposes that there isn't a personal and a social unconscious, but one underlying process. These positions were put forward in a special edition of *Group Analysis* published in 2001. As the concept of the social unconscious became increasingly important in group analysis literature, Weinberg (2007) attempted to clarify some misunderstandings and misconceptions about it. Even-tzur (2016) brings the study of transgenerational effects and the idea of post-memory and social unconscious full circle by tackling the paradox of Israeli attempts to silence the memory of the Palestinian Nakba minority.

Matrices, Memory and Attachment

The idea of matrices is used in both Group Analytic and Group Relations (Tavistock) thinking. Foulkes makes the distinction between foundation matrices which concern formative social influences, and dynamic matrices which form in the context of real-time attempts to work with issues and problems in groups (Foulkes 1975, p. 65). These dynamic matrices can be associated with processes of attachment (Montgomery 2002). Bion (1961, p. 8) refers to the 'Sphinx' in his characterisation of the intellectual problems and knowledge appropriate to group work, and to Oedipus where pairing in group work or the dyadic relationship in analysis is concerned. Julian Manley (2018, pp. 12–13) explains how Gordon Lawrence's innovation of social dreaming rested on a working distinction between group dynamics and matrices. The matrix is a mystical entity that exists beyond individuals or groups, but which emerges, according to Susan Long and Manley (2019, p. 19) via mental networks that build up in communities of practitioners who have activated and work with their 'associative unconscious'. In this situation, a shift from the individual to the social and interacting community is described. This does not account for memory across longer spans of time but represents an important contribution to thinking about social memory and how it might work. It is, however, clear that if the idea of the social unconscious is valid and useful, then multigenerational memory will be a key feature of it.

The Individual Psychoanalytic Contributions

Discontent Civilisation

Freud, at his end-of-life thinking, was grappling again with the fraught and complex relationship between individual psychoanalytic work and group psychology. He felt there was little gain in the concept of a collective unconscious; for him the unconscious was anyway collective, each individual having universal collective traces and being a unique expression of a phylogeny of drives and defences. By implication, the longer-term cycles of repetition between the generations in history are based on universal human tendencies and conflicts.

For Freud, civilisation's discontents are re-enacted in each generation in an intrapsychic drama of development. Freud's choice of the Oedipus myth to name an aspect of this complex developmental process is significant here, because despite recognition of and atonement for his guilt of patricide, Oedipus plays a significant part in his children's going to war with each other (Sophocles, 497BC, Watling, 1973). In the area of Greek myth, Dorothy Willner (1982) gives an important feminist critique in which Antigone breaks the phallic mould of authority. This is taken up by De Sanctis (2012) and Cavanagh (2017). Generational conflict may have a five-generation antecedent: Lévi-Strauss traces back Oedipus's problems to his great-great-grandfather, documented in Willner (1982, p. 59). Would a matriarchy in its radical equality break or modify the Oedipal pattern of repetition? Would there be less intergenerational trauma? It's a theme that D. H. Lawrence (1989) explored in The Rainbow, and in his later writings on the Etruscans. Perhaps for Freud it is religion (Freud, 2001) that is the ultimate transgenerational expression of suffering in that it represents the repetition of unresolved trauma foisted by the primal horde of sons on the father.

Phantoms and Generation Hoppers

From Freud onwards, clinicians of the unconscious have made commentary on the social and the multigenerational. The nature of trauma has been a contested subject within psychoanalysis, with the relationship between Freud and Ferenczi (Haynal, 2002) caught up in that debate. A working distinction between the neuroses of war and peace holds something of that tension. While childhood psychological developments are inherently traumatic, like the shift from a two-person to a three-person perspective—the arena of Oedipal dynamics—any impingement powerful enough to break the continuity of the ego is traumatic. Here war trauma and abuse, two of Ferenczi's key interests, tended to run against Freud's view that it was the intrapsychic realm of trauma that should concern us. Freud's views on this changed towards the end of his life, probably as a result of experiencing the gathering wave of human destructiveness around him (Davoine and Gaudillière, 2004, p. 234). There wasn't time enough for him to consider what it is that is internalised from one traumatised generation to another.

This task fell to two of Ferenczi's analysands, Abraham and Torok (1994), who proposed a new process about longer-term and possibly transgenerational transmission that revolved around the idea of the appearance of a foreign presence in the psyche which they refer to as a 'phantom'. The phantom is an incoherent introject from a parent or significant other. It is without developed symbolic content and is essentially unassimilable. It acts across one or several generations, hopping from individual to individual but robbing more and more psychic energy from each generational host. The resultant states of mind are persecutory. This eventually creates potential for psychotic disturbance. There is a further description of the conditions that sustain the phantom: that of a crypt as a container of some kind. The causes of such haunting generational entities are secrets, the inter- and transgenerational consequence of silences. These events, if they persist, lead to a self living outside of time. The solution is the therapist who knows about cryptology and can read its mute signs. Here a collective psychology comprising several generations is present in each individual and the therapist must listen for the voices of one generation in the unconscious of another. There is an interesting potential link to epigenetics where states of arousal from a previous generation may be switching genes on and off in the next.

At this level of transmission, Abraham and Torok (1994) claim that the unspoken familial and social history are present in each individual in this phantom form. They could be said to be calling for a psychoanalytic cult of the ancestors where the dead might finally be recognised and honoured with rightful burial (the peaceful solution that eluded Oedipus and his children). However, doing this involves disinterring the secrets, shame and suffering of the ancestors. This both extends and contrasts Freud's idea of phylogenetic traces. For Abraham and Torok, the phantom is more specific: it is to do with the secrets of a particular family, or a particular society or time in which the ancestors suffered and may have been perpetrators, victims, witnesses or bystanders. It accounts for both individual and cultural repetitions. There are a few hints as to how the ancestor lives on in the individual: 'The Phantom is therefore also a meta psychological fact: what haunts are not the dead, but the gaps left within us by the secrets of others' (Abraham and Torok, 1994, p. 171). They also add that the phantom presence is not related to a failure to mourn a lost love object but is one which creates a 'tomb-like' quality in the individual (melancholia rather than mourning). It is rather a haunting of the tombs of others, or the burial of an unspeakable fact within the love object. The potent and poetic idea of Freud's (1917) is that in loss, the shadow of the object falls on the ego and is then modified; the shadow cast by the ancestors onto the ego is different— indeed it is deeply other and consequently difficult to recognise. This leads to the problem faced by many children whose parents have been abused in some way: in questioning what happened, they risk losing all mothering and fathering, all chance of care and solace. There is a horror surrounding secrets, and a deep fear of loss and abandonment which can create obstacles to therapy. For Abraham and Torok, the phantom in the parent breaks up normal introjection that the child needs to make. There are parts of the parent's psyche that are just too alien for the child to introject: 'the phantom which returns to haunt bears witness to the experience of the dead buried within the other' (Abraham and Torok 1994, p. 175).

An example of a phantom is the introjected experience of post-war children I spoke about in Chapter 2. Here what should be recognisable as sadness at loss is unrecognisable; instead, it frightens and oppresses. The therapist needs to distinguish between the stranger which is familiar and something to do with love, and the phantom as stranger. In the same way that Malan (1979, p. 80) implored early brief work specialists to read the family story in the story of the 'others' in the patient's life, Abraham suggests that the therapist needs to speak with a care that allows a communication to the patient that there are 'others' in their psyche who are difficult to recognise. For Abraham and Torok (1994, p. 181), a key sign of the presence of ancestors in psychopathology is in the phobic patient. The indirectness of phobias and the sometimes underlying presence of dissociation can be indicators of an endless struggle to master an alien introject.

Time Stands Still in Madness and War: A Self Living Outside of Time?

Davoine and Gaudillière (2004) develop a different but in some ways parallel theory concerning the return of the transgenerational repressed. There is Lacanian theme in that inchoate signs emerge in proto-transferences that can be picked up from "the real" by the sensitive and prepared practitioner. The essential qualification for this is the therapist's openness to their own ancestral and social heritage, echoing Abraham and Torok (1994, p. 253) and Torok's comments in her short essay *Theoretra* (Torok, 1999), and to their own professional genealogy with its rivalries, conflicts and secrets. I speak about this theme in Chapter 7.

It is often the activation of this layer that can allow the therapist to either respond to or shut down the ancestral and historical-seeking expression in the patient. It also has implications for the therapist's supervisory introjects which may clash and split under certain kinds of pressures in clinical work. Davoine and Gaudillière (2004) characterise the kind of resurging transgenerational experiences as having been silenced when an individual or a group has been turned against. Here the genocidal and warlike elements of time-travelling trauma come to the fore; the signs are enactment, acting out, madness or psychosis ripping through a well-adjusted persona.

Davoine and Gaudillière (2004, p. xxiii) draw on Bion (1982) to show how time suffused with trauma collapses into the 'long weekend'—in Bion's case the gap between the two world wars. This is elaborated and expanded: 'Long ago wars form a precipitate in the sessions on the basis of resonances with the analyst's historical bearing or lineage' (Davoine and Gaudillière, 2004, p. xxiii) and this historicisation results in change and improvement for individuals in the therapeutic space (ibid., pp. xxii–xxiii). It's a big claim. Why the patient feels better is a mystery if viewed in intrapsychic terms. What has changed, according to Davoine and Gaudillière (2004), is that because a different language has been found that de-pathologises madness, the missing social acceptance and witnessing can return the patient to themselves or to a sense of themselves in a lost or new contemporary group. This re-witnessing of the self after major social trauma can be profoundly humanising. We have respondents talking about this kind of experience in the research, which I will cover in Chapter 8.

Social Dreaming

Davoine and Gaudillière (2004) make reference to Charlotte Beradt's *Third Reich of Dreams* (Beradt, 1985). Beradt feels that these dreams collected during Hitler's rise to power in Germany give evidence for the presence of an underlying process of private processing in the absence of or breakdown of social solidarity. The dreams, unanalysed and in no way connected to the attempt to give therapy or gain insight, all document how people were hiding from what they knew and were also beginning to internalise and, in some sense, normalise authoritarian rule. These dreams demonstrate the process of identification with the aggressor and they are, as such, prophetic (and, of course to some extent, self-fulfilling prophecies!). Davoine and Gaudillière (2004) argue that all social and historical process can be inscribed in this way in dreams and in the emergence of transference if it can be 'picked up' by the ancestrally and socially attuned practitioner. Bettelheim (1985, p. 154), in his afterword to Beradt's (1985) book, acknowledges that dreams can portray how easily authoritarianism is internalised, but raises reservations about the theory due in part to the absence of the dreamer's latent dream content. He thus refers the dreams back into an intrapsychic frame of reference, removing the key significance of the dreams as a sign of the rapidly breaking social links in interwar Germany. Individual psychotherapy is vulnerable to this mistake, encouraging a retreat into internalisation when a social response is what is needed. The breaking of social links is a key to understanding how hauntings occur and what they mean, a key theme for this book.

Beradt's (1985) approach returns us to the power of oral history and the potency of speaking what has never been said before (Davoine and Gaudillière, 2004, p. xxii). It also alerts us to the ease with which psychoanalysis and other forms of therapy can become co-opted by various forms of state and social repression by keeping alive the illusion that individuals are islands. There is some evidence that Freud himself may have started to change his mind about dreams always being libidinal when his books started to be burned.

Koselleck (2002, p. 336), in the translation of the afterword of the German edition of *The Third Reich of Dreams*, says that the dreams Beradt recorded were not just about terror but were 'dreams dreamed in terror'. For him, the latent and manifest content of the dreams coincide, the personal and the political are fused, and the evidence for the rapid emergence of an apparatus of social terror is clear.

Beradt's dream collection is a poignant reminder that the subject who feels mad and terrified in their dream world may well be at the start of being cut off from their social and historical roots. Their dreams register that social violence is stirring. All Beradt's dreamers had this fate awaiting them. To my knowledge, no one has been able to find out how many survived or for those who did, whether their dreams helped them do it.

Psychosis for Davoine and Gaudillière (2004) is a frantic attempt to bring a foreclosed social connection into being. Madness is response to social calamity, a breaking or loss of the social link. What cannot be spoken is told through another, but that other must be open to the huge disturbance of that telling and to having the capacity to have their own archaic heritage activated. I have referred to this as working with inter- and transgenerational countertransference in Chapters 7 and 8.

When conditions of danger and conflict dominate, all these initial and urgent representations get delayed, and war traumas are made to wait on the threshold 'of a possible inscription' (Davoine and Gaudillière, 2004, p. 237). Beradt's dreams hover on this border. Totalitarianism freezes these out, people emigrate, die or go mad. Another generation must pick up the consequences; something that could have been heard as a clear warning of social danger has been internalised and privatised. We don't yet have a culture that values dream life as an important part of social life. We have turned our backs collectively on one of our best early-warning systems. It leaves open another important question for this book: whether dreaming is a significant part of the relationship between the generations. For First Nations it is, but less so in the West.

Mania, Reparation, Memorials and Haunting

Christopher Bollas (1987, pp. 101–102) links his idea of special states of mood to dreaming. Like dreams, the mood (which by implication is social) works as an environment in which object-relating gets elaborated. Bollas distinguishes between malignant and generative moods and suggests that our capacity to work through or work at the 'unthought known' that comes at us from the social unconscious as much as from individual unconscious identification, will vary when 'aspects of history that have yet to be properly articulated, processed and worked through' block our capacity to integrate change that is occurring. He takes this theme up in more recent work (Bollas, 2018), suggesting that a large-scale difficulty with mourning is threatening our current social contract. He points to the power and significance of manic processes in recent history: the crashing down of the optimism of the Victorian era by two world wars and postcolonial conflict has led to a crisis about the need to understand destructiveness. Late capitalism's offer of mass consumption and short-term psychological fixes as a new source of identity has turned people against the process of deep introspection. This makes the social capacity to mourn losses of all kinds increasingly unavailable. The consequences are alarming, leading us back in some way to the situation of Beradt's (1985) dreamers who can only privately and in sleep think about what might be happening socially and politically. The background is a society and a culture that has become distorted and degraded.

Karl Figlio (2017), in his study of German memorialisation, points to how the attempt to repair and resolve conflict gets undermined by the problem of 'manic reparation' or simulated resolution. If intellectuals or a whole society make partial reparation and fail to take full responsibility, people then cannot offer acceptance of the damage done to both victim and perpetrator in descendant generations. Mourning that is personal is avoided, and depressive positions and genuinely reparative impulses in the Kleinian sense remain beyond grasp. Repeated manic responses lead individuals and whole societies closer to repetition rather than healing or resolution. These could be some of the psychological conditions that lie behind the propensity for intergenerational trauma turning into transgenerational trauma. They are, in this frame, signs of repetition and link back to Bollas's (2018) idea that malignant moods block proper mourning and leave whole societies vulnerable to traumatic repetition.

Stephen Frosh (2019) thinks about different kinds of continuities in death and endings. He prioritises the idea of haunting over the idea of post-memory that promotes the retention of an element of embodiment and connection. Haunting for Frosh gives a timeless sense of change and disturbance running back and forth between the generations. In this sense, haunting is like traffic between inter- and transgenerational trauma and memory. The past is in a state of eternal return, but we need to be aware of the deep and far-reaching transgenerational distortions of colonialism and racism that make hauntings turn either into silences or return as frightening persecutions and accusations.

> If a spirit haunts, then it is not fully lost; the opportunity for repair exists, for settling what needs to be settled and provoking change where that is what has to be done. As the various strands of what is termed psychosocial studies remind us, this is a process involving a human subject that is a meeting point between social and psychological layers. (Frosh, 2019, p. 167)

This echoes the core theme of this chapter: the exercise in developing and maintaining a binocular psychosocial vision.

Psychotherapy, Attachment and Internalisation

The idea of internalisation is central to much therapeutic work. The idea that childrearing and childcare are transmitted from parents to children is at the heart of attachment theory (Dallos, 2006). Patterns of attachment are our first internal working models of relationship. When we do therapeutic work with these, we do intergenerational work. It's a working assumption that the kind of memory that underpins early attachment is procedural and body-based. It is memory laid down as a result of early experiences of soothing, arousal and anxiety; rupture and repair. At its best, these early experiences form the basis for developing affect regulation and occur both before and while we are acquiring language. When the generations first talk to each other, it is body to body, right brain to right brain, womb to foetus.

The recent discovery of the importance of microchimerism in humans takes this relationship deeper still: the baby's genes entering the mother's body to strengthen her heart for childbirth and alter her brain for attunement. As Shildrick (2019) informs us, we don't know for how long these genes express in the mother's body, but it may be several years after the child has been born. This may implicate siblings in complex embodied hauntings: the offspring exists within the self of the mother, and yet any semblance of self is externalised in the becoming of the offspring, carrying with it the remnants or echoes of any antecedent sibling, remembered in the make-up of the mother. These microchimerisms may remain for the whole of life. Complex molecules pass back and forth through the placenta. Does information pass as well? The importance of foetus–placenta–mother relationships is also important for thinking about how epigenetic transmission may work through the mother. This is in contrast to the epigenetic process for men which may work through the methylation of the sperm (Science Daily, 2019).

I mention these things to underline how much current biological science and psychotherapy are in alignment. Another important theme is how much memory and attachment are related. Persons, places and things haunt the interviews of my research participants. Friends, parents, siblings, landscapes, tools and paintings form networks in people's minds and across the research. Each memory has a charge associated with it. I think this confirms a very close link between attachment, memory and deeper time. This book bears witness to some of these connections.

Summary of Academic Sources

In summary, the scope of work related to intergenerational and transgenerational transmissions, ancestries and effects runs across a continuum from the highly technical specialisms of genomic studies and molecular biology to considerations of ideas within economic, political, cultural and psychological disciplines. While there is a wealth of material on memory and the Holocaust, this survey has revealed some apparent gaps in the study of migration, slavery and gendered effects. Even less well-covered are creative transmissions and artistic processes of healing, and very little material has a strong future- or problem-solving focus. There is currently little genuinely interdisciplinary work in the area of multigenerational memory and social memory. Transgenerational transmission remains the hardest to understand, but clearly catches the imagination of many writers, and as the least understood, maybe the most important to grapple with.

Psychosocial Implications

> Psychoanalysis is not a method of treatment applied by one person to another, it is a process engaged in by two people on behalf of one of them – and on behalf of all those family members and ancestors represented by that person. (Eric Fromm quoted in Davoine and Gaudillière, 2004, p. xiv)

Fromm's comment eloquently covers the ethical implications for therapists adopting a multigenerational perspective with a more intergenerational focus. It leaves open the ways in which therapists can do this work of ancestral recognition. Is there something different required by way of technique, assessment, training or supervision? Is a different role required, adjunct to therapy, like a genealogist or generational consultant? Is the intergenerational work best done in one-to-one therapy in a separate and specialised relationship? Or is that work better done in a group or across a wider community? I take these issues up in Chapter 7.

A similar set of questions can be asked of a transgenerational perspective. Here the psychosocial intervention may be more important. This can take the form of research focused on largely transgenerational issues like slavery, using social dreaming as methodology (Manley and Trustram, 2018) or longer-term effects of migration, using genealogy and autoethnography (Williams, 2015). The intervention can be aimed at memorialisation, as with the 9/11 museum in New York, but informed by trauma theory and therapeutic practice. This can help to promote a socially beneficent cycle where relationally informed memorialisation can be a resource for subsequent generations (Pivnick, 2017). If, however, the museum becomes a cultural signifier of unworked-through rage and loss, it further compounds problematic intercommunal and international relations in the future. Memorialisation is always ambiguous and is at its best but most controversial when it encompasses inter- and transgenerational elements. Perhaps memorials are most effective when tripped over, as with the *stolpersteine* in city pavements in some European cities commemorating individual or whole-family victims of Nazi persecution (Figlio, 2017, p. 214).

Returning to the theme of mapping the generations, I hope that this apparently disparate field can now be seen as more joined up. The typology offered in Chapter 2 (Fig. 2.1) allows the practitioner/researcher to begin to orient towards the kind of issues and problems they might be working with and what sorts of knowledge and traditions of intervention may be relevant. It is, in the broadest sense, diagnostic. The thematic map of memory (Fig. 2.2) also provides a way of tuning into what may be going on in any one individual or group troubled by multigenerational issues. Like any heuristic devices, these typologies and maps have limits, but they remind us that in understanding generational relations and conflicts, we need a deeply interdisciplinary base located in both shorter and longer spans of time.

References

Abraham, N. and Torok, M. (1994) *The Shell and the Kernel.* Translated from the French by Nicolas T. Rand. Chicago: University of Chicago Press.

Adelman, A. (1995) Traumatic memory and the intergenerational transmission of Holocaust narratives. *The Psychoanalytic Study of the Child* [online]. 50 (1), pp. 343–367 [Accessed 22 September 2019].

Adonis, C.K. (2008) Trans-generational trauma and humiliation, its potential implications for political forgiveness in post-apartheid South Africa. *International Peace Research Association Global Conference*, University of Leuven, Belgium, 2008.

Agrawal, A.A., Laforsch, C. and Tollrian, R. (1999) Transgenerational induction of defences in animals and plants. *Nature* [online]. 401 (6748), pp. 60–63 [Accessed 22 September 2019].

Alexander, D.H., Novembre, J. and Lange, K. (2009) Fast model-based estimation of ancestry in unrelated individuals. *Genome Research* [online]. 19 (9), pp. 1655–1664 [Accessed 22 September 2019].

Alves-Silva, J., Da Silva Santos, M., Guimarães, P.E.M., Ferreira, A.C.S., Bandelt, H.-J., Pena, S.D.J. and Prado, V.F. (2000) The ancestry of Brazilian Mtdna lineages. *American Journal of Human Genetics* [online]. 67 (2), pp. 444–461 [Accessed 22 September 2019].

Amato, P.R. (1996) Explaining the intergenerational transmission of divorce. *Journal of Marriage and Family* [online]. 58 (3), pp. 628–640 [Accessed 22 September 2019].

Anderson, B. (1983) *Imagined Communities: Reflections on the Origin and Spread of Nationalism.* London: Verso.

Anway, M.D., Cupp, A.S., Uzumuc, M. and Skinner, M.K. (2005) Epigenetic transgenerational actions of endocrine disruptors and male fertility. *Science* [online]. 308 (5727), pp. 1466–1469 [Accessed 22 September 2019].

Apprey, M. (1993) The African-American experience: Transgenerational trauma and forced immigration. *Mind and Human Interaction* [online]. 4 (no issue no.), pp. 70–75 [Accessed 22 September 2019].

Armstrong, D. (2005) *Organization in the Mind: Psychoanalysis, Group Relations and Organizational Consultancy.* London: Karnac.

Atkinson, J. (2001) *Lifting the Blankets: The Transgenerational Effects of Trauma in Indigenous Australia.* PhD, Queensland University of Technology.

Atkinson, J. (2002) *Trauma Trails, Recreating Song Lines: The Transgenerational Effects of Trauma in Indigenous Australia.* North Melbourne: Spinifex Press.

Atkinson, J., Nelson, J., Brooks, R., Atkinson, C. and Ryan, K. (2014) Addressing individual and community transgenerational trauma. In: Dudgeon, P., Milroy, H. and Walker, R., (Eds.). *Working Together: Aboriginal and Torres Strait Islander Mental Health and Wellbeing Principles and Practice.* 2nd ed. Canberra: Commonwealth of Australia, pp. 289–307.

Auerhahn, N.C. and Laub, D. (1998) Intergenerational memory of the Holocaust. In: Danieli, Y. (Ed.). (1998) *International Handbook of Multigenerational Legacies of Trauma.* New York: Plenum Press, pp. 43–68.

Baker, R. (1993) Traditional Aboriginal land use in the Borroloola Region. In: Williams, N.M. and Baines, G. (Ed.) *Traditional Ecological Knowledge: Wisdom for Sustainable Development.* Canberra: Australian National University, pp. 126–143.

Bargh, J.A. (1997) The automaticity of everyday life. In: Wyer, R.S. Jr., (Ed.). (1997) *Advances in Social Cognition, Vol. 10.* Mahwah, NJ: Lawrence Erlbaum Associates, pp. 1–61.

Bargh, J.A., (Ed.) (2013) *Social Psychology and the Unconscious: The Automaticity of Higher Mental Processes* [online]. New York: Psychology Press [Accessed 22 September 2019].

Bataille, G. (1995) Concerning the accounts given by the residents of Hiroshima. In: Caruth, C. (1995) *Trauma: Explorations in Memory.* Baltimore: John Hopkins University Press, pp. 221–235.

Bauman, Z. (2000) *Liquid Modernity.* Cambridge: Polity Press.

Becker, D. and Díaz, M. (1998) The social process and the transgenerational transmission of trauma in Chile. In: Danieli, Y. (Ed.). (1998) *International Handbook of Multigenerational Legacies of Trauma.* New York: Plenum Press, pp. 435–445.

Beiner, G. (2008) In anticipation of a post-memory boom syndrome. *Cultural Analysis* [online]. 7 (no issue no.), pp. 107–112 [Accessed 22 September 2019].

Beiner, G. (2014) Probing the boundaries of Irish memory: From postmemory to prememory and back. *Irish Historical Studies* [online]. 39 (154), pp. 296–307 [Accessed 22 September 2019].

Bengtson, V.L. and Roberts, R.E.L. (1991) Intergenerational solidarity in aging families: An example of formal theory construction. *Journal of Marriage and Family* [online]. 53 (4), pp. 856–870 [Accessed 22 September 2019].

Beradt, C. (1985) *The Third Reich of Dreams: The Nightmares of a Nation 1933–1939.* Translated from the German by Bruno Bettelheim. Wellingborough: Aquarian Press.

Berghahn, D. (2006) Post-1990 screen memories: How east and west German cinema remembers the Third Reich and the Holocaust. *German Life and Letters* [online]. 59 (2), pp. 294–308 [Accessed 22 September 2019].

Bettelheim, B. (1985) Afterword. In: Beradt, C. (Ed.). (1985) *The Third Reich of Dreams: The Nightmares of a Nation 1933–1939*. Translated from the German by Bruno Bettelheim. Wellingborough: Aquarian Press.

Bion, W.R. (1961) *Experiences in Groups*. Tavistock: Tavistock Publications.

Bion, W.R. (1982) *The Long Weekend 1897–1919: Part of a Life*. Reprint. London: Karnac Books, 2005.

Björklund, A. and Jäntti, M. (1997) Intergenerational income mobility in Sweden compared to the United States. *American Economic Review* [online]. 87 (5), pp. 1009–1018 [Accessed 22 September 2019].

Black, S.E., Devereux, P.J. and Salvanes, K.G. (2005) Why the apple doesn't fall far: Understanding intergenerational transmission of human capital. *American Economic Review* [online]. 95 (1), pp. 437–449 [Accessed 22 September 2019].

Bollas, C. (1987) *The Shadow of the Object: Psychoanalysis of the Unthought Known*. London: Free Association Books.

Bollas, C. (2018) *Meaning and Melancholia: Life in the Age of Bewilderment*. Abingdon-on-Thames: Routledge.

Bretherton, I. (1990) Communication patterns, internal working models, and the intergenerational transmission of attachment relationships. *Infant Mental Health Journal* [online]. 11 (3), pp. 237–252 [Accessed 22 September 2019].

Brewster, F. (2019) *Archetypal Grief: Slavery's Legacy of Intergenerational Child Loss*. Abingdon-on-Thames: Routledge.

Bristow, J. (2016) *The Sociology of Generations: New Directions and Challenges*. Basingstoke: Palgrave.

Brookfield, H., Brown, S.D. and Reavey, P. (2008) Vicarious and post-memory practices in adopting families: The re-production of the past through photography and narrative. *Journal of Community & Applied Social* [online]. 18 (5), pp. 474–491 [Accessed 22 September 2019].

Brown, D. (2016) A contribution to the understanding of the social unconscious. *Group Analysis* [online]. 34 (1), pp. 29–38 [Accessed 22 September 2019].

Bus, A.G., Van Ijzendoorn, M.H. and Pellegrini, A.D. (2016) Joint book reading makes for success in learning to read: A meta-analysis on intergenerational transmission of literacy. *Review of Educational Research* [online]. 65 (1), pp. 1–21 [Accessed 22 September 2019].

Cavanagh, S.L. (2017) Antigone's legacy: A feminist psychoanalytic of an other sexual difference. *Studies in the Maternal* [online]. 9 (1), p. 4 [Accessed 22 September 2019].

Champagne, F.A. (2008) Epigenetic mechanisms and the transgenerational effects of maternal care. *Frontiers in Neuroendocrinology* [online]. 19 (3), pp. 386–397 [Accessed 22 September 2019].

Connerton, P. (1989) *How Societies Remember*. Cambridge: Cambridge University Press.

Connolly, A. (2011) Healing the wounds of our fathers: Intergenerational trauma, memory, symbolization and narrative. *Journal of Analytical Psychology* [online]. 56 (5), pp. 607–626 [Accessed 22 September 2019].

Crosnoe, R., Johnson, M.K. and Elder Jr, G.H. (2016) Intergenerational bonding in school: The behavioral and contextual correlates of student-teacher relationships. *Sociology of Education* [online]. 77 (1), pp. 60–81 [Accessed 22 September 2019].

Crownshaw, R. (2004) Reconsidering postmemory: Photography, the archive, and post-Holocaust memory in WG Sebald's *Austerlitz*. *Mosaic: A Journal for the Interdisciplinary Study of Literature* [online]. 37 (4), pp. 215–236 [Accessed 22 September 2019].

Currie, J. and Moretti, E. (2003) Mother's education and the intergenerational transmission of human capital: Evidence from college openings. *Quarterly Journal of Economics* [online]. 118 (4), pp. 1495–1532 [Accessed 22 September 2019].

Dalal, F. (2001) The social unconscious: A post-Foulkesian perspective. *Group Analysis* [online]. 34 (4), pp. 539–555 [Accessed 22 September 2019].

Dallos, R. (2006) *Attachment Narrative Therapy Integrating Narrative, Systemic and Attachment Therapies*. Berkshire: Open University Press.

Daud, A., Skoglund, E. and Rydelius, P.-A. (2005) Children in families of torture victims: Transgenerational transmission of parents' traumatic experiences to their children. *International Journal of Social Welfare* [online]. 14 (1), pp. 23–32 [Accessed 22 September 2019].

Davidson, A.C. and Mellor, D.J. (2001) The adjustment of children of Australian Vietnam veterans: Is there evidence for the transgenerational transmission of the effects of war-related trauma? *Australian and New Zealand Journal of Psychiatry* [online]. 35 (3), pp. 345–351 [Accessed 22 September 2019].

Davies, N. (2011) *Vanished Kingdoms: The History of Half-forgotten Europe*. London: Penguin Books.

Davoine, F. and Gaudillière, J.-M. (2004) *History Beyond Trauma*. New York: Other Press.
De Sanctis, S. (2012) From psychoanalysis to politics: Antigone as revolutionary in Judith Butler and Žižek. *Opticon1826* [online]. (no Volume no.) (14), pp. 27–36 [Accessed 22 September 2019].
Doolittle, R. (1981) Similar amino acid sequences: Chance or common ancestry? *Science* [online]. 214 (4517), pp. 149–159 [Accessed 22 September 2019].
Dunn, T. and Holtz-Eakin, D. (2000) Financial capital, human capital, and the transition to self-employment: Evidence from intergenerational links. *Journal of Labor Economics* [online]. 18 (2), pp. 282–305 [Accessed 22 September 2019].
Ehrensaft, M.K., Cohen, P., Brown, J., Smailes, E., Chen, H. and Johnson, J.G. (2003) Intergenerational transmission of partner violence: A 20-year prospective study. *Journal of Consulting and Clinical Psychology* [online]. 71 (4), pp. 741–753 [Accessed 22 September 2019].
Even-tzur, E. (2016) 'The road to the village': Israeli social unconscious and the Palestinian Nakba. *International Journal of Applied Psychoanalytic Studies* [online]. 13 (4), pp. 305–322 [Accessed 22 September 2019].
Felsen, I. (1998) Transgenerational transmission of effects of the Holocaust. In: Danieli, Y. (Ed.). (1998) *International Handbook of Multigenerational Legacies of Trauma*. New York: Plenum Press, pp. 43–68.
Figlio, K. (2017) *Remembering as Reparation: Psychoanalysis and Historical Memory*. Basingstoke: Palgrave Macmillan.
Fonagy, P. (1999) The transgenerational transmission of Holocaust trauma: Lessons learned from the analysis of an adolescent with obsessive-compulsive disorder. *Attachment & Human Development* [online]. 1 (1), pp. 92–114 [Accessed 22 September 2019].
Foulkes, S.H. (1975) *Group-Analytic Psychotherapy, Method and Principles*. London: Gordon & Breach.
Freud, S. (1917) Mourning and melancholia. In: Freud, S. (Ed.). (2001) *The Standard Edition of the Complete Psychological Works of Sigmund Freud, Volume XIV (1914–1916): On the History of the Psycho-Analytic Movement*. Translated from the German by James Strachey, ed. London: Vintage, pp. 237–258.
Freud, S. (2001) *Moses and Monotheism*. Reprint. London: Vintage Books
Frosh, S. (2019) *Those Who Come After: Postmemory, Acknowledgement and Forgiveness*. Basingstoke: Palgrave Macmillan.

Gapp, K., et al. (2014) Implication of sperm RNAs in transgenerational inheritance of the effects of early trauma in mice. *Nature Neuroscience* [online]. 17 (5), pp. 667–669 [Accessed 22 September 2019].

Gigerenzer, G. (2007) *Gut Feelings: The Intelligence of the Unconscious*. London: Penguin.

Goertz, K. (1998) Transgenerational representations of the Holocaust: From memory to 'post-memory'. *World Literature Today* [online]. 72 (1), pp. 33–38 [Accessed 22 September 2019].

Goodman, R.D. (2013) The transgenerational trauma and resilience genogram. *Counselling Psychology Quarterly* [online]. 26, pp. 386–405 [Accessed 22 September 2019].

Goodman, R. and West-Olatunji, C. (2008) Transgenerational trauma and resilience: Improving mental health counseling for survivors of Hurricane Katrina. *Journal of Mental Health Counseling* [online]. 30 (2), pp. 121–136 [Accessed 22 September 2019].

Hamburger, A., (Ed.). (2018) *Trauma, Trust and Memory: Social Trauma and Reconciliation in Psychoanalysis, Psychotherapy and Cultural Memory*. Abingdon-on-Thames: Routledge.

Harding, R.M., Fullerton, S.M., Griffiths, R.C., Bond, J., Cox, M.J., Schneider, J.A., Moulin, D.S. and Clegg, J.B. (1997) Archaic African and Asian lineages in the genetic ancestry of modern humans. *American Journal of Human Genetics* [online]. 60 (4), pp. 772–789 [Accessed 22 September 2019].

Harkness, L.L. (1993) Transgenerational transmission of war-related trauma. In: Wilson, J.P. and Raphael B., (Ed.). (1993) *International Handbook of Traumatic Stress Syndromes*. Boston, MA: Springer, pp. 635–634.

Hartwick, J.M. (1977) Intergenerational equity and the intergenerational equity and the investing of rents from exhaustible resources. *American Economic Review* [online]. 67 (5), pp. 972–974 [Accessed 22 September 2019].

Harvey, J.-F. (2012) Managing organizational memory with intergenerational knowledge transfer. *Journal of Knowledge Management* [online]. 16 (3), pp. 400–417 [Accessed 22 September 2019].

Haynal, A.E. (2002) *Disappearing and Reviving: Sandor Ferenczi in the History of Psychoanalysis*. Reprint, Abingdon-on-Thames: Routledge. 2018.

Heard, E. and Martienssen, R.A. (2014) Transgenerational epigenetic inheritance: Myths and mechanisms. *Cell* [online]. 157 (1), pp. 95–109 [Accessed 22 September 2019].

Hirsch, M. (1997) *Family Frames: Photography, Narrative, and Postmemory.* Cambridge, MA: Harvard University Press.

Hirsch, M. (1999) Projected memory: Holocaust photographs in personal and public fantasy. In: Bal, M., Crewe, J. and Spitzer, L., (Ed.). (1998) *Acts of Memory: Cultural Recall in the Present.* Hanover, NH: University Press of New England, pp. 3–23.

Hirsch, M. (2008) The generation of postmemory. *Poetics Today* [online]. 29 (1), pp. 103–128 [Accessed 22 September 2019].

Hopper, E. (2003) *The Social Unconscious: Selected Papers* (22 vols.). London: Jessica Kingsley Publishers.

Hopper, E. and Weinberg, H. (2011) *Social Unconscious in Persons, Groups and Societies, the, Volume 1: Mainly Theory.* Abingdon-on-Thames: Routledge.

Hopper, E. and Weinberg, H., (Ed.). (2016) *The Social Unconscious in Persons, Groups, and Societies Volume 2: Mainly Foundation Matrixes.* London: Karnac.

Jeffries, S. (2005) Modern lover. *The Guardian,* 12 November. Available at https://www.theguardian.com/books/2005/nov/12/shopping.society [Accessed 17 September 2020].

Kaitz, M., Levy, M., Ebstein, R., Faraone, S.V. and Mankuta, D. (2009) The intergenerational effects of trauma from terror: A real possibility. *Infant Mental Health Journal* [online]. 30 (2), pp. 158–179 [Accessed 22 September 2019].

Kalmuss, D. (1984) The intergenerational transmission of marital aggression. *Journal of Marriage and Family* [online]. 46 (1), pp. 11–19 [Accessed 22 September 2019].

Karenian, H., Livaditis, M., Karenian, S., Zafiriadis, K., Bochtsou, V. and Xenitidis, K. (2011) Collective trauma transmission and traumatic reactions among descendants of Armenian refugees. *International Journal of Social Psychiatry* [online]. 57 (4), pp. 327–337 [Accessed 22 September 2019].

Kasakoff, A. (1974) Idea of the social unconscious: The problem of elementary and complex structures in Gitksan marriage choice. In: Rossi, I., (Ed.). (1974) *The Unconscious in Culture: The Structuralism of Claude Levi-Strauss in Perspective.* New York: E.P. Dutton & Co., pp. 143–169.

Kaufman, D. (2007) Post-memory and post-Holocaust Jewish identity narratives. In: Gerson, J. and Wolf, D., (Ed.). (2007) *Sociology Confronts the Holocaust.* USA: Duke University Press, pp. 39–54.

Kingstone, H. and Broughton, T. (2019) Roundtable: Victoria's Victorians and the idea of generation. *Journal of Victorian Culture* [online]. 24 (3), pp. 277–281 [Accessed 22 September 2019].

Kleinot, P. (2011) Transgenerational trauma and forgiveness: Looking at the Israeli–Palestinian families forum through a group analytic lens. *Group Analysis* [online]. 44 (1), pp. 97–111 [Accessed 22 September 2019].

Kooner, J.S., et al. (2011) Genome-wide association study in individuals of South Asian ancestry identifies six new type 2 diabetes susceptibility loci. *Nature Genetics* [online]. 43 (10), pp. 984–989 [Accessed 22 September 2019].

Koselleck, R. (2002) *The Practice of Conceptual History, Timing History, Spacing Concepts*. Stanford, CA: Stanford University Press.

Kosoy, R., et al. (2009) Ancestry informative marker sets for determining continental origin and admixture proportions in common populations in America. *Human Mutation* [online]. 30 (1), pp. 69–78 [Accessed 22 September 2019].

Lawrence, D.H. (1989) *The Rainbow*. Cambridge: Cambridge University Press.

Lazzara, M.J. (2009) Filming loss: (Post-)memory, subjectivity, and the performance of failure in recent Argentine documentary films. *Latin American Perspectives* [online]. 36 (5), pp. 147–157 [Accessed 22 September 2019].

Long, S. and Manley, J., (Ed.) (2019) *Social Dreaming Philosophy, Research, Theory and Practice*. Abingdon-on-Thames: Routledge.

McGregor, K.E. (2013) Memory studies and human rights in Indonesia. *Asian Studies Review* [online]. 37 (3), pp. 350–361 [Accessed 22 September 2019].

McLanahan, S. and Bumpass, L. (1988) Intergenerational consequences of family disruption. *American Journal of Sociology* [online]. 94 (1), pp. 130–152 [Accessed 22 September 2019].

Mahajan, A., Go, M.J., Zhang, W., et al. (2014) Genome-wide trans-ancestry meta-analysis provides insight into the genetic architecture of type 2 diabetes susceptibility. *Nature Genetics* [online]. 46 (3), pp. 234–244 [Accessed 22 September 2019].

Malan, D. (1979) *Individual Psychotherapy and the Science of Psychodynamics*. London: Butterworths.

Manley, J. (2018) *Social Dreaming, Associative Thinking and Intensities of Affect*. London: Palgrave

Manley, J. and Trustram, M. (2018) 'Such endings that are not over': The slave trade, social dreaming and affect in a museum. *Psychoanalysis, Culture & Society* [online]. 23 (1), pp. 77–96 [Accessed 22 September 2019].

Mannheim, K. (1952) *Essays on the Sociology of Knowledge*. Reprint. Kecskemeti, P., ed. Abingdon-on-Thames: Routledge, 1972, pp. 22–24, 276–322.

Marques, J., Paez, D. and Serra, A.F. (1997) Social sharing, emotional climate, and the transgenerational transmission of memories: The Portuguese Colonial War. In: Pennebaker, J.W., Rim, B. and Paez, D., (Ed.). (1997) *Collective Memory of Political Events: Social Psychological Perspectives.* Mahwah, NJ: Lawrence Erlbaum Associates, Inc., pp. 253–275.

Marsh, T.-N., Cote-Meek, S., Toulouse, P., Najavits, L.M. and Young, N.L. (2015) The application of Two-Eyed Seeing decolonizing methodology in qualitative and quantitative research for the treatment of intergenerational trauma and substance use disorders. *International Journal of Qualitative Methods* [online]. 14 (5), pp. 1–13 [Accessed 22 September 2019].

Marshall, E.A. (2004) *Institute for Integrative Science and Health.* Available from: http://www.integrativescience.ca/Principles/TwoEyedSeeing/ [Accessed 12 September 2020].

Marx, K. (1967) *Writings of the Young Marx on Philosophy and Society.* Reprint. Indianapolis IN: Hackett Publishing, 1997.

Mills, C.W. (1959) *The Sociological Imagination.* Reprint. New York: Oxford University Press, 2000.

Montgomery, C. (2002) Role of dynamic group therapy in psychiatry. *Advances in Psychiatric Treatment* [online]. 8 (1), pp. 34–41 [Accessed 22 September 2019].

Morrow, E.M., et al. (2008) Identifying autism loci and genes by tracing recent shared ancestry. *Science* [online]. 321 (5886), pp. 218–223 [Accessed 22 September 2019].

Moscovici, S. (1981) On social representations. *Social Cognition: Perspectives on Everyday Understanding* [online]. 8 (12), pp. 181–209 [Accessed 22 September 2019].

Muller, R.T. (2010) *Trauma and the Avoidant Client: Attachment-Based Strategies for Healing.* New York: Norton.

Murray, E. (2018) Children's imagined journeys: Representations of parenting and gender in children's essay competition writings in 1950s England. Presented at the Children's History Society Conference, University of Greenwich, London, 21–23 June.

Nagata, D.K. and Cheng, W.J.Y. (2003) Intergenerational communication of race-related trauma by Japanese American former internees. *American Journal of Orthopsychiatry* [online]. 73 (3), pp. 266–278 [Accessed 22 September 2019].

Nomura, A.M.Y., Stemmermann, G.N., Heibrun, L.K., Salkeld, R.M. and Vuilleumier, J.P. (1985) Serum vitamin levels and the risk of cancer of specific sites in men of Japanese ancestry in Hawaii. *Cancer Research* [online]. 45 (5), pp. 2369–2372 [Accessed 22 September 2019].

O' Loughlin, M. (Ed.). (2015) *The Ethics of Remembering and the Consequences of Forgetting. Essays in Trauma History and Memory*. Lanham, MD: Rowman & Littlefield.

O' Loughlin, M. and Charles, M., (Ed.). (2015) *Fragments of Trauma and the Social Production of Suffering, Trauma, History and Memory*. Lanham, MD: Rowman & Littlefield.

Pearrow, M. and Cosgrove, L. (2009) The aftermath of combat-related PTSD: Toward an understanding of transgenerational trauma. *Communication Disorders Quarterly* [online]. 30 (2), pp. 77–82 [Accessed 22 September 2019].

Peltier, C. (2018) An application of two-eyed seeing: Indigenous research methods with participatory action research. *International Journal of Qualitative Methods* [online]. 17 (1) [Accessed 11 September 2020].

Pennebaker, J.W., Rim, B. and Paez, D. (Ed.). (1997) *Collective Memory of Political Events: Social Psychological Perspectives*. Mahwah, NJ: Lawrence Erlbaum Associates, Inc.

Perroud, N., Rutembesa, E., Paoloni-Giacobino, A., Mutabaruka, J., Mutesa, L., Stenz, L., Malafosse, A. and Karege, F. (2014) The Tutsi genocide and transgenerational transmission of maternal stress: Epigenetics and biology of the HPA axis. *The World Journal of Biological Psychiatry* [online]. 15 (4), pp. 334–345 [Accessed 22 September 2019].

Peterson, K.J. and Eernisse, D.J. (2001) Animal phylogeny and the ancestry of bilaterians: Inferences from morphology and 18s rDNA gene sequences. *Evolution & Development* [online]. 3 (3), pp. 170–205 [Accessed 22 September 2019].

Phipps, R.M. and Degges-White, S. (2014) A new look at transgenerational trauma transmission: Second-generation Latino immigrant youth. *Journal of Multicultural Counseling and Development* [online]. 42 (3), pp. 174–187 [Accessed 22 September 2019].

Pivnick, B.A. (2017) Transforming collapse: Applying clinical psychoanalysis to the relational design of the National September 11 Memorial Museum. *International Forum of Psychoanalysis* [online]. 26 (4), pp. 248–257 [Accessed 22 September 2019].

Portuges, C. (2003) Intergenerational memory: Transmitting the past in Hungarian cinema. *Spectator: The University of Southern California Journal of Film and Television* [online]. 23 (2), pp. 44–52 [Accessed 22 September 2019].

Raghavan, M., et al. (2013) Upper Palaeolithic Siberian genome reveals dual ancestry of Native Americans. *Nature* [online]. 505 (7481), pp. 87–91 [Accessed 22 September 2019].

Rakoff, V., Sigal, J.J. and Epstein, N.B. (1966) Children and families of concentration camp survivors. *Canada's Mental Health* [online]. 14 (4), pp. 24–26 [Accessed 22 September 2019].

Ralph, N, Hamaguchi, K. and Cox, M. (2006) Transgenerational trauma, suicide and healing from sexual abuse in the Kimberley region, Australia. *Pimatisiwin: A Journal of Aboriginal and Indigenous Community Health* [online]. 4 (2), pp. 117–136 [Accessed 22 September 2019].

Richards, B. (2019) Beyond the angers of populism: A psychosocial inquiry. *Journal of Psychosocial Studies* [online]. 12 (1), pp. 171–183 [Accessed 22 September 2019].

Rosenberg, N.A., Li, L.M., Ward, R. and Pritchard, J.K. (2003) Informativeness of genetic markers for inference of ancestry. *American Journal of Human Genetics* [online]. 73 (6), pp. 1402–1422 [Accessed 22 September 2019].

Sanders, A.R. (2008) No significant association of 14 candidate genes with schizophrenia in a large European ancestry sample: Implications For psychiatric genetics. *American Journal of Psychiatry* [online]. 165 (4), pp. 497–506 [Accessed 22 September 2019].

Sankararaman, S., Mallick, S., Dannemann, M., Prüfer, K., Kelso, J., Pääbo, S., Patterson, N. and Reich, D. (2014) The genomic landscape of neanderthal ancestry in present-day humans. *Nature* [online]. 507 (7492), pp. 354–357 [Accessed 22 September 2019].

Schulberg, C.H. (1997) An unwanted inheritance: Healing transgenerational trauma of the Nazi Holocaust through the Bonny method of guided imagery and music. *The Arts in Psychotherapy* [online]. 24 (4), pp. 323–345 [Accessed 22 September 2019].

Schwab, G. (2010) *Haunting Legacies: Violent Histories and Transgenerational Trauma*. New York: Columbia University Press.

Science Daily (2019) Effects on offspring of epigenetic inheritance via sperm. University of California Santa Cruz. *Science Daily*. 20 March. Available at https://www.sciencedaily.com/releases/2019/03/190320102114.htm [Accessed 23 September 2020].

Severson, R.K., Nomura, A.M.Y., Grove, J.S. and Stemmermann, G.N. (1989) A prospective study of demographics, diet, and prostate cancer among men of Japanese ancestry in Hawaii. *Cancer Research* [online]. 49 (7), pp. 1857–1860 [Accessed 22 September 2019].

Shamtoub, Y. (2013) *Intergenerational Transmission of Trauma and Attachment in Adult Children of Iranian Immigrants*. PhD, Alliant International University.

Shevlin, M. and McGuigan, K. (2003) The Long-term psychological impact of Bloody Sunday on families of the victims as measured by the revised impact of event scale. *British Journal of Clinical Psychology* [online]. 42 (4), pp. 427–432 [Accessed 22 September 2019].

Shildrick, M. (2019) (Micro)chimerism, immunity and temporality: Rethinking the ecology of life and death. *Australian Feminist Studies* [online]. 34 (99), pp. 10–24 [Accessed 22 September 2019].

Solon, G. (2002) Cross-country differences in intergenerational earnings mobility. *Journal of Economic Perspectives* [online]. 16 (3), pp. 59–66 [Accessed 22 September 2019].

Solow, R.M. (1986) On the intergenerational allocation of natural resources. *Scandinavian Journal of Economics* [online]. 88 (1), pp. 141–149 [Accessed 22 September 2019].

Sophocles (1974) *The Theban Plays*. Translated from the Greek by E.F. Watling. 2nd ed. London: Penguin Books.

Sosa, C. (2012) Queering kinship. The performance of blood and the attires of memory. *Journal of Latin American Cultural Studies* [online]. 21 (2), pp. 221–233 [Accessed 22 September 2019].

Stanley, L. and Dampier, H. (2005) Aftermaths: Post/memory, commemoration and the concentration camps of the South African War 1899–1902. *European Review of History: Revue Européenne d'Histoire* [online]. 12 (1), pp. 91–119 [Accessed 22 September 2019].

Stanley, E. and Stanley, L. (2006) *Mourning Become...: Post/memory and Commemoration of the Concentration Camps of the South African War 1899–1902*. Manchester: Manchester University Press.

Sykes, B. (2010) *The Seven Daughters of Eve: The Science that Reveals our Genetic Ancestry*. London: WW Norton & Company.

Till, K.E. (2012) Wounded cities: Memory-work and a place-based ethics of care. *Political Geography* [online]. 31 (1), pp. 3–14 [Accessed 22 September 2019].

Torok, M. (1999) Theoretra. *Psyche: Zeitschrift Für Psychoanalyse Und Ihre Anwendungen* [online]. 53 (3), pp. 211–214 [Accessed 22 September 2019].

Tschuggnall, K. and Welzer, H. (2002) Rewriting memories: Family recollections of the National Socialist past in Germany. *Culture & Psychology* [online]. 8 (1), pp. 130–145 [Accessed 22 September 2019].

Tubert-Oklander, J. and Hernández-Tubert, Reyna, R. (2014) The social unconscious and the large group Part Ii: A context that becomes text. *Group Analysis* [online]. 47 (3), pp. 329–344 [Accessed 22 September 2019].

Tucker, W.T. (1965) Max Weber's Verstehen. *The Sociological Quarterly* [online]. 6 (2), pp. 157–165 [Accessed 22 September 2019].

Vogel, M.L. (1994) Gender as a factor in the transgenerational transmission of trauma. *Women & Therapy* [online]. 15 (2), pp. 35–47 [Accessed 22 September 2019].

Volkan, V. (1998) *Bloodlines: From Ethnic Pride to Ethnic Terrorism*. Boulder, CO: Westview Press.

Waterland, R.A., Travisano, M., Tahiliani, K.G., Rached, M.T. and Mirza, S. (2008) Methyl donor supplementation prevents transgenerational amplification of obesity. *International Journal of Obesity* [online]. 32 (9), pp. 1373–1379 [Accessed 22 September 2019].

Watling, E.F. (1947 [1973]) *The Theban Plays*. Reprint. London: Penguin.

Weber-Stadlbauer, U., Richetto, J., Labouesse, M.A., Bohacek, J., Mansuy, I.M. and Meyer, U. (2017) Transgenerational transmission and modification of pathological traits induced by prenatal immune activation. *Molecular Psychiatry* [online]. 22 (1), pp. 102–112 [Accessed 22 September 2019].

Weinberg, H. (2007) So what is this social unconscious anyway? *Group Analysis* [online]. 40 (3), pp. 307–322 [Accessed 22 September 2019].

Williams, A. (1997) Intergenerational equity: An exploration of the 'fair innings' argument. *Health Economics* [online]. 6 (2), pp. 117–132 [Accessed 22 September 2019].

Williams, N. (2015) Anglo-German diaspora and displacement in early twentieth century history: An intergenerational haunting. In: O'Loughlin, M., (Ed.). (2015) *The Ethics of Remembering and the Consequences of Forgetting, Essays on Trauma, History and Memory*. Lanham, MD: Rowman & Littlefield, pp. 125–142.

Willner, D. (1982) The Oedipus Complex, Antigone, and Electra: The woman as hero and victim. *American Anthropologist* [online]. 84 (1), pp. 58–78 [Accessed 22 September 2019].

Yehuda, R., Bell, A., Bierer, L.M. and Schmeidler, J. (2008) Maternal, not paternal, PTSD is related to increased risk for PTSD in offspring of Holocaust survivors. *Journal of Psychiatric Research* [online]. 42 (13), pp. 1104–1111 [Accessed 22 September 2019].

Yehuda, R. and Bierer, L.M. (2007) Transgenerational transmission of Cortisol and PTSD risk. *Progress in Brain Research* [online]. 167 (no issue no.), pp. 121–135 [Accessed 22 September 2019].

Yehuda, R., Daskalakis, N.P., Bierer, L.M., Bader, H.N., Klengel, T., Holsboer, F. and Binder, E.B. (2016) Holocaust exposure induced intergenerational effects on FKBP5 methylation. *Biological Psychiatry* [online]. 80 (5), pp. 372–380 [Accessed 22 September 2019].

Yehuda, R., Engel, S.M., Brand, S.R., Seckl, J., Marcus, S.M. and Berkowitz, G.S. (2005) Transgenerational effects of Post Traumatic Stress Disorder in babies of mothers exposed to the World Trade Center attacks during pregnancy. *Journal of Clinical Endocrinology and Metabolism* [online]. 90 (7), pp. 4115–4118 [Accessed 22 September 2019].

Zalme, A.M. (2017) *Kurdish Generational Diasporic Identities. Perceptions of 'Home' and 'Sense of Belonging' within Families among Iraqi Kurds in the UK*. PhD, University of the West of England.

4

Reconceptualising Loss and Reaching for Creativity

Reconceptualising Loss

A mother recounted her decision a few years ago to write a set of notes for her young son, to pass on some memories that her mother had passed onto her. Mother and grandson do not speak the same language. Loss is anticipated through this act—both her mother's death and her own eventual death too. Yet loss of another kind is also being tackled: that of the loss of a shared language between one generation and the next. This private preparatory activity, which had been going on for some time, came to light through a research conversation on memory. What this first very ordinary example introduces is that people anticipate and prepare for loss. In this example, there is something quite complex about passing on a story: it must be translated into another language. Within this act is a further story, one of migration, forming one narrative inside another. This communication into the future involves being able to explain the presence of a connecting thread through the maternal line which might otherwise not be known about. It also anticipates a time when the son will be interested enough to become a bearer and holder of these stories.

© The Author(s), under exclusive license to Springer Nature Switzerland AG 2021
N. Williams, *Mapping Social Memory*, Studies in the Psychosocial, https://doi.org/10.1007/978-3-030-66157-1_4

The impulse behind the story is also important: it is for a specific person. It counters in a small way the loss of continuity that death always brings, and that migration and language also accentuate. It is a way of actively yet privately reconceptualising loss. It involves gift-giving to the next generation.

Another respondent said that in responding to her grandchild's request to tell her story, the grandmother experiences a tension between what is expected and hoped for—a personal account—and her deep desire to tell the story of her nation. She wants to tell a story about what happened 'to us', a shared collective past. This comes with a sense of pride and urgency. There are different kinds of losses. The personal narrative of a grandmother and her life is one; the life of her nation is another. They are valued differently, yet the two are vital. Can they be told in a way that weaves them together so that the child can hear both? How can a migrant grandmother embody the life and pride of a nation in which she no longer lives?

Reconceptualising loss often also refers to places and networks that have almost disappeared. The adjustment from a face-to-face community, in which the past is remembered orally, to one in which something gets written down is fraught with problems. One respondent contemplated a future time when her son will not be able to meet people who remember his past or indeed remember his mother. What is being lost here is a mechanism of keeping the past present as a community passes out of time. It isn't clear what can be done, or even whether the next generation will be interested.

Sometimes an inheritance from the past is negative and dangerous. Another respondent described how as a child she was always alert to, but troubled by, what was wrong in the world. In adult life, she realised that suffering interested her and that the experience of loss was what lay behind it. This insight was built on during psychotherapy so that it was possible to think about that constant sense of loss as something to do with all her forebears who had lost home and country. None had escaped this sense of loss, despite positive outcomes of migration and better lives for them in the present. This example is very different from the first three. Here the respondent is telling us that something that was always inside her from childhood, a pervasive feeling of disaster, trouble and loss, came from her people, her group. It is closer to what I have defined as a transgenerational issue: here the impulse to understand and alleviate suffering comes from a massive social loss and diaspora. This is another form that reconceptualising loss takes. Here it is a response of intense interest in severances, and an abiding questioning of why and how this happened. What does it mean? What should happen in light of these social losses? There is an insistent and restless probing that presages a life's work. In this sense, it is also a creative response, something which I will explore in the next section of this chapter.

This respondent also said that meeting others helped to transform the overwhelming feeling of dread; the subsequent embracing of ideas was necessary to address and tackle the problem of abject social loss that accompanies calamities touching whole communities. This process of recognition through comparison was a central way of building a new understanding of loss that was not internalised/individualised as shame and depression. This is a reconceptualisation of the idea that all loss is individual, turning it into something more social, an insight that is in itself liberatory and therapeutic. But do things get better or are they just better described? How can reparative action arise from reconceptualising loss in this way? How can post-diaspora peoples come to terms with what has happened to them? Tracing back ancestry only leads to lost records. An intergenerational enquiry is blocked by the catastrophe that has been undergone. There is an absence of narrative. Another kind of intervention is needed beyond one-to-one therapy. The shape this can take is varied but the important idea is that a conversation or action needs to happen with and within groups. Action needs to be pro-social as well as involve individual insight.

Reconceptualising loss when diasporic experience is involved can lead to profound but puzzling communication between one generation and the next. One respondent described a family acquiring different languages and practical skills on a long journey in which only a few members survived. People who are desperate can do incredible (and terrible) things: these actions become an invisible template for future generations. Diasporic loss involves developing survival techniques, but these can then run through a family so that the third generation can be disorientated and struggle with a set of values and practices that seem to have no purpose. This dichotomy can cause conflict and a stand-off between members of the last generation who knew why you must have a bag packed and need to be armed, and those who 'just don't get it'.

For people who have had these experiences, losses of heirlooms or significant belongings are diminished in importance, as are large items of material security like houses or cars, which can easily be destroyed or disappear. What remains is the knowledge of what to do when this happens and how to notice the warning signs. There is a kind of 'wire in the blood' alertness that gets promoted alongside a personal resourcefulness. Loss and action are closely connected. The loss of possessions and home is only the start of the diasporic experience; there is much worse to come. This sense of readiness for the next turn of events swings between dread and further mobilisation. It is a definite state of mind akin perhaps to continual low-level anxiety.

I have avoided the word 'trauma' in this chapter up to now. For every dislocation of population, there is massive and widespread trauma, and I look at this more closely in the chapter on hauntings. Suffice it to say at this point that respondents who reported experiences of migration in their family also spoke of their difficulties in grieving: they felt 'hardened'. It is hard to cry, especially after three generations. Some felt that those of the generation subjected to the diaspora, although dead, were still there in an ever-constant presence. In this sense, we are no longer talking about loss as reconceptualised but are moving towards experiences of haunting which I will describe in the next chapter. This presages a basic shift from one sort of memory to another.

What happens after the diaspora? How do families touched by such experiences manage in second, third and fourth generations if they have some remaining or developing capacity to reconceptualise loss? Often if this capacity has been impaired it leads to the kind of consequences that I describe next.

The birth of children can be problematic. Perhaps surprisingly, not all new life is welcome. Likenesses to lost ones can cause deep ambivalence to parents trying to start afresh in a foreign country. Anything that reminds them of the losses they have undergone can confuse and disturb. In the third generation, the group most explored in this research, there is a reaching out and a curiosity about people with the same names who are obviously important to their parents but who are now dead. As children, these third-generation survivors are prone to feeling that those children or young adults who didn't survive are more valued than they are. They reach out to them in their imaginations to try and understand what it must have been like to be them and die so young. Typically, this goes on in private: it's an intensity that their parents cannot be told about or be party to.

When miracles of survival do happen, the survivors are not always welcome. While this was a well-known phenomenon in Israel where survivors of Nazi concentration camps sometimes struggled to feel accepted, its incidence inside migrant families is more hidden. The tendency to arbitrarily reject or bar certain family members echoes the harsh and deadly rejection meted out by the perpetrators, yet its reasons are less clear, fickle and more arbitrary. Who will be favoured and who will feel like the one on the outside? Who will live and who will die emotionally? There is a primitive tendency to blame the victim for not having looked after themselves properly: How could you have let this happen to you? Didn't you see it coming? These post hoc rationalisations are common in traumatic dislocations.

For these post-diaspora families, it is often left to the third- and fourth-generation children to begin to reconceptualise loss and start to make sense of the maddening disturbance in attachment and failures in solidarity to which they have been subject. It can be a lifetime's work.

One of the problems that all post-diaspora children have is that they are the first generation fully of the new land, its customs and languages. This means that in some ways they are parents to their parents who may be unable to integrate as well or at all. It's a sense of being brought up by people who were emotionally and culturally living somewhere else. This can cause huge strains on identity and can generate a loneliness that cannot be spoken of, because disclosing it would be a betrayal of their parents' efforts to parent them.

Some economists have noticed what they call the 'migration potential' (Ivlevs, 2015) for the children of migrants to migrate again. This can be construed as a positive availability of globalised labour market mobility, and therefore a resilience factor specific to children of migrants. However, the accounts I have from third-generation migrants suggest that the push to move on comes instead from a self-identified need to find a landscape and society that they can make their own. Wanting to migrate again is a reaction to the migration of their parents or grandparents. While it might be expected that families who have survived a relocation might want to stick together and settle down (and indeed many do), we also see a desire for the opposite: to get as far away from each other as possible.

Post-diaspora families are often on the cusp of acting out and repetition. They have seen the worst that humanity can do and consequently know it can happen again. In that sense, they carry a difficult but important 'canary in the coal mine' function for their host nations. They have unwelcome insights into how social order can break down and where that may lead. It can also mean they value what they have more deeply than their host country's natives do, knowing what it is like to lose everything.

Reconceptualising loss puts demands on an individual throughout every phase of their life. The role of therapy is considerable for some of our respondents both as patients and as practitioners. It informs how they think about themselves. It is clear though from our participants that much questioning about the past had happened before a significant therapeutic encounter had occurred. I also received reports that the therapy available was only partially relevant, a further feature of post-migration identity. Something new is needed for each migrant group, and it must be invented. I take this up in more detail in Chapter 7 on the intergenerational implications for psychotherapy.

A respondent talked about the effect of losses in her childhood. This laid the ground for a professional life working both with young people and with people who are dying. How can people be helped to die well or gracefully? How can people learn to let go of this life? How can younger people be supported to overcome the traumas that accompany a bad or difficult start in life? These questions are usually asked separately, and such support offered by different organisations. To carry out this work with both age groups, loss has to be reconceptualised. Developing an interest in troubled teenagers as well as struggling older people eventually engendered an idea of the generations helping each other. So here we see the start of a social invention/intervention: put these two groups together. The question arises of whether they can be absorbed in a single organisation (or community), or if the relationship between youngness and oldness needs to be put together 'in the mind' by the individual practitioner/carer/citizen. In the richness of the notion of what young and old people can learn from each other came an idea about how the generations might connect differently. This respondent felt that new communities were needed to promote a mutual support between people at different stages of life. The most obvious outcome of such a stance for later generations is a fuller passing on of varied and age-appropriate capacities and skills to care for people. Transmitting the gift of caring from one generation to the next (beyond the family) is the key idea here. The various ways in which this can happen are elaborated in some of the examples that follow, showing how creativity between the generations (and its shutting down) takes place.

People plan and prepare for endings in a private way. This involves informal gifts of stories, records and photographs. The disappearance of communities in which relations of kinship and friendship are remembered is often a stimulus. The stories that are offered are not necessarily easily welcomed or understood. There is tension between moving on into the future, spurred by peer pressure on youngsters, and their parents' and grandparents' concerns with change and endings. By contrast, in families and groups who have experienced diasporic loss, the social trauma is refracted through the individual families that undergo it. In such cases, the situation is almost reversed: it is the parental generation which strives to minimise thoughts about losses, while the children and grandchildren try to do the work of mourning. These diasporic states of mind are characterised by disturbed attachments and extremes of isolation between generations. The onus of completing the process and forgetting the trauma that has been undergone tends to fall on the third generation. In this way, there is a dynamic tension between remembering and forgetting that also underpins a developing capacity to intergenerationally mentalise, making it possible to imagine the worlds of different generations separated by time, age and death. Sometimes the process of reconceptualisation proves too difficult. In these instances, the memory process becomes characterised by haunting and experiences that are unhappily interred. This requires a different kind of response for either the forgetting to become 'successful', or for new experiences that are reparative to emerge.

Creativity and Shutting Down

Tensions and conflicts in inter- and transgenerational relationships express themselves through the struggle between creativity and its shutting down. The talents and traumas of each generation inform each other and are often closely connected. These themes are present in the whole process of reconceptualising loss, yet in these examples we can see what came forth and what was harder or impossible to express. This expression or non-expression has effects on the generations that follow.

One participant in the research knows he is good at art. He can paint but he doesn't know why. He can fix, design and build things. He senses that he has always had this gift; it's not clear whether it is learned from someone, and if so, from whom. The normal way of describing this aptitude is 'self-taught'. It's an end to thought. However, through a process of family-based storytelling, the respondent learns of an inventor several generations back in his maternal line. He feels proud and inspired by the story. By another chance encounter, he discovers that he shares a surname with a significant but little-known seventeenth-century French painter.

Delusions of grandeur could follow but they don't. Instead, stories such as this offer an explanation and legitimacy for a creativity that might otherwise be seen as 'strange', without valid educational status. The family history provides an antidote to shame; it allows him to experience pride and to enjoy his unexpected talents.

How can creativity get shut down? Other respondents spoke of difficult experiences within organisations where creativity should have been 'on tap' and part of the job but which was always hard to find. A respondent talked of years of frustration and anger about not being able to get things done or make any changes within a community dominated by an older generation. He described how a lack of confidence turned individual silence into a group silence, whereby no one dared to challenge how things were done. Eventually the younger workers left, feeling unable to contribute, and the organisation died. This is an example of an intergenerational failure within an organisation, but it is also an expression of a wider malaise in the West about renewal, and the nature of the settlement between the generations that is both economic, cultural and political.

The issue of creativity and its frustration is closely tied to relationships between the generations. Yet these conflicts are often described in terms that are personal: crises of mid-life, later life, the need to retrain, reassess, feeling depressed and so on. Yet the consequences are stark: skills and expertise all disappear with the death of an organisation. Something is lost that could have been preserved and developed in a new way.

Yet this problem occurs in families too. One respondent explained the tensions that her interest in the past had set up between herself and her mother. Her mother wanted to shut down the conversation about the family's difficult past and the effect of migration on them. Shutting down happens in the hidden and private spaces of families, as well as within the more public spheres of organisations. This respondent bemoaned the loss of narrative and story connecting the generations and felt the barrier of an immovable cultural force. Family and cultural context were conspiring against the expression of her own creativity.

Taboos loom large in this section of the data. A respondent talked about feeling stifled by an inability to speak of her experiences as a post-Second World War child in Germany. She had to move away before she could start to ask the questions that were constantly on her mind. This is an example of the push for creativity coming from children and young people. The adults involved in the war don't talk about it. It took the post-war generation to begin to change this block, in a battle between two generations. Another respondent spoke of how hard it was to find parents in the UK to participate in her children's school projects on the war. Even the victorious side's older generation didn't want to speak. Again, something is shut down, being flagged as dangerous, misguided and unwanted.

Another respondent from one of these post-war and post-migration families lamented the unavailability of freely told stories from the parental generation. This left her as an imaginative child holding partial stories inside her that could not be told because she lacked an inter-generational companion. As a consequence, much remained a mystery. Storytelling gets shut down. The idea of intergenerational companionship is related to the idea of intergenerational mentalising. The retelling and elaboration of stories require relationships devoted to that task. In the family, these may be between particular family members, but we can see that this happens in professional intergenerational relationships as well.

Some adults recognise that they mustn't shut down socially if they are going to carry out intergenerational work. A participant described the struggle to make a contribution in his work with children while suffering from extreme lifelong social anxiety. This personal determination not to shut down had other positive effects for the individuals and organisations encountered within this person's professional life.

Another respondent spoke of Hannah Arendt's ideas about the natal process in history (Durst, 2004), the tension between the emergence and the suppression of the new. Here intergenerational dynamics are caught between creativity on the one side and trauma on the other. There can be periods where the creative has the upper hand and others where trauma and shutting down predominate.

The question this observation raises is whether creativity and shutting down are in fact binary states that can be identified as predominant in different periods of time or whether they operate in parallel within individuals and in culture all the time. One respondent described the period 1912–1945 as characterised by a shutting down in libertarian/emancipatory politics. A suggestion from the data is that children of traumatised families must hold their creativity inside them until they can find better conditions for its expression. Another possibility is that creativity and shutting down constantly change place. My discussion of Charlotte Beradt's (1985) work on social dreams (see Chapter 3) shows that when a culture is shutting down and taking an authoritarian turn, people dream what they feel they can no longer speak. Whole groups or societies may do the same.

Looking for roots can embody this ambivalence. Coming to know what one's ancestors did can be inspiring, giving a sense of continuity for personal qualities or talents. It can uncover or confirm deep hurts and traumas. Equally it can, as another respondent observed, be an avoidance of political and social action, a replacement for the painful activity of finding identity and creativity in the present. This idea suggests that in conditions of cultural powerlessness, people turn inwards to their dreams and to their imagined past. This links both to Anderson's (1983) ideas about 'imagined communities' and to Volkan's (1998) 'chosen trauma'. Another contributor argued the opposite: that an unexamined past combined with a desire to live in the present is individually and socially pathological, and leaves us prone to repetition, both socially and psychologically.

This leads onto a discussion that occurred in one of the focus groups about the nature of research using online genealogical databases such as Ancestry as a search for the identity of dead people, rather than for a current network of relationships. With the former as motivation, the past is passive, delving into which shuts down creativity, whereas attention paid to the present and to one's community opens up a world of choices and options. These divergences and polar opposite views were more commonly expressed in the focus group which tends to be a forum more suited to expressing the tensions in contemporary culture.

The current pattern of relationships was very important for other respondents talking about their role in helping or blocking the creativity of people younger than themselves. These observations have a strong future focus but show that if the generations engage with less fear and defensiveness, a different prospect can emerge. It takes the idea of knowing how crucial staying open to one's own creativity can be at a social level (see Chapter 7). A new set of intergenerational relationships needs to be built to support this effort.

A respondent spoke of the fear she experienced when approached by a younger woman who insisted that she could help her with her work. A professional arrangement might have been to offer clinical supervision (both were psychotherapists). What was set up was a project to look at how people of different generations can learn to co-mentor each other. This also had a political context in terms of women mentoring women rather than maintaining the hierarchical professional relationship borrowed from clinical/academic work. The (older) respondent talked about finding the places where she is still hiding because she didn't expect to be valued by her peers. This taps into the creative potential of exchanges between living generations and between older and younger people.

Another respondent talked about a trauma that had not been healed in psychotherapy. In this experience, a difficult-to-grieve loss became more available and took a different form through art. In this example, an existing identity with profound professional loyalties had to be put to one side for something new to happen. Here is the other aspect of the dilemma of intergenerational change between living generations. If it can be done, then perhaps the next generation doesn't have to wait for a funeral before they can usher in their own creativity.

Several therapists in the survey talked about needing to expand and change their sense of what the therapeutic was in order to accommodate their own experiences of finding a way to pull creative intergenerational threads together. The theme of storytelling seems key here. Yet the tension between facilitating insight and joint collaboration remained a feature, as if the expert clinical role is nearly impossible to relinquish for many practitioners. Sometimes these creative educational processes are presented as clandestine activities smuggled into the everyday institution whether it be clinical or academic. Sometimes the older generation facilitators cultivate something for their students from which they themselves were never able to benefit in their own training.

The importance of stories in finding creativity or shutting down was spoken about extensively. One respondent obsessively read accounts of people who had died in extermination camps. What happened to that person? Did this person's fate have something to do with mine? Could this happen to me? These stark stories from young people who died are a very clear example of a creative force overcoming the attempt to shut down a whole people. Yet a reader in another generation must tell the stories again, or stories of the stories, so that something can come into the imagination that can be passed on. It looks like it might be an intergenerational mentalisation process (see Chapter 7 for elaboration) that takes three generations to get established against the shutting down of the first trauma-informed generation.

There are other kinds of marginalisation that, while not murderous and diasporic, can still completely freeze out and silence. Respondents talked about how their initial academic or professional training made them unable to think about vital issues in their own identity and about how to carry out research on it. Many spoke about the importance of first-wave feminism in finding a voice (Heilbrun, 1974) and this connected the theme of lost voices, from both personal and social histories (Rowbotham, 1992). Some reported this marginalisation being mirrored in colleagues or managers who did not understand them. Racism is the most emphatic of the breakdowns in mirroring and empathy. Here the shutting down and silencing properties of the educational system or the training institute come to the fore in the experience of some of our respondents with important inter- or transgenerational issues of identity. Some therapists felt unable to integrate experiences of migration and the trauma associated with it into their training. Some speculated that they may have been trained by a generation of migrant therapists who had somehow used psychotherapy as a defence against their own experiences of abject personal and cultural loss.

The post-war culture of the 'new start' that echoes the generation that doesn't want to talk was a strong theme that arose through the research. This suggests that the social defences of institutions at least in these post-war periods function quite like those of the individual family members. Eyes are set firmly on the future. Stories of conflict are minimised or not told. The war is idealised or laden with shame, a subject of manic reparation or depression (Figlio, 2015).

Beyond academia, in the struggle to bring experience-based learning and autobiographical memory into research, the world of psychotherapy is referred to as 'better' in that it offers emotional containment. Nevertheless, it is also talked about as another closed system when it is blind to cultural and social difference rooted in deeper family and social history. A key generation of therapists were migrants. The emphasis on the inner world could be seen as a defence against the traumas of migration.

Other participants described lifelong cycles of creativity and shutting down as an alternation of states. People discussed finding their own voice over a lifetime, separate from that of their family or profession. Many talked about the possibility of giving back, but without the preoccupation of survival that earlier working and professional life entailed. This also echoes the experience of Holocaust survivors' third-generation children who at last feel safe enough to ask what really happened. This feeding back cannot happen in a vacuum. Yet finding contexts in which to do it are thin on the ground. It's perhaps something that, as a culture, we don't do very well or sufficiently.

In this section on creativity and its attenuation, the problem of both social and individual defences comes to the fore. References to the role of intergenerational relationships within people's professional lives occurred frequently because the relationships between the generations are often mediated through work and social productivity.

Talents, skills and capacities are seen as being passed down the generations. They are not learned. This can be a source of intergenerational pride, but it is a hidden and perhaps mysterious process. This represents a kind of long-term continuity of creativity in families where skills appear in one generation and emerge again in the next. By contrast, organisations can die if younger workers' talents can't be promoted or their ideas recognised.

History is prone to phases, some in which creativity is more possible and others in which shutting down and limitation prevail. Creativity and shutting down also constantly change place within the lifetime of an individual and an organisation. Sometimes one generation can be seen to be more creative than another. Spurts of creativity require periods of consolidation. The creative work of one generation may be consolidated by another. In revolutionary and reactionary periods, the work of a generation may be torn down by another.

The repeating and elaborating of stories lead to new intergenerational relationships in which the past and future can be reimagined. This capacity to mentalise across the generations requires altered forms of companionship and more open professional systems. It requires risk-taking and innovative methods of collaboration between different age groups.

An extended run of creativity is more likely if intergenerational mentalisation has developed in society. This is based on a good settlement economically between the generations and the presence of different forms of intergenerational companionship (by definition absent in conditions of revolution and reaction). These may be between the different generations within families but also in the context of one's professional life. New forms of collaboration are required, specially designed to let the old and young learn from each other, less encumbered by set roles of seniority and authority.

Another form of creativity comes out of wartime and diasporic displacement where, in parallel to post-war reconstruction, individuals, families or groups create anew from the rubble of what is left culturally and physically. Perhaps the greatest creativity can come from the most comprehensive destruction and loss. The reconstruction of postwar Japan and Germany are examples of this, but many others exist, as do parallels with families who have 'lost everything' but are living as migrants within relatively normal, albeit alien, surroundings.

The form that this reconstruction can take is critical to what happens two to three generations later. For instance, the amount of denial or acknowledgement in the group or nation that is rebuilding, and the degrees and type of trauma will have a major bearing on the sort of culture that emerges. While this is a separate subject, it is clear that several of the stories that emerged from the research are touched by this attempt to construct a post-diaspora identity.

References

Anderson, B. (1983) *Imagined Communities: Reflections on the Origin and Spread of Nationalism*. London: Verso.
Beradt, C. (1985) *The Third Reich of Dreams: The Nightmares of a Nation 1933–1939*. Translated from the German by Bruno Bettelheim. Wellingborough: Aquarian Press.
Durst, M. (2004) Birth and natality in Hannah Arendt. In: Tymieniecka, A, T. (Eds.). (2004) *Analecta Husserliana (The Yearbook of Phenomenological Research) Vol 79*. [online] Dordrecht: Springer, pp. 777–797.
Figlio, K. (2015) *Remembering as Reparation: Psychoanalysis and Historical Memory*. Basingstoke: Palgrave Macmillan.
Heilbrun, C.G. (1974) *Toward a Recognition of Androgyny*. London: W. W. Norton & Company.
Ivlevs, A. (2015) Happy moves? Assessing the link between life satisfaction and emigration intentions. *Kyklos International Journal for Social Sciences* [online]. 68 (3), pp. 335–356 [Accessed 18 September 2020].
Rowbotham, S. (1992) *Hidden from History: 300 Years of Women's Oppression and the Fight Against It*. London: Pluto Press.
Volkan, V. (1998) *Bloodlines: From Ethnic Pride to Ethnic Terrorism*. London: Karnac.

5

Haunting

Hauntings Are Personal and Social

Our participants told us of losses that disturb, losses on the edge of conscious experience that haunt and trouble. This area of experience is often connected with trauma, shame and secrets. There are also experiences of trauma or suffering so extreme that people have attached to them the question 'where does that go?' The answer that this research suggests is that there is a cycle or movement of experiences that may have a frozen or unrepresentable phase that can move into personal or social awareness if certain conditions are met. The most significant of these are the passage of time and the survival of group members or descendants. Intergenerational trauma appears to be a process that needs to be resolved across two to three generations, during which an experience of haunting can be converted in a process of reconceptualising loss. This process of forgetting and remembering can run in one direction and then another, suggesting a dynamic relationship between being able to recover and represent memories on the one hand and losing all trace of them on the other.

It is also possible that if an event becomes completely lost in time, via transgenerational memory, it can be represented in future generations by social, cultural or epigenetic processes, as I discussed more fully in Chapter 3. Examples of such events are mass migrations or social displacement (such as the process of migration to towns in eighteenth-century Britain) and mass extermination. Memories of these may be held informally within ethnic and group memory or become more formally represented via social movements, civic societies, museums, drama and film. I suggest that every culture has its limits and that the nature and duration of transgenerational memory varies between cultures and across the world. The evidence suggests that smaller-scale societies are the most successful at preserving important memories. As these societies are more family-like, gaining their solidarity from filial or community ties, it is often the family that contains significant traces of previous events beyond its current individuals and through which certain talents as well as traumas are transmitted. It is also true that long-lasting social institutions can be containers for hauntings. The Church, the armed services and the state have their fair share of secrets.

Memories in the form of haunting share a key element: a quality of incompleteness that troubles and perplexes. It is also not clear what will happen to the haunting in future generations. Will it fade or become elaborated? Who will do this work of memory and what form will it take? Respondents spoke about memories that hinted at or pointed towards events experienced by their ancestors. Sometimes the recollection is based within the family; at others it is more social, suggesting a prevalent mood of a people or group. At other moments, the accounts indicate experiences that are somatic, involving panic, anxiety and dread. There is also a suggestion that hauntings can often be a sign or trace of trauma. Sometimes a haunting can appear in a historical text, awaiting discovery. Self-help societies can be haunted by aspects of what they were formed to commemorate or cope with.

I found many occurrences of haunting in our participants' narratives. I have grouped these around particular sub-themes which emerged across several accounts and give one or two examples from each.

A respondent spoke of a genealogy society formed to research the families of a particular migrant group. He told the story of a meeting during which a row erupted about the lack of interest in more contemporary migration, as if nothing had happened after the First World War. He went on to explain that this group's primary trauma was the loss of identity during the First World War and that this had been the abiding focus of the society since its formation. The society is an expression of the trauma and shame of identity loss; had the members' families managed to keep their identity, the group wouldn't have been needed.

Another respondent talked about the current mood of gloom pervading French society, likening it to that of the 1940s. She went on to speculate that the extent of unprocessed trauma from the experience of the Occupation has caused depression to predominate and creativity to be in short supply.

Names can haunt. A single first name, passed down the generations from a survivor of the First World War within a family which lost many of its members, becomes a talisman of survival. It is an unwelcome reminder of suffering including subsequent war-related mental illness. Each son in subsequent generations carries it: both the name and quite possibly the pangs of its significance.

Whole societies can be haunted by traumas. One respondent said that for her and for many Irish people, the famine happened 'yesterday'. This past is like a person 'standing right behind you'. She went on to add that it interested her how different cultures hold onto or relate to the past. This alludes to the short memory of the British in matters of Empire occupation and partition. While it's vital to ask why some cultures remember and some don't, here it is clear that the massive trauma and diaspora caused by the Irish Famine created a multifaceted haunting, which on a large scale is like the first example of the genealogy society's members living largely at a single point of time in the past.

Moods haunt and suggest an underlying malaise, yet it is sometimes hard to know what that malaise is. At other times it is very clear, but no one is talking about it.

Hauntings of Time and Place

A respondent spoke of his father's experience of being expelled from his Polish homeland during the clash of the German and Russian armies in 1941. In his story, we get the sense that time hasn't passed. The threat of becoming a victim of war is still lively. This man is like a ghost at a party: his children don't listen to him, even though he knows something that they don't, something which could save their lives. He feels his children are not interested enough in how to deal with a war—for instance how to shelter from bombs, be prepared for sudden departure and recognise the signs of danger in time to deal with them.

From a perspective of intergenerational memory, something ghost-like haunts here. What will its fate be? Maybe it will fade through the third generation or perhaps some interest may develop in reconceptualising the loss.

A respondent recounted his family's reluctance to celebrate a youngest child's birthday, the day also marking the anniversary of an aerial chemical attack which they survived but which killed many. Their habit of postponing the birthday celebrations for a few days remained into later years. This arrangement, where one kind of remembering is put off because of another, is a way of managing trauma that has yet to find its place. Some initial psychic and social trading has been done. This is a haunting of the future and its direction of travel is unclear. Its fate will depend on many factors yet to play out in the life of this young girl, her family and her people.

This last example shows how trauma spreads out through social space and in time so that in this instance it could become both an inter- and transgenerational haunting. Much depends on how family and international events play out in the future.

Closely linked to hauntings in time are hauntings of place. Perhaps the most archetypal experience of place is that of the burial ground. Is the interment settled or 'unhappy' and is some sense of disturbance associated with it? The following accounts of haunting of place show how respondents appear to be affected by events that did not happen to them. A place somehow becomes the focus or the trigger for an experience.

A woman rents a car and drives to the West of Ireland to find the location of her ancestors' house, which is a ruin. Her daughter has a panic attack when she stands on the land. In this story, something inexplicable happens in an apparently unfamiliar place. It is a visceral experience of fear that seems to spring from nowhere. The conscious action is a family seeking an ancestral home, which gives a context for a search for roots and meaning, but what occurs to this child is an entirely physical and unexpected experience. This could be how a transgenerational memory initially registers, but how can it be followed up?

A mining accident is remembered and recounted by the granddaughter of a survivor. The disaster devastated a whole village. The participant went on to describe how she'd recently returned to her home area. A chance meeting with a stranger led to the discovery that her uncle, with whom the family had lost contact, was in a local nursing home. Pictures of the mine covered the wall of his room. In this unexpected visit, he wept about the event to the respondent. The sense of an unprocessed loss resonates in this participant's story. It is as if she knew the facts of the pit disaster, but not the feelings of it. In her account of her return to the area and reunion with her dying uncle, we sense how close to the surface the trauma of the disaster still was, after all the years. The faces of fellow mineworkers in the pictures reveal how tight community ties can be, especially when sharing a dangerous, close connection to the very earth under one's feet. This haunting of place is at once individual, familial and communal.

Places can haunt in other ways as well. One participant said of his attempts to find his family's origin that he couldn't find the village names until he found a mediaeval map. In modern maps, all the old names were absent, suggesting the replacing of one social order by another. This old map communicates complex ideas under the guise of being a representation. It is a view of a social and a political world that has passed out of time. Even the place names have changed, yet are held in a family's memory as being part of its identity. This map felt to the respondent like a voice coming across the generations that embodied at once a lost past, a haunting and a nightmare (it is the site of a major the post-Second World War diaspora and change of nation state boundaries). It is an example of how the past might be haunting the present and offers the possibility of transforming the haunting into understanding. This map contained clues to both a lost genealogical family identity but also a profound and contemporary social issue of contested nationhood. Maps are haunted by colonial pasts. Another respondent described an almost identical experience when looking at an early twentieth-century military map—the first time he had seen the village and town names of his childhood printed on any map at all, so complete had been the erasure of his people's culture by a more recently created nation.

Another respondent thought his migrant father's affection for Britain might have had something to do with its island status, with the surrounding sea representing something of a safety barrier. The open expanse of Europe across which armies can march and refugees flee is in contrast to the imagined safety of a physically separate and delineated country. Britain and Europe haunt this respondent and his father, through an ancestral knowledge of the propensity for human aggression and destructiveness.

Hauntings of Faces and Names

One respondent said that she was haunted by photographs that showed similarities of facial features carried down the female line in her family. The pictures iterate like a fractal: she is like her grandmother, her mother as child is like herself as a child. Her daughter repeats the pattern of similarity from both previous generations. She calls this uncanny resemblance a good haunting, but it makes her think of ghosts that can't be exorcised, and reminds us of other aspects of genetic inheritance that haunt such as particular diseases or predispositions. Here, the haunting is one of self-similarity. The reiteration in face after face through time is an example of the search for recognition and of how the psychological aspect of the fascination with genealogy works: we are seeking ourselves through our ancestors.

While faces and shared names can hint at connections across time, broken connections also have the power to haunt. When Anglo-German relations in the First World War London became volatile, the Schoenfelds, German-Jewish immigrants who for many years had run a local tobacco business in Poplar, East London, escaped into their next-door neighbour's house to hide from the rioting mob bent on destroying their business premises (Liverpool Remembrance, 2009). They survived, but their name did not: they took the decision to become the Sheffields instead. Much German ancestry in the UK was disguised through name changes. This holds for other migrant groups needing to integrate urgently. Names can haunt, they can contain secrets, they can identify you. Names link us to the past. Taking up a name, or keeping a name, means keeping something from the past in the present (and into the future, potentially). Replacing or changing a name does the opposite, breaking the links socially and on into the future. Some German-Jewish respondents recalled altering their Jewish-sounding names to more Germanic or British ones. Some immigrants arriving in early twentieth-century British ports lost their surnames altogether, being recorded by the direction of their arrival as Eastman or Westman in the ships' passenger lists.

Hauntings of Objects

Objects can be filled with affective charge, significance and meaning. Objects have functions that themselves signify a meaning and purpose. They are also more likely to have been produced by artisans the further back in time they originate. One of the respondents was brought up surrounded by guns and archery; bows that had been 'passed down'. Although he still used them, he noted that these objects that had been passed on with a sense of pride could be quite shaming in contemporary culture. The participant is also holding onto something else: a different cultural understanding of what it means to be armed from the commonly held views in society today. Without a weapon you are unprepared and therefore unsafe. This seemed to link very powerfully to an ancestral past involving violent social dislocation.

Personal journals can haunt. A respondent spoke of the journal from her fourth-time great aunt giving her a window into the life of a creative unmarried woman. The act of writing the journal seemed significant: Who was it written for? Was a fourth-generation descendant a voyeur or a welcome companion? The respondent described the journal as a 'jewel', explaining how reading it had helped her to value the hidden side of women's creativity and how much has had to change socially for this to come into the open. This feels like a communication down the ages. It opens up the possibility that these unmarried women might have had different kinds of 'jewels'—different kinds of opportunities which are not visible at first glance. We might make assumptions about their lives having been less rich than those of their married sisters, but they had another life, hidden beneath the contemporary social radar. The journal writer of today can identify with, and delight in, the work of her unknown ancestor. This haunting across time holds an important element of sisterly intergenerational companionship.

Haunting by Shock and Dissociation

A respondent described the immediate aftermath of war, focusing on the experience of a young child taken from the breast of her dead mother. The situation is unbearable for the witness. Someone saves the child who goes on to be adopted. The respondent asks where an experience like that goes? What happens to the suffering of the survivors? This notion of 'where does it go?' reminds me of how people make sense of life after death, as if something has to *go* somewhere. There is a haunting quality, yet no one seems to know what happens after unspeakable trauma when the self prior to the traumatic experience has died, but the body lives on.

Another story was of a soup-kitchen volunteer suffering a breakdown. She had long felt a compulsion to feed people. Her grandmother had been a child migrant put on a coffin ship (a vessel used to carry refugees from the Irish Famine or from the Scottish Highland clearances) with little more than a name tag. During her final illness, the grandmother had delusions of people coming to her door begging for food. Her granddaughter begins to make links between her own involvement in hunger-relief work and her grandmother's experience of famine in Ireland. This might be seen as a haunting manifestation of intergenerational deprivation and famine. The respondent is thinking about the mechanics of intergenerational transmission. What may underpin hauntings of these extreme kinds are epigenetic states linked to famine and to PTSD. This ties into the theme of extended heredity discussed in Chapter 3.

Hauntings that cannot be processed stay right on the edge of experience. The artist Arshile Gorky was a child of six when his mother died of starvation and he joined the march of dispossessed Armenians leaving Turkey. A generation later, following the artist's suicide, his American granddaughter 'found' the iconic landscape that had featured in his art and that showed exactly where his childhood home had been. Much of his adult life had rested on a shaky disavowal of his refugee identity. His family had felt deeply haunted by this past and the 2011 film *Without Gorky* was an attempt to lay some of this to rest. The idyllic rural background of some of his pictures is a haunting of a time during which he had felt safe, before the death of his mother. In finding the geographical spot featured in his paintings, the family experienced some release from the complex spell of a difficult and tragic life.

Perhaps what this data tells us is that trauma and the unspeakable will *go* where it can. Into the background of a picture, into a compulsion to feed others, but also when a self is interrupted and broken by a traumatic event, then it is to the post-traumatic growth that we have to look. It is in the recovered life of the migrant in these examples that we must search for the inchoate hauntings from a previous time. I explore this further in Chapter 8.

These examples are of haunting before experience takes shape. Perhaps they represent the moment of dissociation in a trauma before the dust of the explosion has settled. They mark a sense of urgency and alarm, a question without an answer. We don't know what happens next.

Haunting by Imitation and 'Picking Up'

The phrase 'picking up' appears in respondents' transcripts and sheds light on an everyday haunting that people experience. It elucidates how survival skills are passed onto future generations. These experiences are sometimes close to the body, involving the acquisition of skills through watching or being around one's elders. One respondent described how his migrant father, traumatised by his wartime experiences, met his mother and settled down. Many years later, when members of his father's family came to visit, he didn't know who they were, but while listening to stories of their exploits, 'picked up' bits and pieces, fragments of what these strangers said and did. Unusual levels of physical strength and skill demonstrated by these strangers fascinated him.

This is also where the past starts to impinge on the present and something gets *picked up*. It is something that also involves curiosity, imitation and identification.

The respondent felt there was something genetic involved in picking up traces of experience, a practical sensibility that came from both his parents. He accounts for the creativity found in different branches of the family in this way. The skills are not learned at school but picked up from one generation by the next.

These thoughts hint at the idea that the skills of our forebears are there in our bones; we take up the rhythm of them by imitation. A family trait such as practicality or business acumen needs to be picked up and engaged with in order to be activated into a unit of cultural transmission which might then be passed on in turn. What we learn from our family and, more broadly, from our social milieu, is important.

In this story, there are three generations picking up skills in order to survive the extremes of diaspora. The father has just picked these things up and by implication passed them on, alongside the all-important 'knack' of picking up which seems to be a kind of watchfulness coupled with an attention to detail. By implication, survival skills are not taught as such to the respondent's children but are passed on by being 'picked up'; they remain close to the body in the form of implicit memory.

It is unclear how bodily haunting of this kind can be shifted to either loss that is identifiable or capacities that are recognised and that belonged to specific ancestors. There is a molecular (Deleuze and Guattari, 2004) quality to these memories. This body-based level of experience is also a source of unbidden creativity if it can be recognised or used in some way.

Haunting by Absence

Respondents told several stories of an absence haunting them or their family members.

One respondent talked about being haunted by a nameless dread that eventually took her into therapy. Part of her ancestral story is the Irish Famine and how her family survived this. Implicit within survival of such a life-threatening episode is the capacity to shut down and focus on the next task ahead and not to connect with the plethora of losses around you.

For this respondent, therapy offered the possibility of letting go of the struggle to formulate or explain. This is an interesting approach of losing focus and direction, a kind of falling apart leading to a reconnection with affect and body-based experience. This seems to be concerned with exploring and possibly reconceptualising loss, yet it is shot through hauntings from previous generations. It requires much psychological work, social support and validation.

The respondent tried to take advantage of having a generation above her to glean more information about what might have happened to her predecessors, but her mother possessed a deep stoicism which she renames as a philosophy of 'unspeakability'. Rejecting a creative engagement with the difficult past, her mother always focused on the next thing, rather than looking back. As a result, the respondent felt she was entirely isolated and left alone with her thoughts and feelings. With the help of therapy, she began to find a capacity to write as a way of coming to terms both with her childhood and with the Irish diaspora. Her family's reaction was negative. Initially, she felt so ashamed she even withdrew a paper about the subject for a conference.

She described eloquently how in shame she silenced herself and that it took another year before she was able to present the paper and thereby risk sharing her past with colleagues. What is visible in this story is how she repeatedly comes up against the haunting quality of an absence, and initially is silenced by it, but persists in engaging with the experience. The significant breakthrough she experienced in finally presenting the paper was validated by a positive and non-judgemental reaction. She described the experience of having been accepted as 'having found my people'.

This reinforces another theme associated with the shame of poverty and diaspora: not only is the past experience silenced, but the respondent's own particular capacities and talents cannot find their reflection. It's as if those who 'made it' are dispersed and no longer available to her. This is a process of social severance that reinforces silencing. It's like a double blow.

As she gains confidence, the respondent's engagement with haunting by absence takes on the quality of a detective tracking back from the scene of a crime to identify the motive. She's trying to locate the enactment, or resistance to an enactment, that is visible in a later generation and then work back to see what the original deprivation or trauma might have been. She develops ideas about the unspeakable, linking to affectual rather than intellectual knowledge.

The respondent described how severance and absence can occur after a major social trauma even when individuals and families can survive such events. There is a shame associated with poverty and deprivation which is enacted through silencing and thus breaks the familial and social links. There is also her experience of needing to find a new social group, or 'people', which can provide a supportive and appropriately curious environment for the personal exploration of haunting by absence. From this creative space, she developed her ideas on how to spot the enactment of an earlier trauma, and then track back to unearth its origins. The role of therapy alongside creative professional and social action figures large in this story.

This example also highlights a route by which a haunting, if worked on and enquired after, can shift into a new form of creativity. The historical lack of recognition from this respondent's ancestors can shift into a profound experience of recognition amongst a new group of colleagues and friends in another generation. This important recognition is a form that intergenerational healing can take. I discuss this in more detail in Chapter 8.

Haunting and Active Forgetting

Haunting suggests a ghost, a tenuous connection or an association which we don't necessarily invite, but which gives us the potential to generate communication and to make meaning. Active forgetting, by contrast, is concerned with experiences, memories, people or places being locked away. There is a barrier to connection or communication—the contents are not meant to be found, not meant to allow meaning to be made. Active forgetting can also be thought of as a desire to bring 'closure' as well as to cover up and conceal.

The intention to forget things is often a positive one. If there is something dangerous around, it behoves us well to see it locked away. The anthropologist Mary Douglas (1966, p. 119) cited Van Gennep's (1960) sociological insights into danger:

> He saw society as a house with rooms and corridors in which passage from one to another is dangerous. Danger lies in transitional states, simply because transition is neither one state nor the next, it is undefinable. The person who must pass from one to another is himself in danger and emanates danger to others.

The idea of a person in transition emanating danger to others might unconsciously underpin one of the central tenets of active forgetting: the unwillingness, or apparent lack of capacity for people who have endured horrors, to speak of these to others. Sometimes it is those around the traumatised person who don't dare ask. Either way, communication is locked away. The liminal quality of a person who has had dangerous and frightening experiences accompanies them like a haunting. They have something about them that is uncanny, reminiscent of the return of the dead. This fear can inhibit relatives, partners and therapists in being interested or enquiring further.

In the research data, I found a distinction between active forgetting, which was known and could be consciously thought about, and forgetting, which hovered on the edge of consciousness. Sometimes respondents felt they were locked out, at other times there was a secret concealed from them.

Locked Out from the Known

One respondent, reflecting on his own professional life, recounted a period of hospitalisation, during which he thought he would not be allowed back to resume his career after his recovery. He feared being locked out of his chosen profession because his mental state would deem him 'dangerous'. He is 'dangerous' in Van Gennep's (1960) terms and is literally and metaphorically interred from society. In this story, he knows he is being locked out and the pain of that is apparent, like being imprisoned for a crime he hasn't committed. With skill and determination, he returns, but the impetus is not so much an improvement in his health, but rather the horror of losing everything through being temporarily unwell. In this example, there is a struggle for survival with life or death consequences. People who leave their work with mental health issues are often seen to 'disappear' to their colleagues: like shell-shocked soldiers they fall into the liminal area of burnout, breakdown and disability.

A focus group respondent spoke about being struck by the intense discomfort of a family who were descendants of a Nazi prison camp commandant. Always fearing a public revelation of its historical connection to an extermination camp, the family had wanted to forget about it. The past was exposed by the TV ancestry programme *Who Do you Think You Are?* (2007) which featured a third-generation relative. This example shows how the perpetrator experience gets locked away in the following generations. A known atrocity committed by an ancestor brought feelings of contamination or toxicity which were dealt with by active forgetting. The actions of the few spread both down and across the genetic line, leaving an ever-widening fan of descendants picking up the shame of the shared family history. The pull to simply lock away this difficult and unwanted inheritance is strong.

In a connected example from the 2012 documentary *Hitler's Children* (re-broadcast on the BBC on 2 September 2020), several third-generation children of perpetrators described a struggle to reverse the type of silencing described above. Most had to counter the denial of their parents and siblings. Each bore witness to wanting a different future for their children. The daughter of one third-generation witness described feeling protected by her uncompromising and outspoken father; another said his understanding of his purpose in life was to bear the guilt that no one in his family had yet shouldered. These examples of third-generation witnesses combine a reparative action with another: neutralising evil.

In contrast, another respondent spoke of a different kind of survivor experience. To hide his lack of means, his ancestor would rent a suite during his annual trip back to his homeland to visit relatives. The pain of poverty, of an abject and non-flourishing life, must be hidden. Yet everyone knew the suite was rented.

In these examples, the fearful and shaming actions are known and the cover-up is known. The only question is whether it can be maintained. In both cases, the active forgetting is about intense shame and loss of face. Yet others in these families fight back. It would take a finer-textured analysis to understand why, but the siblings of these perpetrator families illustrate clearly the third-generation role, to witness or to forget. They play a pivotal role for the memory of the generations.

Another respondent gave a further illustration of the problem of being locked out of the 'known'. Talking about James Joyce's rejection of honorary Irish citizenship when Ireland became independent in 1920, he illustrates how this dilemma was faced by thousands of ordinary citizens after the end of the First World War. Empires had fallen, national boundaries had changed, people with one identity suddenly had another to cope with. Joyce chose to remain British. Most had no choice and were locked out of their previous identity. This tightening of identities was a foretaste of events leading up to the Second World War where loyalty to a single nation state started to take precedence over belonging to a particular family, region or ethnic group.

The issue here is that by making the 'wrong' choice, one can be left with a profoundly unhappy loss of identity: the loss of nationhood, state or family. A contemporary example might be the teenage fighters who left Britain to join the Islamic State of Iraq and the Levant (ISIL) in Syria and now wish to return home to their families. Their rights to British citizenship are in question. They sit like a ghost on our consciousness, locked out from home but not going away.

Another respondent, talking about contemporary South Africa, said that the inspiring idea of a 'rainbow nation' when repeated enough times could sound like a defence against social fragmentation. The underlying fear of social violence leading to civil war is adopted to silence people, with a hopeful image covering up corruption and lack of progress.

This is a silence that is a choice, conscious or unconscious, to edit the immediate experience, by removing and getting rid of the difficult material. I speculate that moves to enforce political correctness, to silence unhappiness or dissent however crassly expressed, can have the effect of pushing nationalism or racism underground until it emerges as a political statement such as Brexit. This is an example of being unhappily interred—either subsumed within the European Union or left out in the cold as a single nation, depending on your point of view.

Locked Out from the Unknown

Experiences of being locked out from the unknown are harder to grasp. We need some kind of revelation, cypher or sign to reveal the presence of something that is unknown. This suggests that the memory is close to the body and is implicit in nature. Abraham and Torok's (1994) ideas about transgenerational 'generation hopping' experiences caused by secrets and silencing might fit here, although the evidence, just like the experience, is hard to describe and define.

One respondent described how she was given a clue to her persistent unhappiness: her mother eventually told her that she had not been wanted. Her parents had tried to bury their feelings about having had her, but ultimately the feelings had not been walled off effectively and she had sensed them without knowing the details. It seemed in this story that her parents felt that by editing the truth they could escape the consequences. Sometimes it's better to simply know, rather than be haunted by the idea that something is not as it should be.

Another respondent spoke of the impact her illegitimacy had: a cover-up of her birth and her concealment from one side of her family for many of her early years led to her continually putting herself in positions of invisibility as an adult. She became very sensitised to the issues of validity and authenticity through art and through citizenship. Knowing what was genuine and what was counterfeit became central organising principles for her.

Others described different ways of getting 'locked out' of themselves. A respondent recalled imagining prison bars all around her, early on in personal therapy, and felt they were her failed attempts to free himself from her past. She knew that there was so much she couldn't get to. However, she persisted with her therapy and described a state of mind which she called 'dread' breaking down into a profound experience of vulnerability.

The fear that she described is what can lead to interment rather than recuperation and recovery, if not given time, space and containment. Her way out of her unhappy interment came through being able to engage slowly with the nameless dread. Consequently, she reported being able to teach differently at depth, holding her students in a similar way to that in which her therapist had held her. This feels like a very embodied engagement in how she allows her students to meet their own difficult feelings, much as she has been allowed to in her therapy. This seems to be a key to enabling an unknown unhappy interment to be processed; there needs to be creative enactment that allows for the associated feelings, affects and unthought knowns to be perceived in a way that is bearable. This links to the role of therapy in working with intergenerational trauma that I take up in Chapter 7, and also to the idea that shorter generational cycles are very significant in the workplace and in professions).

Some respondents were directly affected by Holocaust and other genocide testimony. These stories often contained examples of things which won't remain interred. Experiences of horror, genocide, war, torture, famine and cruelty abound. These memories are often without very much context: 'My father stabbed him twelve times'; 'I recognised my sister's face amongst the girls' bodies floating downstream'; 'they were taken to the camp and were killed on the first day'. Suffice it to say that in catastrophes, both man-made and natural, it is often the fate of the human body that is the focus. Perhaps the focus on the body, its condition, its absence or presence can be the start of questioning and witnessing. Families without the bodies of loved ones find grieving even more difficult.

Therapists with high caseloads of traumatised people will know how certain events described by their patients will stay in their minds for years and decades. For some, it can be difficult to stop digging up bones; the sense of outrage is so strong and the presence of haunting so ubiquitous, while answers are often in short supply.

Given the prevalence of the Irish Famine in some of my respondents' stories and the problem of the presence and absence of bodies in hauntings, I am put in mind of a peculiar aspect of English Civil War history. In 1660, the Indemnity and Oblivion Act was passed, aiming to give closure to the conflict, but the burial location of parts of Oliver Cromwell's body remains secret to this day. Perhaps the fear of civil war is still great. It is also interesting that English pamphlets from the period detailing alleged Catholic atrocities against Protestants in Ireland used European iconography from the earlier Hundred Years' War. It's as if the attempt to quell and end a conflict both suppresses and conserves the main elements of strife without resolving them. They are packed and ready for transmission to another generation. Given the right conditions (mainly the suppression or non-resolution of conflict), something that was intergenerational turns into a transgenerational problem.

The violent and toxic legacies of the Atlantic slave trade and the genocide of indigenous peoples are examples of conflicts that are largely unresolved and continue to trouble oppressor and oppressed. These in the current period are often colonial hauntings, as the unexpected presence of the Irish diaspora in our research data demonstrates.

Summary

In this chapter, I have described hauntings and active forgetting. The hauntings take a myriad of forms (time, place, person, objects) and can be experienced as shock and dissociation, a capacity to 'pick up' something, an absence. Not all hauntings are bad—many respondents spoke of being usefully informed by the haunting about how to live their life now. Active forgetting comes in two main states: things we know about which are locked away, and things we are unaware of consciously which, were we to know about them, might explain a current unease or a repeated pattern of behaviour in one's life or society.

Bringing together the idea from haunting by shock and dissociation with our understanding that forgetting can be an active process, we might think of the states of deep dissociation which polyvagal theory Porges describes (2018), combined with a need to protect others by splitting off difficult experiences (Van Gennep's ideas of danger and transition). The result is something so locked away that it evades conscious awareness. We could speculate that when it evades the unconscious as well, that forgetting is successful because it is apparently complete. This must be the outcome for many traumas, or we would all be incapacitated by awareness of our inter- and transgenerational horrors. It may be that we are haunted or troubled by thoughts, ideas or experiences in which the dissociative affect resonates in an unhelpful way, so our capacity to segregate is impacted. When this happens the traumas which our forebears have encountered fail to be forgotten and are passed on as hauntings for subsequent generations to face.

This links back to the idea of generation-hopping experiences that have a life of their own between and inside individuals (see Chapter 3). While this is a difficult idea to work with, it does also suggest that in situations where there has been a progressive failure to think about, acknowledge and represent events and actions, forgetting can lead to an extinction of an experience at least in an individual or a family line. In societies that are interconnected, complete erasure is probably unlikely, given the ongoing existence of victim and perpetrator dynamics and more subtle processes of cultural appropriation. Hauntings and active forgetting show how, as experiences pass out of intergenerational knowing, they may remain available transgenerationally in physical culture and in the memories of other groups.

If explored with courage, curiosity and openness, hauntings suggest stories of endless connections, objects that remind and bear witness, an archaeology of experiences as well as things (Bennett, 2010).

References

Abraham, N. and Torok, M. (1994) *The Shell and the Kernel*. Translated from the French by Nicolas T. Rand. Chicago: University of Chicago Press.

Bennett, J. (2010) *Vibrant Matter: A Political Ecology of Things*. London: Duke University Press.
Deleuze, G. and Guattari, F. A. (2004) A *Thousand Plateaus: Capitalism and Schizophrenia*. Reprint London: Continuum. 2012.
Douglas, M. (1966) *Purity and Danger*. London: Routledge.
Hitler's Children (2012) [TV]. Directed by Chanoch Ze'evi. BBC Two, 23 May.
Liverpool Remembrance (2009) *Liverpool And Merseyside Remembered*. Available from: http://liverpoolremembrance.weebly.com/anti-german-riots.html# [Accessed 20 September 2020].
Porges, S.W. and Dana, D. (2018) *Clinical Applications of the Polyvagal Theory: The Emergence of Polyvagal-informed Therapies*. New York: W. W. Norton and Company.
Van Gennep, A. (1960) *The Rites of Passage*. Translated from the French by Monika B. Vizedom and Gabrielle, L. Caffee. (missing edition number) London: Routledge.
Who Do You Think You Are? (2007) [TV]. BBC Two, 27 December.
Without Gorky (2011) [TV]. Directed by Cosima Spender. BBC Four, 12 March.

6

Images of Nature in Multigenerational Memory

Beyond Human Nature, Nature as Guide and Healer

I'd be better if I were a willow rather than an oak.

The quote above was used to illustrate the important quality of adaptability being in tension with a more determined, stubborn or fixed sense of self. The respondent spoke of his desire to tell truth to power and demonstrate leadership that stood up for the rights and voices of the less powerful, especially those of the child. It alludes to the lifelong tension between two types of resilience, the oak relating to the first phase of a professional life involving leadership in an organisation, and a second 'willow phase' focused more on listening flexibly and responsively to individual experiences through a career in counselling.

The oak/willow image speaks of the dilemma of how to focus and in what way to take action. For instance, if deep unfairness and injustice are a fundamental feature of the lives of our parents, then what does the next generation do with this? If our parents have had to be vigilant and uncompromising, we may be without a model for flexibility that isn't seen as weak or made of 'inferior wood'.

The respondent who coined this phrase bemoaned how little change he had been able to make in a lifetime. This referred both to professional achievements but also to his own personal patterns.

This ushers in a basic and fundamental question about intergenerational change: Are there identifiable ways in which one generation builds the foundations for the next? Or are we vulnerable to the cultural 'wipe clean' so beloved of Darwinian genetics? (see Chapter 3, on epigenetics.)

A natural image of two types of tree forms a notion of a trajectory that is both personal to one lifetime and yet suggestive of a sequence of growth development, decay and regrowth across two or more generations. These images of different woods allow us to reflect on how we are who we are: in this instance more oak than willow.

Another respondent described a working life spent at one location rich in natural and architectural features. Fitting new buildings into old landscapes and responding to the loss of large trees through disease led to a lifelong sensitivity to what an environment might be asking of the human communities that live in it.

This then connects to a developing professional and spiritual identity that is both individual and community based, offering custodianship and guardianship to a working landscape. The mystery of care is also articulated in that nature and the non-human world may have ways of indicating 'what they need' if we are sufficiently attuned. Designs may arise not from architects' papers or planning committees but from following a sight line in a landscape, or respecting a spring or old pond long located at a particular spot.

The respondent continued by telling us that the presence of large trees in a landscape were an important reminder that human affairs were by comparison very short term. By asking questions a gardener might ask, such as 'what does this landscape want?' or 'what will work here?', it became possible for him to formulate a social project that put young and old people together, creating a collaborative connection around the theme of care across the generations. This was one of the few ecological views offered in this research of the relationship between the generations.

Suggesting a relationship between nature and personal development bestows on the natural world its own life and intelligence, so that while standing outside human affairs, nature could also interact creatively with human issues in subtle but direct ways. Death of trees or the passing out of life of a whole species could help humans think about facing their own death and ending, both individually and collectively.

Speaking of the role of gardener, the respondent explained how the landscape could listen and respond to his efforts to alter and enhance the garden. He described it as process whereby as he gardened he would always move between deep involvement in what he was doing and stepping back from it and learning to see in it the exact things he was doing in relation to the environment. By implication, this model was also applied to the process of counselling or therapy, which becomes a kind of gardening of the mind or soul.

The natural world also helped to chart a connection to the mythic where certain trees were seen as representing primal forces of vitality, transpiration and regeneration. This was seen as the mystery of transforming something heavy and dense into the light and vital, a quality embodied by this ideal human community of the social project as it looked after its younger and older members through time.

Another respondent spoke at length about the natural world—and wilderness in particular—as linked to personal healing. Images of castles of rock and profound isolation in wild places were followed by the revelation that this somehow allowed her to conceive a child, something that was unimaginable until this immersion in nature. This points to the healing of what feels to be beyond human holding or care. She alludes to something miraculous where wilderness gives birth also to imagination. The discovery or rediscovery of imagination turned out to be a key theme for our respondents and links to one of our overarching themes: the development of intergenerational mentalisation.

Nature of Place, Physical Environments and Haunting

A respondent recounted an experience of illness and depression which she could recognise through the way she experienced nature at that time, being more aware of processes of decay, illness and death. She came to realise via a process of introspection that the landscape and her own identity were deeply connected.

Place can provide a long-term way of identifying and working with change in the self. Landscape becomes like a long-lived parent, partner or teacher. The respondent said that she didn't talk about this experience for many years, and felt it was bizarre but perhaps also shameful, something that should be associated with people rather than places. The revelation, however, led to an understanding about the rest of her life: that her deep attachment to land was a way of identifying and transforming herself; nature became her therapist and lifelong companion. She no longer felt trapped by her past, and being in the landscape became a resource where it was possible to recognise her feelings and thereby clear and renew herself.

Here the relationship with nature is experienced as a reciprocal one, characterised by mutual influence and care.

Greater Nature

Is there one long river in England? Well in Ireland we've got the Shannon.

This comment by a respondent alludes to a transgenerational theme of how collective traumatic 'dammed up' experience finds its own way through all kinds of ground and watercourses into the present generation and beyond. The power of a mighty river is unstoppable despite human attempts to control it for short-term gain. This restless and insistent image of water doesn't require scientific explanation or justification, it just is. The inexorable flow of human experience will push its way through. Water in mighty rivers will filter into a million tributaries and will still find its path, whatever its destination.

Some countries of course have fewer rivers than others, some have more or less rain, so even here the life of different nations is in the hands of their geography and resources. We are challenged here to think about the generations as a river flowing through us, impervious to our attempts to control who we think we are. Nothing will stop this transgenerational flow; it is larger than the individuals through whom it is transmitted who form its course and who make its riverbed.

This a reference to transgenerational processes as opposed to intergenerational ones. The image of water seems important in articulating a complex idea, one which was repeatedly used by my respondents.

This transgenerational image of watercourses is one that portrays a movement through time in which a whole social experience flows. This leads us to think about historical and social events and a history of the land. A respondent spoke about the Irish Famine, describing the intertwining of the sentiment that the land had failed and its powerful political context. Here the respondent spotlighted the way in which something described as natural—a famine—can have human agency hidden inside it. This is a powerful reference to a depopulation that literally cleared the ground for enclosure and brought about the death and diaspora of a whole social class of people. Future generations of famine survivors are, in this respondent's view, 'haunted by hunger'.

Another respondent talked about the dangers of perceiving beauty in a landscape: he described a bucolic scene in a Central European beauty spot and a meeting with a group of old women. They laugh at him for saying that he finds the landscape moving in its splendour and rebuke him by pointing out that those kinds of feeling of attachment to place are dangerous. It's a painful and puzzling moment for him. They explain that if you are stupid enough to be in love with a place then you will have even more pain when you are dispossessed. This is a poignant intergenerational moment mediated by a pastoral image of nature. The women view the land as the site of a major ethnic cleansing campaign, and one which is now 'occupied' by 'another people'. To even refer to beauty risks the whole cycle of war starting again. It is a powerful warning given by a group of elderly women who have 'seen it all'.

Practical Nature

Rural pursuits performed by ancestors for countless generations are accounted as the source of a respondent's practicality, his ability to turn his hand to anything. The approach to hunting is one of survival and domination over nature. He says of his forebears that they used to go out on the sea bank, on the mudflat and shoot conger eel with 2.2 rifles. Further back in this respondent's intergenerational family story there are tales of cruelty, competition and everyday exposure to life-threatening risk: floods, wild crocodiles and also dangerous practical jokes amongst family, friends and neighbours. The social context of these stories was intercommunal competitiveness followed by military invasion and diaspora for his family and community.

Here nature stands in as a model for how to relate to other humans: expect to be attacked, so counter-attack and dominate in return. In these stories, other humans are treated 'like animals' and expect such treatment back. Accounts abound of intercommunal violence and beatings witnessed by children. This brutalised pre-social order breakdown then gives way to further images of cruelty at the start of a diasporic journey, people 'loaded into trucks like cattle' where 'many died'. This respondent also talked about his forbears eating dead animals to survive. Family members also 'fell by the wayside' and were left behind. In their long journey through mountains and deserts, only the youngest and fittest got through to the end.

There were images of drowning in this survey of memory. They convey the arbitrariness of accidents and portray nature as pitiless executioner. They occurred in the context of a journey of forced migration and involved tragic loss of friends and family. In relation to the forces of water, humans are abject and defenceless, and yet, as with famine, there is some human agency hidden inside these tragic natural events.

On a positive note, another former migrant spoke about a means of survival on a long journey by foot (one amongst many). While walking at night to avoid detection, arrest and torture, he staved off dehydration and starvation by recognising the smell of watermelons. Coming from a farming family, he knew the signs of harvest and where to look for leftover or discarded fruit. It happened only a few years ago. Yet something now haunts this respondent about the smell of watermelons.

The Trouble with Big Landmasses and the Advantages of Islands

Using images drawn from geography, another respondent encapsulated a post hoc summary and explanation for migration and that of his family in particular. Migration across a big land mass, on which anything can and does happen, makes people search for an island or safe space which is also like a castle; a place of imagined or actual safety. He felt that the British are complacent because of their sea barrier. In Europe, by contrast, it's easier for things to go wrong 'all of a sudden'.

The question about whether islands are ever really islands is alluded to poetically by John Donne in Meditation 17 (1623):

> No man is an island entire of itself; every man
> is a piece of the continent, a part of the main;
> if a clod be washed away by the sea, Europe
> is the less, as well as if a promontory were, as
> well as any manner of thy friends or of thine
> own were; any man's death diminishes me,
> because I am involved in mankind.
> And therefore never send to know for whom
> the bell tolls; it tolls for thee.

Donne turns nature into culture and makes the case for the interconnectedness of all people. This is an example of something that all respondents reached for when evoking nature in their explanations of the relationship between the generations. Some aspect of the natural and physical world offers a connection, however fleeting or strange, to something 'other' or greater than personal experience. Nature becomes a means of inferring connection between past, present and future, a way of referring to deeper time or duration. Nature is also one way of referring to processes that operate beyond the everyday and to connections between the generations.

By contrast, nature also appears in the personal romantic mode of explaining something human: a sense of limitation, connection, threat or opportunity. In these examples, I have given of 'do or be done to', of the safety of islands, of the role of the teacher, of different qualities of wood, the healing power of landscape and water are ways of making links between nature and identity. In the background, these examples offer a naturalistic way of describing how personal qualities emerge, are passed on and fade away in processes of development and decay between the generations. By referring to the mystery of agency in the natural world, and time beyond human time, respondents point to forms of creativity and problem-solving that reach forward into an unknown future, thus extending recognition, empathy and enquiry beyond the immediate generation in which we are located. These images and experiences in and of nature can be the seed for forms of intergenerational companionship which I discuss in more detail in Chapters 7 and 8.

Reference

Donne, J. (2012) *Collected Poetry*. London: Penguin Books.

7

Therapeutic Implications of Working with Multigenerational Memory

Intergenerational Companionship

One of the most striking themes that come out of this research is that of intergenerational companionship. While the model for this came originally from the idea of promoting intergenerational awareness by putting young people who had had a difficult start in life in the position of caring for older people, several practitioners talked about intergenerational experiments that involved stepping outside existing professional roles to bring about new forms of collaboration between younger and older practitioners. The traditional arena for this in therapy is clinical supervision, but this relationship was then repurposed to one of companionship, beyond the hierarchical passing down of clinical wisdom.

One respondent described how modifying a traditional supervisory role with a younger therapist led to another kind of collaboration that involved a two-way mentoring. Collaborative work followed, with each seeing the other as having the potential to help their work. Our respondent spoke of the acknowledgement shown by a younger colleague that allowed her to open up about certain subjects that she had previously kept hidden because of prior experiences of not being valued by seniors in the profession. This is an example of intergenerational repair within a profession, allowing a discharge of creativity albeit requiring a daring re-evaluation of traditional clinical roles. Multimedia artwork provided a means of exploring complex and traumatic loss that couldn't be expressed through words. Interestingly, it is the validation and encouragement by the younger colleague that allows the older practitioner to open up, take risks and overcome some of the hurts of previous supervisory relationships when *they* were the younger and abject party.

Another respondent with responsibilities for training and education referred to the fear of self-disclosure that trainee therapists share, that is the trepidation of being seen as pathological. He suggests that despite the nuances in training, the take-home message tends to be that as a therapist you must be seen to be able to hold yourself together. This is in tension with another value held by the respondent which is a capacity to 'fall apart' and be moved by experiences 'beyond words'. While falling apart may sound alarming, it is more in the spirit of developing a capacity to disintegrate and reintegrate. There is some evidence from attachment theory that storytelling—and by implication working with autobiography—may help cultivate this capacity to crack up while not falling apart (Stuthbridge, 2017).

Courses that are autobiographical and use mixed media encourage trainees to connect broader family and social historical issues that sensitise candidates to intergenerational problems. By promoting training elements such as these in which trainees/students can explore their biographies freely and without judgement, the respondent has tried to counter the tendency to intellectualise experience which he feels is common in psychotherapy training. By bringing in a strong autobiographical element to his own training work, the respondent feels he helps to create a new way of establishing context that is essential if the 'otherness' and beyond-language aspect of intergenerational experiences can be recognised. Storytelling as a pedagogy can help trauma be thought about in a less clinical way and more part of personal and social experience (O'Loughlin and McLeod, 2015).

The background to this struggle is the culture of technical diagnosis combined with the attenuating power of the training establishment. The idea that psychotherapy training institutes are social defences against anxiety is not a new one; but an intergenerational autobiographical aspect included in training might counter some issues that are known to have occurred around, for instance, migrant psychotherapists (the majority in certain periods of time), de-emphasising the social and political, and prioritising the 'inner world' as a means of managing their own traumatic diasporic experiences. This also connects to the evidence that the experience of migration may be experienced as shameful as well as traumatic. A more psychosocial stance in training would be about enabling an inner-world response to the social and political. Tutors and trainers offering to share aspects of their own autobiographies could also create a stronger sense of the whole training group as a community of learners. This would also allow some of the troublesome power differentials between trainees and trainers to be talked about so that early- and late-career dynamics could be anticipated and better understood. Storytelling can help participants in the therapy training witness each other beyond the roles that they occupy and sometimes use defensively.

Storytelling: Intergenerational Companionship and Mentalisation

One respondent told us that she knows from childhood how a story may be all that is left of murdered family members; the horror and loss are simply and starkly reported by a cousin, but they are also given as characters in a story. Here, we see the creative force holding more sway than any push to shut down. The story, bearing witness to genocide, stops this truth being silenced, yet also begins a relationship with family members who will never be known to the child reader. She explains the power of this stark story: that the pain is raw, unmediated by a parent, told by someone like her—a cousin and a young woman. The story became her story, one that belonged to her. She felt haunted by these unknown relatives, yet they are also her ancestors: they could be her; she could be them. Time stands still in the starkness of the account.

Several other respondents spoke about how to fashion stories that would travel from one generation to the next. They spoke of the creative tension between speaking freely about what they would like their grandchildren to know and striving to gain the curiosity and collaboration needed across the generations.

An important process in storytelling emerged: reminiscences could engage and calm an older person telling a story to a younger one; elements of affect regulation are involved. There is some evidence (Hepper et al., 2020) that reminiscences involving nostalgia especially in the social process of storytelling soothe both younger and older parties. Significantly, something similar was reported in the shift from an individual telling a story as a child and then telling it again as an adult. This suggests an intergenerational mentalisation function for storytelling where elements of reverie and imagination come to the fore. Mentalisation has also been characterised as a form of mostly preconscious mental activity (Bateman and Fonagy, 2010). This is important for a practice of therapy that is intergenerationally informed. The idea of intergenerational mentalisation that grows out this natural exercise of the imagination may be quite rare, or alternatively, perhaps it is hidden. The widespread interest in ancestry and family history could be a positive sign, but it depends on how it is made sense of and with whose support. Many of the participants in this research had an interest in ancestry. Some have applied it socially, but for others it has been a solitary or inner-world activity.

Therapy as a Preparation for Multigenerational Work

Some respondents spoke about the contribution therapy made to their capacity to tolerate and work with dissociative and very disturbed states of mind. While the general understanding is that these states of mind are formed early and are sometimes trauma-related, they seemed to help people deal with a profound sense of otherness that encounters with their ancestors' experiences stirred up in them. Over a decade of giving talks to various audiences and sharing these findings with colleagues, we have noticed the emergence of very strong feelings either in ourselves or in audience members during events. This is in contrast to my experience of other public speaking on therapy-related issues. While initially we felt we hadn't had enough therapy ourselves or were too identified with the material, we now think that this ancestral multigenerational material is deeply disturbing and in each meeting many hauntings are stirred up. Over the years, we have developed a more open meeting style in which the emergence of feelings in a larger public space is acknowledged and thereby normalised. This seems to help. The meeting seems to be able to respond to people's distress sometimes in very specific ways, but also through the sharing of parallel or similar stories and experiences. This links back to the earlier finding of the value of sharing autobiography in training. More often, the emergence of traumatic feeling is amplified and distorted by gender resentments, racial oppression and in a public space can cause fear and confusion, as witnessed during the opening session of the Truth and Reconciliation Commission in South Africa (Oboe, 2007). Throughout the duration of the innovative and creative TRC, staff members and participants suffered vicarious trauma (Haupt and Malcolm, 2001). While I don't think we have solved the problem that all large groups are prone to—surges in affect and contagion of feeling (Kreeger, 1975; Agazarian and Carter, 1993)—I think there is some evidence that it is possible to bring about trauma-informed large-group responses that are particularly creative and helpful for multigenerational work. One of the strengths is the multiplicity of voices that ancestral work implies (Blackman, 2012) and I discuss this more fully in Chapter 8 on the psychosocial.

As well as helping people attend to fractured and dissociated states of mind, therapeutic work helps multigenerational work through the light it can shed on family secrets, and the power of silencing. Much intergenerational work is informed by the idea of secrets having a longer history than the individuals who needed to keep them. Within a single generation where a significant secret has been enacted (e.g., 'we didn't really want you' or 'we were so ashamed of illegitimacy we hid you'), therapy helped uncover and make sense of the pain and maladaptation each secret bequeathed, allowing something to change in the next generation. The need to repeat lessens, and in transforming these hurts, the individuals involved become hubs for education and communication for others who were similarly afflicted. Therapy can therefore be seen to play a key role in transforming intergenerational relationships and in lessening the damage caused by secrets and unprocessed trauma.

Therapy also offers new possibilities for attachment and working through trauma. The knowledge of postpartum psychosis, for instance, can be traced three generations back through the disturbed attachment patterns in the descendant children, but when and how does anything change? How can new reparative patterns of attachment be found in an age before therapy and John Bowlby? The answer in my own family was the presence of significant friendships amongst the women through which childrearing was shared, going far beyond babysitting into lifelong multiple attachments, where friends of the family offered parenting (or aspects of it) that the parents could not. The wills of these damaged nineteenth-century parents attest to the gratitude they felt to others beyond their family for helping to bring up their children.

Attachment and trauma-informed therapy developed after the main psychoanalytic therapies. Trauma-informed work is still developing rapidly, and while I have used some of these frameworks (Bowlby, 2005; Dallos, 2006; Shevlin and McGuigan, 2003), it is clear that another level and type of intervention is also relevant to working with multigenerational issues.

A key idea is that attachment dynamics are the mainstream of connection (or lack of) between the generations. A secure attachment achieved in a subsequent generation can stem the tide of trauma in the future. This is important as it is easy to slip into the assumption that a traumatised generation of parents cannot parent well and will tend to transmit the traumas they have had rather than contain or mitigate their effects. This idea sits behind Abraham and Torok's (1994) work. It may be true in certain circumstances, but there is also evidence, for instance, that Holocaust-affected parents formed secure attachments with their children (Alford, 2019). This is important because it suggests that there is an inherent tendency towards seeking secure base-type attachment; even Harlow's monkeys chose softness and warmth over food (Harlow, 1958). The question for the generations then becomes how intergenerational arrangements typically help disturbed attachment problems. Adoption is perhaps the most obvious example. This is as old as humanity and there is evidence for adoption elsewhere in the animal kingdom. The more integrated the generations are, the greater capacity to lessen the devastating effects of parental and child separations. In pre-adoption-agency eras, adoption was managed within the extended family. Genealogists are familiar with its sometimes puzzling signature. I have two known adoptions in my family system, two and three generations back. Both saved the individual involved from something far worse, yet bequeathed problems of identity that ran through a subsequent generation.

Before the age of therapy, families worked out how to cope with traumatic loss and alleviate the problems of poor parenting based on insecure attachment. If attachment theory is right, there is a prediction sitting behind this, which is that individuals, families and societies that are more successful at these kinds of repair will have better intergenerational mentalisation.

I'm now in a position to define more fully what this term means. The evidence from the current research is that the generations are better known to each other if stories exist that connect them and the telling of these stories is either based on or seeking intergenerational companionship. This companionship isn't necessarily between parent and child (although it may be) but exists between individuals who are intergenerationally charged or potentialised to each other. This can happen in any relationship. For instance, in the professions and world of work, it is often between senior and less experienced individuals; in families it may be between aunts, uncles and other related children. It can also be across generations through the identification of family members who were of a similar age or situation to the person researching them. One respondent spoke of the deep connection she felt to girls and young women who did not survive to adulthood.

The definition is extended by thinking about the implication that increased levels of mentalisation between the generations might have. At its most general it is similar to successful or effective therapy: conflict is managed better and hence relationships of all kinds last longer and so have a better chance of fulfilling both their purpose and potential (Beutler et al., 2018). This is very specific and rests on the attachment-based understanding of managing rupture–repair dynamics in relationships and developing a reflective capacity from this. This in turn entails skills and capacities to soothe and recognise the other and be soothed and validated in turn and this links back to the therapeutic role of narrative and storytelling.

A creative nexus of skills and capacities is developed, such that more is passed on, less is lost and change is informed by respect for the living and mourning for the dead. It sounds like an ideal society. In truth, these things have traditionally happened more in smaller-scale face-to-face societies and communities bound by tradition and stabilised by territory. It does not mean, however, that it does not happen now.

Intergenerational companionship is not normally part of written or recorded history. It has few written records, because it is more to do with intimacy and relationships between bodies. It is in essence a state of being. A quote from George Elliot in *Middlemarch* (1871–1872, p. 873) encapsulates it:

> But the effect of her being on those around her was incalculably diffusive: for the growing good of the world is partly dependent on unhistoric acts; and that things are not so ill with you and me as they might have been, is half owing to the number who lived faithfully a hidden life, and rest in unvisited tombs.

One could of course pen another formulation about what troubles us being those other unhistoric acts that are destructive, secretive or malicious. There is plenty of evidence for that in this research. I have been reminded of George Eliot because of her sensibility for time and the longer term of nurture in relationships. She is a voice at the beginning of modernity prescient to the submersion and denigration of the feminine.

In Chapter 4, I looked at several examples of reaching for intergenerational companionship, each of which gave the respondent a dilemma about how well-received and long-lasting their offer of companionship would be. By contrast, the loss of this intimate but largely hidden connectivity between the generations puts social and psychological continuity at risk. Without it we are less likely to survive and flourish. Something similar happens in organisations.

Several of our respondents spoke about the role that attachment to nature and the ability to think about nature as a partner can play in the connectivity of generations. The idea of an intergenerational project in partnership with nature gives a sense of responsibility for development over much longer time periods than a single life, with organisations intentionally trying to maximise the age range of their participants. Mapping the longevity of organisations was not a part of this research, but is clearly a key issue for multigenerational relationships. Organisations that can balance innovation with continuity can last longer. In human history, organisations that last longer than a few generations are rare.

Paradoxically, it is in the arena of more fluid social dynamics that multigenerational relations are the most stable. Small-scale societies and face-to-face communities are more flexible because of the role that storytelling, ritual and ceremony play. Here, a culture can flourish in perpetuity, continually adapting in tune with and guided by its dreams and ancestors, as I described the Aboriginal communities in Chapter 2. Atkinson (2002) speaks of the 'lore' of ritual being the key to this continuity and 'lorelessness' being the abject state of personal and social breakdown when these practices are attacked and lost. The Oracle at Delphi lasted—depending on definitions—between 1,600 and 5,600 years. Was the priesthood continuous as a body holding the narrative of society? No one now knows. Consultations to ordinary people, potential migrants and colonists defined it as lasting many generations (Wilson, 2010, p. 107). Some of the capacities for multigenerational transmission identified in this research seem to have more in common with these long-lasting, light-footed practices of storytelling and dreaming. Social and group attachment may be the longest-living and most intimate institution of care we have. We need to build on it, rather than away from it. But as the research has shown us, therapy can be as much part of the solution as the problem.

Shortcomings of Therapy Training: Loss of the Generational Other

A respondent felt that his voice had been completely silenced by the end of his training and described the ensuing years as a process of finding how to counter this and the feeling of displacement it had generated.

He commented that this displacement was uncannily like his diasporic experience as a migrant. I speculate that if training is imbued with white and neocolonial assumptions about science and the nature of the psyche, then training for non-white or ethnically different trainees may reproduce their experience of displacement and alienation. If the therapist is also a migrant and has unconsciously used psychotherapy training as part of their own acculturation process, the situation has added complexity. Although experience of one's own diasporic history can have a beneficial effect on helping someone work through their own, for black trainees, it may reinforce the internalisation of a white superego—a step on the way to developing a false self (Alleyne, 2005). On a cultural–relational level, an English therapist may have an unconscious level of assurance and entitlement that subtly undermines someone with a more abject cultural experience, for instance in the Irish diaspora. Some minority ethnic group therapists also report the problem of internalising their client's unconscious racism towards them.

This also represents a fundamental problem for mental health services. Will patients with different ethnic backgrounds struggle to be understood enough to be helped psychologically if practitioners have not gone through and understood the kind of displacement that migration and its multigenerational complexities generate? Practitioners who are not aware of the postcolonial aspects of their culture may not understand the likely transferences they receive from patients from these cultures. Codes of ethics cover the importance of awareness of difference and curiosity on the part of the therapist but it would help if they stressed the value of gaining concrete knowledge about a client's specific culture and generational experiences. This groundwork can be challenging and time-consuming, but without it, much will be missed or misunderstood. These longer assessments can be thought of as a shared exploration of personal and cultural history which gives the therapist time to think about their own ancestral and cultural valency with any particular client presentation.

This means longer-range assessments both in terms of time span (including three generations, if possible), and cultural and ethnic influences. Long assessments have become unpopular and unfashionable in the era of fast results, psychometrics and outcome-focused values.

Another complex assessment—the adult attachment interview—has suffered the same fate despite being very informative and predictive. These encounters lay the ground for a good working alliance partly because they are constructed collaboratively with the client, but also because they show care and interest. The co-construction of a genogram to include past and present family members is something often only carried out by family therapists. An intergenerationally informed therapist needs to understand deep family history, and cultural difference that flows from it.

Therapists also need to be able to read the mute signs of cultural and family others buried in the patient's psyche which I discussed in the context of undisclosed war trauma in Chapter 2. They need to help the patient 'de-individualise' their experience so they can take responsibility for it in new, more inclusive ways. The therapist also needs to be able to spot the unspoken signs of trauma that may not belong directly to the patient but which they have internalised. This connects to the transgenerational aspect of multigenerational dynamics. We don't know how far forward the experience of an ancestor can echo and why it can be pivotal for some individuals and not for others, yet to rule it out is to potentially rule out something important. Addressing slavery has to involve a long memory and much research informing any social response. Why should therapy be any different? Aileen Alleyne's (2019) elaboration of post-slavery syndrome as originally formulated by DeGruy (2005) is an example of a specific assessment framework containing an intergenerational schema of five generations. It is also an example of a multigenerational formulation. Each client and ethnic group will need a formulation specific to their experience as it emerges.

For a therapist to be able to do these things well, they need to have been exposed to these ways of working and forms of insight in their own training. Biographically specific, culturally sensitive and inter- and transgenerationally informed training doesn't really exist at the moment. At best, therapists come at these issues through personal experience and curiosity and are informed by absences in existing training. This falls into the familiar and valuable category of 'continuing professional development'. This piece of research by implication tells of how therapists want to change and alter what they know and how they work. But participants have told us something of their experiments and inventions as well as their struggles at being othered by their training.

Intergenerational Issues in Endings in Clinical and Training Organisations

The closing stages and leave-takings for therapists and their employing organisations is mostly seen as a personal process related to endings, loss and moving on. Here, I show the other side that is intergenerational and full of supplementary tensions and possibilities.

A respondent told us of a deep tension between the generations in his professional and personal life: 'And the older generation continued working very hard, very dedicatedly to what they believed was right. But gradually the new life that needed to sustain it couldn't take hold and would always depart'.

While this could be a projection of the problem of the failing energies of the human body in ageing, it is very consciously about the problem of sustaining creative therapeutic work in the context of fewer younger people entering the profession. A perceived loss of cultural relevance also shrinks this number even further. The business of taking care starts to look too difficult and too demanding for the younger generation of workers and managers. Care work is another example of this. This is a recipe for despair and for social breakdown between one professional generation and the next. We can imagine these to be present-day conditions for a breaking of the social link in the not-too-distant future, not caused by war or famine, but by the failure to care and to imagine how good care can happen. The tension here is whether the skilled therapist just carries on working, or if they stop to imagine what the world will look like without people like them in the future. One respondent asked: 'How do I die creatively to the work?' It recontextualises what a good ending might be, as this is often framed as a personal issue. If the leave-taking is in the context of a breakdown between the generations, this will be internalised as failure if it is not thought about. Interestingly, some respondents also talked about battling depression during and after leave-taking which may be an internalisation of deeply social conflicts like these.

Respondents talked about the importance of retraining and personal renewal when working with the problem of intergenerational change. The older generation needs renewal to continue to contribute, but also needs to be able to come and go, or to work on a part-time basis, a creative arrangement that improves self-esteem and work efficacy. Fortunately for our respondent, this was possible, but for many employers it is not attractive. Not all managers recognise the importance of the intergenerational issue. This example also underlines the importance of education and training in creating a place that aspires to maintain a deeply therapeutic function, something all but lost in some NHS contexts.

Another respondent again spelled out the consequences of not thinking intergenerationally. He spoke of having observed many people, not just from his generation, but succeeding ones, wanting to offer something and then eventually leaving the profession with a great sense of disappointment and frustration.

The tensions between younger and older work in two directions. There will be losses, one way or the other. If everyone leaves the older generation unchallenged, they do not have to face displacement of their ideals, values and practices. But this may be at the cost of the creativity and energy of the younger generation which ultimately means the loss of a community of practice and therefore, at some point, capacity. This process has happened very dramatically in many institutions in British society.

There is a later-life developmental issue here: if there is still room for growth in the older practitioner that can allow the space for and curiosity about the challenges to values and roles that younger practitioners bring, then a kind of intergenerational 'relational turn' can happen.

Another respondent noticed how the organisation lingered inside him after leaving. The organisation had percolated through him and in subsequent work he found his own individual expression of it. While this is a normal feature of leave-taking—where something of the previous workplace and profession has been internalised—it also illustrates that the organisation that has been left doesn't get the benefit of this integration and further learning.

One of the key features of these mature professional contributions is the holding of the organisation in mind (Armstrong, 2005) which often includes the essence of professional learning from years of creative work. This is a difficult thing to get hold of, requiring mutual recognition between different generations of professionals within an organisation. The value of extended and open-case multi-role discussions can be another kind of narrative that can help bind an organisation with a historical narrative about how to help its users. It is happening less and less, and its absence is not without consequences: organisations may simply be unable to provide the services they say they can. In other organisations and professions, wars for control have gone on, of which members of the public may be completely unaware. It may take the form of a move towards evidence-based practice but is also a way of displacing an older generation of workers. It can be a symptom of intergenerational breakdown.

Specific Features of Multigenerationally Informed Therapy

Multigenerational memory is by definition 'distributed' in that it does not strictly belong to any one individual. Therapists need therefore to be aware of the illusion of the self as unitary while holding the presence of the many in their dyadic work. This is an aspect that therapy can contribute to our personal experience of ancestry but can be complicated when therapists (and clients) think that all 'personal' experience is developmentally located within the individual. In these instances, states of fear, loss of sense of self and dissociation can be interpreted as 'split off', in other words are defences against issues such as abandonment, intrusion and parental failure that are intrinsically familial and personal. While therapy is the best place to begin to help search beneath the surface of experience, it equally may foreclose messages and voices from earlier generations and wider social influences, thus becoming a therapy that functions as a defence against social and political anxieties rather than a gateway to exploring them. Joy DeGruy's (2005) idea of Post-Traumatic Slavery Syndrome rests on a 'both/and' perspective: the recognition of the trauma of slavery is of little use without tackling racism, its perpetration and its internalisation. Like the findings on Holocaust survivor parents (Alford, 2019), great caution is required not to assume that a PSTD-like experience in one generation will lead to poor parenting in the next.

When thinking about multigenerationally informed therapy, it is helpful to consider a kind of unitary multigenerational self. This multigenerational self comprises a collective psychology of several generations present in each individual, wherein the therapist must listen for the voices of one generation in the unconscious of another. Multigenerational memory has continuities and discontinuities. Moving from a one-generational/individual focus to a two- and potentially three-generation one helps to make new experience available, not all of which is directly the patient's/client's yet is nonetheless inside them or available to them in some way.

The idea of an extended multigenerational self also rests on the idea of intergenerationally passed-on talents, trauma and values arriving in a largely unsorted package from our parents or guardians and to them, previously, from theirs. We are often unaware of them. They are akin to what John Bowlby calls Unconscious Working Models (Bretherton and Munholland, 2008). Some aspects of this intergenerational package remain closed, either permanently, or until they are activated by lifecycle challenges or traumatic or challenging social events. What emerges at these junctures comes from the extended generational self, for better or worse. One of the key social and therapeutic challenges is finding recognition for this process of 'being someone other' and accepting that it might be okay to parent in certain ways, or that untoward feelings such as depression may not be fully one's own. Taking an unpopular decision, for example, or taking direct action and suffering for it may echo war or other traumas that involved aggression and violence.

Inter- to Transgenerational Switch in Therapeutic Work

This shift is most radically described by Davoine and Gaudillière (2004) in a scenario where patients suffering from recurrent psychotic symptoms and behaviours are helped by an intervention that is on the lookout for the mute signs of social rejection and violence, those that imply life or death issues of survival, not just for the patient but for his or her parents and forebears. They indicate that for a therapist there must be a resonance from such a level of disturbance.

This description creates a basic model of working, which is that the therapist needs to be transgenerationally attuned to their own material just as in current therapeutic practice where the point of 'training therapy' or 'training analysis' is to familiarise the therapist with enough of their personality and unconscious to acquire the capacity to learn from personal experience at a deep intrapsychic level. For transgenerational work, what is required beyond this is an ongoing capacity to deepen the assessment in collaboration with the patient, coupled with a social and historical sensibility and interest. Then, in the process of therapy, it is about recognising the unspoken signs of the other in the self. Sometimes these aspects feel too alien to approach, yet Malan's (1979) brief work model gives a reliable guide for thinking about the significance of the 'other' as therapeutic work evolves.

I have described the consequences of missing these clues in my description of my early work, as a therapist unaware of the power of the trauma of previous wars (see Chapter 2). While writing this book, I have become aware of other communications I missed from clients, involving a historical trauma so significant when I came across its social counterpart that it fitted like a missing jigsaw piece. Without letting myself off the hook, I think that this points to the importance of missing things and how this is handled. Winnicott (1971) describes how the therapist has to fail in order for the client to really do the work. Therapy in this sense needs to be good enough. However, good enough is premised on having acquired the knack of returning to or refinding the internalised other that can recognise and contain. What the therapist provides is a working model for exploration and problem-solving. The work of the intergenerationally informed therapist is to ensure that this knowledge is firmly established in the mix somewhere. Multigenerational awareness is part of a psychosocial toolkit for therapist and clients. Looking again at the chart I first presented in Chapter 2, it is possible to think about any piece of psychotherapeutic work as moving through or being informed by the key features of this cycle of memory. I have added some new terms that particularly aid therapeutic thinking (see Fig. 7.1).

Much therapeutic work will occur across the upper arc and is likely to involve shorter-term intergenerational issues and problems. Losses are being identified and worked at, creativity is being contacted and shut down and new aspects of the self can emerge. Deeper down and further into time or trauma, we come to the layer of hauntings and broken social links. This is more the realm of the transgenerational; the presence of issues that have hopped the generations start to predominate. These may be signalled by frozen histories: the past (of a famine, for example) is 'standing right behind you'.

Creative

Reconceptualising loss   **Creativity and shutting down**

Memories intact enough   *Action possible but sometimes thwarted*
Relationships knowable/discoverable   *Presence of learning relationships*

Reintegration **The natural world, cycles, complexity and imagination** *Disintegration*

Move towards nature and social   *Breaking the link with nature and place*
imagination

Developing mentalisation across the generations increases adaptability

Loss/breaking of the social link   **Hauntings and unhappy interment**

Deep trauma and dislocation   *Trauma but some memory – secrets*
False selves and frozen histories   *Generation-hopping, trance states and the*
                                                   uncanny

Destructive

Fig. 7.1 A typology of multigenerational memory: Intergenerational emphasis

Standing at the centre of the map is imagination and nature, reminding us of the work involved in developing mentalisation across the generations that increases recognition, acceptance and adaptability and ameliorates suffering. The lower arc of the chart represents the limits of memory and the limit of our survival heuristic at any one time. The further we can extend this area, the better our capacity to deal with social conflict will be, and we get a corresponding deepening of our collective social memory. We could imagine the shape of the chart changing like a cell boundary at different times. In periods of social shutdown, our memories shorten and our capacity to dream socially reduces. Chosen traumas start to predominate in the lower arc, social violence returns as haunting and our survival heuristic is foreshortened. In more open periods, the boundaries open up and the generations talk to each other better and more fully. Socially and psychologically there are more resources and more solutions to problems. It is likely that our relation to nature and to our imaginations is more open and more complex.

The third generation may be particularly significant in memory work. It is often the watershed between living memory and not. Its members act like gatekeepers—the last chance to play an active part in remembering before transgenerational memory kicks in. My findings suggest they pick up much of the work of reconceptualising loss or complete the process of forgetting trauma and secrets that have gone through preceding generations. In this way in any generation, there is a dynamic tension between remembering and forgetting which underpins any developing capacity to intergenerationally mentalise. It is often a loss—such as a death—that stimulates the imagination of the upcoming generation and initiates reminiscence. The process of remembering or forgetting is always an active one (although not necessarily conscious). The presence of mutual witnessing between the generations is something that therapy can help to promote. Perhaps one of the roles that the third generation plays after trauma is some deeper-level digesting of the experiences of the preceding generations that are still pressing or available in one of the forms suggested in the typology of memory above.

By contrast it could also be said that when the presence of the grandparents is reassuring, they provide a grounding generation, a base for new beginnings. Sometimes an intergenerational transitional space can open out between the generations in which there are thoughts and experiences available that two generations can't access as easily, similar to the way grandparents can ease and leaven relations between parents and their children.

Much multigenerational work that is specifically therapeutic belongs more to the upper arc in the map of memory but also has as its focus the conversion of hauntings to tangible ancestors or experiences that can join contemporary life in some way, repairing broken social links, acknowledging victim and perpetrator dynamics and natural and social catastrophe. The lower arc is also more likely to have psychosocial interventions in it. The upper layer may be more the zone of therapeutic practice. They are, however, not mutually exclusive and creative interventions weave between the two.

States of Mind Associated with Multigenerational Issues

I have covered many of these in each of the main sections on my findings and in the extended case studies given in Chapter 2. The chart of memory above is based on states of mind that have been reported by many people in the research. I think it unlikely that there is a single or even an identifiable cluster of 'issues and symptoms' that characterise multigenerational problems. This may change as we understand the experience better or it may remain 'distributed' because the main quality of the experience is that it never 'belongs' to one individual. I summarise here what seem to be some signs and features. A key feature is the presence of something strange, alien or other in one's sense of self. Everyone has this: we are full of others with whom we have had relationships. Relationships of loss and attachment to place may be important, as are journeys of migration. Social dislocation of any kind may echo other earlier dislocations or diasporas. The presence of violence, war and other trauma in relatives and friends is an indicator of full-blown trauma within a person's historical and social network. They are 'close by', socially and psychologically.

There may be a sense of non-specific dread or depression that recurs. A person may feel haunted or may themselves feel disturbing to others, having something of the uncanny attached to them. Secrets may have cut down or reduced the sense of self, leading to the development of a false self or selves. Difficult-to-manage affects, a range of closer-to-the body symptoms, fears of madness and experiences of dissociation can feature. This latter group of experiences can also link into doer-and-done-to dynamics and consequently the dynamics of abuse. This is always personal but can also include the abuse of one group by another.

While this is a grim list, it needs to be said that the opposite capacity—to contribute that which is creative in difference or in owned and understood perpetrator/victim dynamics—is the key to reparative experiences in this arena. The capacity to explore and find the courage to face what can be known can lead to fuller social and psychological life. Understanding the interplay between social fields distorted by racism/classism/sexism and life spaces that are more personal is key to deinternalising some of the most abject aspects of oppression and misrecognition that are the social legacy of unresolved transgenerational conflicts.

Beyond Words

The issue of how to work with a multigenerational experience for which there are no memories, artefacts or records confounds many respondents. Some of the therapeutic methods described here are an attempt to counter or address this problem of deeply traumatic experience. A working model of building secure attachment as a basis for dealing with the adversity of diasporic life is essential. Having a positive and secure therapeutic base provides the support and safety needed to confront internalised destructive others and turn hauntings into communications or even conversations. This can only build up over time and through several generations, as an antidote to internalised transgenerational trauma. The work is gradual: one generation being perhaps more outwardly focused, another consolidating the gains and yet another critical of what and who has been left out or disadvantaged. One generation may have created or undergone an exceptional number of traumas. It may fall to another to acknowledge and learn from them. Generations of non-acknowledgement will lead to a shallowing of culture and knowledge and decreased capacities to solve social and emotional problems in the present and future.

Respondents who reported experiences of extended transgenerational dislocation spoke of their difficulties in grieving: they felt 'hardened'. Some reported feeling that those of the generation subjected to a diaspora hadn't died but were still there in an ever-constant presence. Haunted people are not happy, nor are haunted societies. A haunted future is not a future at all; more of the same will follow.

Trance Methodologies

The capacity to think 'free associatively', to enter into reverie or mild trance with 'evenly balanced attention' (Freud) or 'without memory or desire' (Bion, 1967) are key elements of the psychoanalytic and psychodynamic tradition. Winnicott's (1971) idea of potential space suggests that these creative states of mind can occur in a dyadic relationship in which many self-states can be explored. In relation to thinking about the ancestors and the grandparental generation, one can see the potential for a kind of relational thirdness re-enlivened so that their imagined presence can inform current relationships. This may explain something of the uncanny experience that some respondents had of their ancestors coming back to life when they researched and thought about them.

This marks the emergence of a recognition of the other in oneself and oneself in the other. Benjamin (2018) stresses that it is the surfacing of analytic thirdness that allows the creation of a transitional space promoting openness to the other. This raises a point (which I take up in Chapter 8) about the relationship between social fields and potential spaces. It is this potential space that therapist and client are contained by over the days, weeks, months and years of their therapeutic journey. The potential space has typically been thought about in the context of the one-to-one encounter typical of psychoanalytic work. The idea of potential space can also be applied to group work, and psychosocially to the research process. The research described in this book has a kind of transitional quality to it, where a range of experiences from different times and across geographical and social spaces have come into relationship. It has a life of its own.

These 'trance' methods can be helpful in thinking about the generations and memory and can be particularly helpful in groups and meetings. They can also be useful in research, the role of intuition being a new element particularly in beneath-the-surface methods (Crociani-Windland 2018).

Blackman (2012, p. 155) talks about mediumistic processes as having to do with the problem of the 'one and the many'. According to Blackman, film can offer a form of distributed perception where traumatic issues that were experienced by many individuals can be refracted into the social, and where traces of them can be discerned even though the individual context is lost or blurred.

Cho's work (2008) describes a diasporic unconscious where experience is trans-subjective and carried by various mediums (particularly women) and communicated by certain affects (especially shame). The story will come out when a receptive medium is present, but the form of expression may not be direct, but instead synaesthetic, taking different sensory forms (Blackman, 2012). If one can hear an ancestor or see an ancestral landscape in shapes or colours as in Maxim Gorky's art (see Chapter 5), then something of the becoming another or finding the other in the self becomes more possible. An experience of shame in the practitioner may alert them to the presence of a diasporic experience in their client, their ancestors or group. Identifying and decoding the synaesthetic in therapeutic communications may be another capacity that the therapist must develop to help recognise the generational other in the self. This involves a sensibility towards communication and expression in different, mixed or alternating sensory modes.

The cultural problem of hearing voices can be perpetuated by therapists who are attached to the idea of an integrated unitary self, and this can be further reinforced by the potential for misdiagnosis psychiatrically. The therapist needs to develop a sensibility towards communication and expression in different and mixed or alternating sensory modes. They also need to be able to cultivate the capacity to dissociate in order to approach the distributed type of consciousness and self-senses that characterise some multigenerational experiences. There is a link between the capacity for medial embodied communication and some of the trance state methods described earlier. Most therapists will have a toe in the door of some kind that helps when working with these issues. There will be much further work to do. We need to reach further towards an expression of the themes beyond the personal, and it is these which I will discuss in Chapter 8.

References

Abraham, N. and Torok, M. (1994) *The Shell and the Kernel.* Translated from the French by Nicolas T. Rand. Chicago: University of Chicago Press.

Agazarian, Y.M. and Carter, F.B. (1993) Discussions on the large group. *Group* [online]. 17, pp. 210–234 [Accessed 20 September 2020].

Alford, C.F. (2019) Intergenerational transmission of trauma: Holocaust survivors, their children and their children's children. *Journal of Psychosocial Studies.* 12 (1–2), pp. 145–155.

Alleyne, A. (2005) The internal oppressor—The veiled companion of external racial oppression. *UKCP Journal* [online] [Accessed 20 September 2020].

Alleyne, A. (2019) Post slavery syndrome and intergenerational trauma [Lecture]. No date. Available from: https://www.confer.uk.com/module/module-slavery.html [Accessed 20 September 2020].

Armstrong, D. (2005) *Organization in the Mind: Psychoanalysis, Group Relations and Organizational Consultancy.* London: Karnac.

Atkinson, J. (2002) *Trauma Trails, Recreating Song Lines: The Transgenerational Effects of Trauma in Indigenous Australia.* North Melbourne: Spinifex Press.

Bateman, A. and Fonagy, P. (2010) Mentalization based treatment for borderline personality disorder. *World Psychiatry* [online]. 9 (1), pp. 11–15 [Accessed 20 September 2020].

Benjamin, J (2018) *Beyond Doer and Done To: Recognition Theory, Intersubjectivity and the Third.* Oxon: Routledge.

Beutler, L.E., Edwards, C. and Someah, K. (2018) Adapting psychotherapy to patient reactance level: A meta-analytic review. *Journal of Clinical Psychology* [online]. 74 (11), pp. 1952–1963 [Accessed 20 September 2020].

Bion, W.R. (1967) Notes on memory and desire. *Psychoanalytic Forum.* 2 (3), pp. 272–280.
Blackman, L. (2012) *Immaterial Bodies: Affect, Embodiment, Meditation.* London: Sage.
Bowlby, J. (2005) *The Making and Breaking of Affectional Bonds.* London and New York: Routledge.
Bretherton, I. and Munholland, K.A. (2008) Internal working models in attachment relationships: Elaborating a central construct in attachment theory. In J. Cassidy & P. R. Shaver (Eds.), *Handbook of Attachment: Theory, Research, and Clinical Applications.* New York: The Guilford Press, pp. 102–127.
Cho, G.M. (2008) *Haunting the Korean Diaspora: Shame, Secrecy, and the Forgotten War.* Minneapolis: University of Minnesota Press.
Crociani-Windland, L. (2018) The researcher's subjectivity as a research instrument—From intuition to surrender. In Cummins, A.-L. and Williams, N. (2018) *Further Researching Beneath the Surface (Volume 2): Psycho-Social Research Methods in Practice.* Oxon: Routledge, pp. 27–48.
Dallos, R. (2006) *Attachment Narrative Therapy Integrating Narrative, Systemic and Attachment Therapies.* Berkshire: Open University Press.
Davoine, F. and Gaudillière, J.-M. (2004) *History Beyond Trauma.* New York: Other Press.
DeGruy, J (2005) *Post Traumatic Slave Syndrome: America's Legacy of Enduring Injury and Healing.* Milwaukie, Oregon: Uptone Press.
Eliot, G. (1871–1872) *Middlemarch.* Reprint. London: Penguin Books, 2003.
Freud, S. (1912) *Wild Analysis.* New Penguin Freud series, Ed. by Adam Phillips. Translated by Adam Blance. London: Penguin Books, 2002.
Harlow, H.F. (1958) The nature of love. *American Psychologist* [online]. 13 (12), pp. 673–685 [Accessed 20 September 2020].
Haupt, P. and Malcolm, C. (2001) Between hell and hope: An organizational case study of the Truth and Reconciliation Commission (TRC) in South Africa. *Organisational and Social Dynamics,* 1 (1), pp. 113–129.
Hepper, E.G., Wildschut, T., Sedikides, C., Robertson, S. and Routledge, C.D. (2020) Time capsule: Nostalgia shields psychological wellbeing from limited time horizons. To be published in *Emotion* [preprint]. Available from: https://psycnet.apa.org/record/2020-19442-001 [Accessed 20 September 2020].
Kreeger, L. (1975) *The Large Group: Dynamics and Therapy.* Reprint. Great Britain: Karnac, 1994.

Malan, D. (1979) *Individual Psychotherapy and the Science of Psychodynamics*. London: Butterworths.

Oboe, A. (2007) The TRC women's hearings as performance and protest in the new South Africa. *Research in African Literatures* [online]. 38 (3), pp. 60–76 [Accessed 20 September 2020].

O'Loughlin, M. and McLeod, B. (2015) 'Thinking beyond our means': Engendering a depth understanding of trauma. In: O'Loughlin, M. and Charles, M. (Eds.) *Fragments of Trauma and the Social Production of Suffering: Trauma, History and Memory*. Lanham, MD: Rowman and Littlefield, pp. 291–308.

Shevlin, M. and McGuigan, K. (2003) The Long-term psychological impact of Bloody Sunday on families of the victims as measured by the revised impact of event scale. *British Journal of Clinical Psychology* [online]. 42 (4), pp. 427–432 [Accessed 22 September 2019].

Stuthridge, J. (2017) Falling apart and getting it together: The dialectics of disintegration and integration in script change and self-development. *Transactional Analysis Journal* [online]. 47 (1), pp. 19–31 [Accessed 20 September 2020].

Wilson, N., Ed. (2010) *Encyclopedia of Ancient Greece*. New York: Routledge.

Winnicott, D. (1971) *Playing and Reality*. London: Routledge.

8

The Psychosocial and the Transgenerational

How the Intergenerational Turns into the Transgenerational

In this chapter, I am looking at the psychosocial aspects of memory. In the transgenerational type of processes such as those described in this chapter, it is important to bear in mind that the quality of memory involved is 'distributed', having cultural as well as embodied qualities. Norbert Elias's (1978) work on the civilising process emphasises the development of a 'sensibility for the long term', that in part relies on a history of manners: bodies over time communicating closeness, acceptable and unacceptable behaviours. It is also related to the development of different forms of state authority and illustrates a link between a long-term socioeconomic history and one of human behaviour and consciousness. Elias's idea of the civilising process isn't based on the progress of modernity; it is more like Freud's (1930) idea that civilisation is always discontent. It is about 'civilising' ebbs and flows. As an example of a transgenerational issue that emerged in my interviews, I quote a respondent talking about an experience related to a social dreaming event held at a slavery museum:

> ...but what came out was how at the same time slavery was getting going, the rural working classes in Britain were losing their livelihoods en masse, and were being utterly dislocated. This was going on at the same time as the same society that was foisting social violence on its own citizens was bringing about the mass dislocation of Africans from their own communities and roots. Instead of the plantation, the slavery at home was a destitute urban poor.

In this extract, there is a sense that a whole world was being lost; parallel social losses and violence were occurring across three continents. Manley and Trustram (2018, p. 86) reported some of their social dreaming participants feeling like they were 'in the same boat' as the enslaved. This is an example of a new identification brought about by a psychosocial methodology, in this case social dreaming. Manley and Trustram have discussed this more fully in their work on social dreaming and slavery.

Frosh (2019) elaborates Christina Sharp's (2016) reflections on blackness—that everyone is now 'in the wake' of the slave boats—saying that this wake continues to spread 'without dissolving' (Frosh, 2019, p. x). This is a powerful transgenerational image, the keywords being 'without dissolving'.

These losses have not been reconceptualised, and thus are difficult to hold in memory in contemporary relationships. In many cases, the traumas that were occurring at the same time in history were known without being able to be thought about consciously as connected; they were a kind of 'unthought known' (Bollas, 1987). These social hauntings could nonetheless be seen to be resurfacing in current times in different ways, such as in white supremacy movements on the one hand, and Black Lives Matter on the other.

Another respondent talked about the loss of what was meant to be:

> The Edwardian generation was haunted by this social destruction after the First World War: they were fun-loving, gregarious, modern, outward-going, not warlike, experimental; male and female identities beginning to melt a little bit, the glimpse of something really modern about it. I think it's one of the things that I do remember from clinical work with clients of a certain age, whose parents went through that war. All of this sense of optimism was destroyed by the war – the loss of a whole culture.

These reflections allow us to think about longer time spans where events of social violence led to new but traumatic histories which have considerable subsequent influence. Slavery has a 400-year history, along with the get-rich-quick societies that brought it about. In Europe, the First World War turned into the Second World War, and untold breaking of social bonds occurred across several continents. Some of the migrations embedded in the accounts of my research subjects are bound up in the dislocations produced by these wars, while others were flights from famine and extreme poverty in Europe in the nineteenth century.

The descendants of these migrants spoke of difficulties in grieving: they felt 'hardened'. Some reported feeling that those of the generation subjected to the diaspora hadn't died but were still there in a perpetual presence. Others reported feeling haunted by knowing that something had happened without being able to identify what it was. In this sense, we are no longer talking about loss as reconceptualised but are moving towards experiences of haunting and unhappy interment which I described in Chapter 5, but in this case related to larger social events in history.

Hidden Migrations and Multigenerational Identities

The gaps in literature and records around any event, be it war, diaspora or mass migration become hauntings in time, if the actual events sink below the surface and cease to be witnessed. This active witnessing is usually inscribed in intergenerational memory held in families, communities and professions. Transgenerational haunting starts when the event is not or ceases to be inscribed in culture.

I had examples in the research of memories being at this tipping point where, for instance, memories of hunger haunted an old person's dying, or people spoke in a foreign language in that moment of passing, and these memories produced hauntings that were just on the verge of going out of intergenerational memory. When enough can be known to give context, memories can be reset in a further generation. The first example links to a discovery by a grandchild that she was descended from a young girl loaded onto a coffin ship (Ramsay, 1997). The second is of someone who had lived a life of assumed Englishness but was in fact of German origin (Williams, 2015, p. 137). Both share a part-repressed and part-unrecorded memory tied up with poorly understood or unrecorded social conflicts. The Irish Famine is the background of the first example and being an enemy alien in a country at war that of the other. There are moments of transition in which the intimate and personal experience of witnessing someone's death is also full of transgenerational memory. In these hauntings, something transgenerational lives on; if it can be heard, then it can take on new form or pass out of time altogether: it is a tipping point of memory. Going back to the example of social dreaming in the slavery museum, showing the emergence of a new identification ('in the same boat', 'in the wake') can be seen as a way of getting to a more depressive position (Roth, 2005) whereby the guilt of an oppressor identification is able to be turned into a more realistic and less defended attitude. This internal shift can be the key to a more compassionate and empathetic understanding of those who were exploited and enslaved. Having a choice like the one afforded by a psychosocial intervention may inspire the third-generation witness to remember and be curious rather than want to forget something that is too painful or puzzling.

In both the Irish and German examples, the third-generation witness found a personal meaning to the social causes they were drawn towards, but also discovered themselves the bearer of a very particular identity. One was concerned with righting the wrongs of hunger and starvation; the other was caught up with the power of hidden identities and injustices. This shows how a psychosocial process is in play where a fear-laden repressed memory that could be seen as entirely personal has a sweep of social history waiting for a receptive host or medium to embody it anew. These experiences are unfinished both on a personal level in the issues of loneliness and attachment that these individuals experienced, but also at the social level such that we could predict that their descendants would have a transgenerational identity that was as complex and specific as any personal one.

The privacy of these moments-of-death recollections are also examples of how a memory that is deeply social becomes purely personal. Yet these memories are charged with hauntings which need further curiosity and work to recover their transgenerational significance.

There is another level to this process of transmission. While it may be that there was a level of choice or at least curiosity in both the third-generation actors wanting to know what might have happened to their ancestor, the compulsion to feed and the anger at political injustice predated that choice and curiosity in these examples. What lies beneath this is hard to understand. It could be thought about as a predisposition towards these transgenerational issues. It may be that it is at this transgenerational level and for this third generation that an epigenetic message can start to loosen and have less effect. Perhaps generations one and two can secure their food supplies and fight for their rights, while the third generation can decide to think about why and make a choice. The form that this choice takes is determined by the link between inter- and transgenerational issues in that third generation. This has to do with the social field and life space of those third-generation individuals. The third generation can hold a kind of integrating/processing function where the extremes of the trauma of the grandparental generation can be better digested. This witnessing at the moment of death can lead those in the next generation to identify and empathise. As with the example of the social dreaming event at the slavery museum, a more depressive kind of witnessing can emerge, a feeling of being in the same boat as a grandparent, in the wake of their famine or ethnic otherness. Perhaps this will be characterised by a life busy with reparative work or, in contrast, a turning away from the past in pursuit of a different future. If being Irish or being German for these third-generation witnesses becomes less transgenerationally complicated, things may change. Similarly, things may change as the fates of each nation alter over time, and a haunting that might be experienced as a dangerous or unwanted memory becomes something that can be welcomed, understood and even cherished. These are also two opposite examples of toxic histories: the Irish being victims of an avoidable famine in a colonised land; Anglo-German migrants being seen as dangerous fifth column aggressors. Cultural representations carry a lot of the stigmatised national identities: the Irish in jokes; Germans given the derogatory nickname of 'Hun', then 'beast' (Williams, 2015, p. 126). This kind of transgenerational mud sticks.

One can see this also as a multigenerational identity and sensibility at work, full of subtle influences and precursor experiences, moving through time with different possibilities available to discrete generational ages and phases. The multigenerational sensibility draws on a very wide social field. Some aspects of the Irish nation rose again in America, and some of the German nation in Britain. Now both migrant groups have nations of origin that survive and are flourishing, despite toxic and difficult histories. These examples are part of an unimaginably large patchwork of multigenerational identity made up of inter- and transgenerational experiences of different groups who have migrated. Here are two groups that after considerable transgenerational issues and trauma have temporarily gained some room or space that has fewer victim or oppressor dynamics contained within it. Much has changed on the transgenerational level that makes for a more creative present moment for them. This may change again in the future.

Other groups are different. The struggle for social emancipation for African-Americans and their descendants is waiting for a radically different level of response from all parts of the white population. There is a European transgenerational problem in play here—not only the institution of chattel slavery but the racism of eighteenth- and nineteenth-century European culture that accompanied many migrants to America. In British terms this has to do with the haunting of colonial history, glorified in terms of power and empire, denying the harm caused and wishing away the consequent multicultural society that erodes white dominance. Something of this still troubles and haunts contemporary race relations in both Britain and the United States.

The transgenerational level of social life can be depressing, but while relations of power predominate, it is the ultimate spirit level for everyone. The transgenerational level is a measure of the possibility for sanity where all ancestors' voices are sought and can be heard. Alongside this, there is a resourceful and creative side of transgenerational memory that speaks to land, place and more intergenerationally integrated groups with enhanced problem-solving capacities and institutions. I approach these issues through the theme of social fields and research as a social intervention.

From Transitional Spaces to Social Fields

Internalisation and Attachment, Empathy and Social Fields

A key implication from this research is that multigenerational memory, if it includes patterns of attachment and care between the generations, is a deep-level source of social affect regulation. When the generations first talk to each other, it is through the language of the body in a right-brain to right-brain dialogue, to paraphrase Schore (2009). I have conceptualised it as intergenerational mentalisation. This term has some parallels with but no exact corollary to three key sociological concepts, those of *verstehen*, cultural capital and *habitus*. Each is helpful in adding an aspect that adds a stronger psychosocial emphasis. Weber's idea of *verstehen* (Tucker, 1965) comprises the understanding of the other on their own terms and in relation to motivation. His sociology is based on a kind of active empathetic method, and one that asserts that the uniqueness of human social experience means we can't reduce the understanding of groups and societies to either social forces or individual psychology alone. It is through *verstehen* that we can know the motivation of others within their particular social circumstances. Weber provided, from the birth of the academic discipline of sociology, a way of approaching social life with a sensitivity to psychosocial issues and in so doing indicated the importance of intergenerational and transgenerational transmission, without specifically thinking in these terms.

Bourdieu's (1984) concept of cultural capital refers to important symbolic assets that include ways in which we assimilate and acquire methods of moving and speaking at an unconscious embodied level from those around us, as part of that specific class and group culture; cultural capital can also be objectified in the specific cultural signifiers embedded in our possessions and can be institutionalised in the acquisition of titles and awards. If we think about these different dimensions of symbolic aspects of culture as being transmitted as well as acquired motivational aspirations, it may be possible to see these as based on inter- and transgenerational transmission.

Bourdieu's (1977) related—but broader—idea of *habitus* is concerned with how individuals embody certain ways of living that lead to the social reproduction of those ways of living. This is an intergenerational process. Ways of living linked to poverty and social class are key examples. These are transmitted from one generation to the next, and cultural capital is closely related to this *habitus*. We have examples of this in the research where respondents talk about an intergenerational learning that they feel is so close to the body it could be genetic. The strength of the idea of *habitus* is that it is based on the idea of social practices, which give rise to certain kinds of capital or potential: *habitus* may have a deep history for some people and groups; it complements the ideas of mentalisation in its closeness to the body and non-verbal communication. *Habitus* also relies on the idea of social fields which inform the work of both Lewin (1997) and Shevlin and McGuigan (2003) who explain how trauma spreads through a social network. The field is itself close to the body and family; it determines our interpretation of what is possible given the circumstances. The social field allows highly adaptive, conservative and self-regulating behaviour. Bourdieu (1984) refers to it as *doxa*, or unconscious learning (see also Deer, 2008).

Fields and Transitional Space

The distinction between field and space may help to understand differences between inter- and transgenerational memory. Transitional space, like mentalisation, grows out of the process of intimate care and development. Yet it is the least concrete expression of it. Winnicott suggests that a measure of any society's depth of culture rests on its capacity to play. For him, culture and play are connected through the ability to sustain illusion promoted in the early playful interactions of mother and infant. This transitional area of experience located in the maternal matrix radiates out into culture, taking many different forms (Lerner, 1992). This socially extended capacity for creativity, the capacity to play with inner meaning and outer forms contracts when society takes an authoritarian turn or when war and social catastrophe descend. This contraction has been documented in Beradt's (1985) book on dreams during the Third

Reich. An increased authoritarianism in society drives people's dreaming inside them and out of sight. By contrast, potential space, as I described in Chapter 7, is transformative. Its function is to bring forth the new worlds of young minds as they grow. This magic of change and development can occur throughout the life cycle: transitional space and its potential is something that can be carried forward in time, but it always needs others for its fruition and expression. This openness is something that can also characterise relationships between the generations.

Lewin's original idea was to think about racism as a field phenomenon, something that could enter the life space of all individuals (Hampden-Turner, 1981, p. 128). Social fields connect individual personalities to their life spaces or immediate social environment, but the field also creates a connection with the larger social and physical environment. Shevlin and McGuigan's (2003) work on trauma in networks illustrates Lewin's basic idea. When something 'big' or pervasive happens in the social field, like trauma (such as Bloody Sunday) or a longer-lasting social process like racism or migration, then the personal element of the field is distorted: the person regresses if they can't overcome the resulting restriction in their social field. Lewin's life space is an early social systems theory view of how personality emerges and how we deal with conflict. For Lewin, the social field is a system that tends towards equilibrium. It changes through crisis or tension. Lewin's later-life work in the American Civil Rights Movement added confirmation of another strand of his ideas, that the researcher had their own active life space, and this interacted with the life space of their research subjects. Research was not a doer/done-to activity but one of action and collaboration. Action-led research is a precursor to psychosocial research.

In relation to potential space, the intergenerational drama of human psychological development and its vicissitudes are key. Mentalisation throughout the life cycle or its lack is the focus. Human development always has a social context. This, according to Lewin (1997), also has certain systemic life properties of protection and self-regulation. The social field is the transmitter of social events through and into the life space of the individual. From a psychosocial perspective, it is through the field that the transgenerational and traumatic enter. Lewin was not

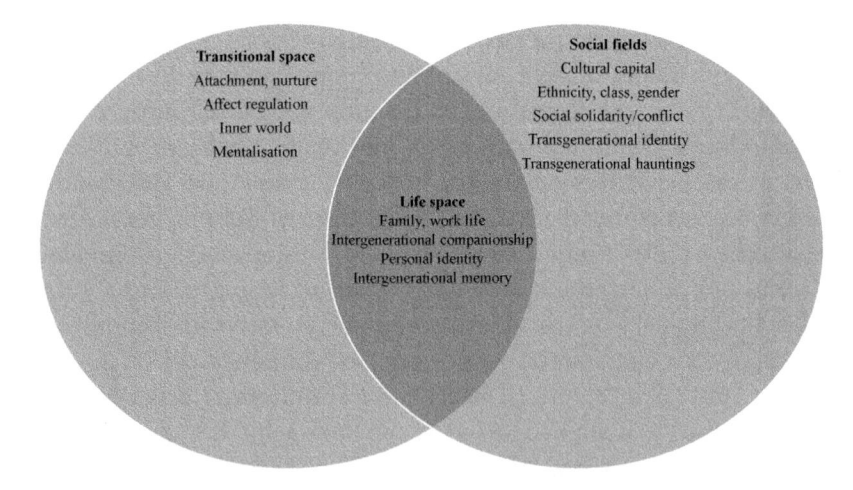

[Figure: Three overlapping circles showing:
- **Transitional space**: Attachment, nurture; Affect regulation; Inner world; Mentalisation
- **Social fields**: Cultural capital; Ethnicity, class, gender; Social solidarity/conflict; Transgenerational identity; Transgenerational hauntings
- **Life space**: Family, work life; Intergenerational companionship; Personal identity; Intergenerational memory]

Fig. 8.1 A psychosocial map of the overlapping dynamic fields in which the generations operate

psychoanalytically informed so did not view the field as 'unconscious' in the way that Bourdieu does.

This interplay of the deeply personal potential space of the inner world and the earliest formative relationships, the intergenerational family life space and the wider social field of class and ethnicity is characterised in Fig. 8.1.

Research as a Social Intervention

At the heart of transgenerational memory is a type of mediumistic sense-making where the ghosts and ancestors can be rejoined and invited back into the mentalising processes of contemporary generations. This decentres the idea of an expert professional like a psychotherapist and replaces it with knowledge that is held in groups and networks that have their own culture, ways of enquiry and healing. Typical leaders hold more transient roles like consultant, facilitator, host, witness or shaman to attend to the work in hand and accompany the process.

This research is a collection and congregation of voices all of whom have had much to say about the generations and memory. To express the conversations with and between these individuals and groups, I have produced a data set that has informed the middle chapters of this book. It is an attempt, however imperfect, to reflect something back. This chapter and Chapter 7 on therapeutic implications have continued to be based quite closely on participants' voices. In this last section, I explain how psychosocial research of this kind is a form of social action, and consequently a register of a particular moment in a particular culture. This can be useful when working with intractable and difficult problems. It can also bring new voices and new perspectives because of the intertwining of personal narrative in deeper time. Each interview and group meeting was conducted as a slow open conversation which allowed the maximum possible amount of reflection, association and 'what if' thinking on the topic of generational memory. Groups, public meetings and individual interviews all had moments of affective intensity. While the public meetings were initially quite small, this changed over time and my colleagues and I had to think about meeting dynamics involving significantly larger numbers. The research seemed to be turning into something else as more and more people wanted to join in, in some way or another. Even now, long after the research project has closed, I receive communications from people wanting to offer their stories and relate ideas that have since occurred to them.

During the research I became curious about the strong presence of feelings, or more likely affects, as I discussed in Chapter 2, in many of the interviews and group meetings. Given the evidence from the research that has emerged around affect regulation and storytelling, it seems to me that the team was getting a confirmation of a wider need to complete unfinished stories that involved the emotional lives of current, but also past generations. At one meeting I was handed a piece of paper written by a young soldier 101 years previously. The person bearing the scribbled note had no shared family connection to this young man but wanted me to connect him with the soldier's mother's family. It seems that in ancestry work there are connections that people want to find but don't know how. Sometimes it seems as if those connections seek us out, and this can feel uncanny.

One of the most striking features coming from the interviews was that of migration. For many participants, it was a known but not frequently contemplated part of their identity, and for others, it was an agonising source of pain. In one meeting, we had an overlap of experiences between those who had contemporary traumatic experiences of migration and those with historical ones. This seems to me to be one of the most creative aspects of this kind of research: contemporary and historical diasporas can be spoken about openly and freely. Alongside any specific trauma, there appears to be a subtle experience of shame about having had to migrate. It became clear in these meetings and was confirmed by the research that the experience of migration casts a long shadow equal in intensity to war and social danger to which it is often connected. Being able to get this into the open is very helpful and liberating.

In talking about their ancestors, many participants wanted to talk about their social conditions, issues of class values and experiences of poverty and hardship. These retrospectively focused conversations had an eerie quality. What became apparent in relation to looking back was also a recognition of the vulnerability of our own progress in terms of modernity, which is pretty paper-thin. Like the participants in the slavery museum social dreaming event, people felt themselves to be all in the same boat as their ancestors. This had a levelling quality where time seemed more open and did not seem to have the reassuring stages of a history book but rather the affective quality and unpredictability of a walk down a nineteenth-century city street.

Research can be a form of social action occurring in the overlapping life fields of researchers and participants. The benefit of the 'action' part of the research is something that holding a psychosocial perspective can promote, even if it is not necessarily intended to be therapeutic. Several participants reported positive changes from participating in the research. These ranged from insights and realisations to changes in relationships in both their personal and social life. Examples of this unintended positive outcome of psychosocial research included a desire to hand on an object being 'caretaken', insights gained in the longer psychosocial interviews that led to new work developments, the relief when a difficult personal haunting changed into knowledge about an actual ancestor which brought about a change in a relationship with a living relative or the relief of the sense of isolation and loneliness once a haunting of a transgenerational nature can be known or acknowledged as a shared experience. In this sense, 'big issues' such as migration, race and class sat alongside personal stories when the groups were communicating well or when an interview had gone deep enough. To go back to the theory, an interplay between transgenerational and intergenerational issues emerged naturally from the intimacy of the research meetings.

These conversations, to the extent that I managed to catch them, form the basis for this book. They can be expressed as 'research findings', but some fall into the arena of consequences. This could take many different forms but a psychosocial approach that emphasises the emotions as evidence and the binocular vision that joins the social and the psychological worlds together can offer a way of engaging the unconscious in social action that is more contained and encouraging of experience-near thinking about the most difficult of human issues. The large group or the social dreaming matrix are two examples. There are clearly many possibilities here and there is no reason why they could not be extended and adopted alongside more familiar forms of social action. They could be used to help different groups to deepen their connection to complex and intractable issues by becoming more familiar with their own hauntings.

Different types of memory require different types of response. Group meetings, if set up correctly, can offer a mixture of emotional containment and issue-based exploration. Bringing together mixed groups with deep and toxic social relationships can offer a kind of therapeutic conflict resolution and research-based activity. An example of a Group Relations event that attempts to link historical to current inter-ethnic conflict is the work done by Partners in Confronting Collective Atrocities in Poland (Brunner, 2019). The conferences have run for over 25 years, bringing together initially Germans, Jews, Palestinians and then others into an arena of experiential learning to confront and learn from atrocities.

One of the major psychosocial issues key to inter- and transgenerational dynamics is how extended mourning lasting several generations can be known about by other groups and peoples. A psychosocial perspective would focus on longer time spans than the lifetime of individuals for the resolution and reworking of loss. A psychoanalytically informed version of this would predict that long-term non-resolution will lead to repetition including cycles of violence and warfare alternating with depressive internalisation and poor individual and social health. The type of response is key, and it needs to be complex and multifaceted. With our depleted international institutions, our capacity to respond to larger problems is diminishing, while the problems themselves increase. This is a sign of a wider malaise and social breakdown. These new conflict resolution skills will need to be spread widely, scattered more like seed than targeted social policies. Everyone needs to know them. This may sound idealistic, but it isn't. Basic therapeutic skills are now much more widespread in the general population due to the influence of 'therapy' at a personal and at a cultural level.

One of the things that a psychosocial approach can do is to help identify the presence of extended multigenerational processes that are informing and complicating contemporary conflicts. Losses must make sense and be deeply understood by all parties to enable a chance of resolution. I offer this imaginary scenario to illustrate just a few of the complexities as well as potentials involved in a psychosocially informed intervention:

> A female descendant of a slave owner begs forgiveness from a contemporary black activist for her family's enslavement of his ancestors. He refuses to give it. He says there is 'too much hurt'. From an individual/couple conflict-resolution perspective, one might try to set up another meeting and do some further preparation with each party, but from a transgenerational perspective this may miss the point that while racism continues unabated, socially there is indeed 'too much hurt'. Had this exchange happened in a large group with a mixed ethnic membership, something else might have happened: participants could have further identified with the very painful conflict and gained some insight into the power and complexity of the reversal over longer periods of time of victim/persecutor dynamics. The black activist's refusal to forgive could have been explored as having the double potential for a broader remembering linked to current injustices, or the beginning of a reversal of the victim/persecutor dynamic by punishing her through a refusal to acknowledge her desire for forgiveness. In a more therapeutic setting this reversal could be explored, but would it be appropriate? At another level of intervention where ancestors are imaginatively involved, one might extend and deepen the issue

by asking: Do I have my ancestors' permission to forgive? The idea of forgiveness needs exploring too. Who benefits from it? Is forgiveness being asked for by the transgressor to relieve their guilt, rather than because of a real wish to do better now? Does forgiving imply the problem has been resolved? Can individuals meaningfully resolve a hurt that is felt by thousands of others? The law of talion may be more appropriate: reparations made and paid, a settlement and a new beginning.

This example of painful historical memory with both parties being informed and affected by a shared heritage of abuse alongside deep contemporary injustices brings me back to different types of memory. This attempt at reconciliation was doomed because one party at least could not reconceptualise loss or was not prepared to. Both were haunted by different kinds of memories. This is really where the rub is: until we know what haunts whom, we lack a reliable basis from which to proceed. Any attempt that is not fully informed by what haunts each party or group will lead to manic reparation (Figlio, 2017). Karl Figlio's idea of remembering as reparation underlines the problem of projection and hallucination in relating to the other. Where hatred and fear form one party's sense of the other, then both parties are deeply haunted by the harm—imagined or real—that they have done to each other. There is in effect nothing to witness, because the desire for forgiveness is too vague or is only relevant to one party and not the other. Coming to know hauntings is complex and demanding psychosocial work. It involves a lot of investment and care if it is to be worthwhile. Kathy Livingston (2010) talks about the issue of disenfranchised grief in relation to descendants of Nazi perpetrators and Holocaust survivors. Working with hauntings does allow the parties to ask what their ancestors and current families might want; it creates a more imaginative process. It also requires the right cultural moment—in this example where black and white people might find a deeper form of collaboration against inequalities, or when descendants of Nazi perpetrators and families of Holocaust survivors find they can collaborate. This change in the social field is critical: without it, this kind of conflict remains beyond personal resolution. Hauntings remain hauntings, and social links may sever more completely. The consequences are further alienation and cycles of acting out, including the construction of false and misleading histories.

Developing a multigenerational sensibility is key to working with these kinds of conflicts. Yet sometimes it is the voice of the child that can give a clue as to how to proceed. In a school playground, a young white boy puts his arm possessively/aggressively around a young black boy and says: 'You are my slave'. They are both seven years old. Is it a moment of play or oppression? One could ask where he learned to say that and think about how he performed an initiation into a lifelong experience of racism for the black child, as it carries an important aspect of the transgenerational memory of black people being the chattels of white people. In a way, the white boy was a hapless carrier of the racism that surrounded him, but it does suggest the need for intervention. Can a school be a school without racism? The team that set up the 2020 Channel 4 series *The School that Tried to End Racism* show it is possible but extremely challenging for all parties. Jane Elliot's (*The Eye of the Storm*, 1970) famous 'Blue eyes brown eyes' anti-racism intervention shows that children with explicit affect-based anti-racist training remain that way in adult life.

These kinds of early intervention affect children's social fields. Friendship patterns are changed and values altered. Far better to have an early social intervention than a teenage psychological one for low self-esteem or an even later one following a criminal offence or adult mental illness. In this sense, a psychosocial intervention at a group level amongst these children and their friends could lessen the baleful power of transgenerational issues and memory that they will all face as they grow up. This type of intervention is future-focused and is done in awareness of the possible consequences of not working with such issues. Can a whole society manage something as far-reaching as this? The postcolonial issues of school curricula loom large here. Without decolonialising the curriculum, this malignant history of slavery and its attendant racism will be muffled. Imagined and chosen trauma are not far behind these scenarios. The difficulty for Britain in continuing to memorialise its victory in the Second World War suggests a problem in coming to terms with a post-imperial past and in finding its place as a significant but small country amongst larger ones, one of which was its recent former enemy, and another the enemy before that.

The following is an example of a postcolonial transgenerational haunting, using a 30-year marker for distinct generations and taking a seven-generation sequence from the planned French invasion of Britain in 1803, via the declaration of the First World War against Germany at 1913 to its part two finish in 1945. Intergenerational memory goes back three and a half generations to just before the First World War. There are some examples of working with memories from this period in Chapter 2. Going back the same number of generations from there to 1803, we would expect to find some of my ancestors shaking in fear at the prospect of invasion and others hoping for a continental liberator. The fond but ambivalent canon of English folk song about Napoleon is widespread enough to evidence the latter. Jane Austen's novels are subtly suffused with the menacing presence of the European battlefield. In short, transgenerational memory arising mainly in the fourth generation is inscribed in culture. Little of it arrives in formal history books. What the seven-generation memory gives is a narrative about the problems of living on an island, being a rising imperial and later neocolonial power and the subsequent process of decline. There are some interesting connections to the research findings.

Some of our respondents reflected on their past migrations. Did they end up in the right place? Do they regret the dislocation? Is their present better than the situation their ancestors were trying to leave behind? Two groups stand out: one that pictures Britain as an island castle and better than any large landmass for that reason; the other bemoaning its racism and carrying a visceral fear of it from previous and current generational experiences. Each group carries very different hauntings which can lead in different directions in terms of the kind of contributions they make in the ensuing generations. Thinking about memory psychosocially, I offer a map that elaborates on the earlier psychological map, focusing on the social dimension and some of the social action-based issues (see Fig. 8.2).

In the top arc, society is essentially integrated and most social groups are known to each other, despite othering and stereotyping. The institutions of society are relatively open, and the voices of the different generations are known and listened to. There is some give and take so that different groups tend to or want to learn from each other.

Creative

Reconceptualising loss	**Creativity and shutting down**
Societies intact enough	*Action possible but sometimes thwarted*
Relationships between groups	*Presence of learning relationships*
knowable/discoverable	*between groups*

Generational voices heard and listened to

Reintegration **The natural world, cycles, complexity and imagination** *Disintegration*

Move towards nature and social imagination	*Breaking the link with nature and place*
Developing mentalisation across the generations increases adaptability	*Increased conflict between ethnic groups and nations*
Loss/breaking of the social link	**Hauntings and unhappy interment**
Deep trauma and dislocation	*Trauma but some social memory; social secrets*
False social identities and frozen histories	
Identity wars based on chosen traumas	*Retreat into dreams away from the social*
Breakdown of social order	*Generation-hopping, 'old new movements'*

Destructive

Fig. 8.2 Typology of multigenerational memory: Transgenerational emphasis

Society is not deeply polarised into different identity groups. As generational conflict increases and social cohesion decreases, hauntings emerge; some are real, some imagined. We start to enter the lower arc. This happens when long-running social conflicts are not resolved and where old behaviours and social movements arise as if unbidden. Social and political secrets become the norm and fear starts to predominate. There is an attendant fear of social breakdown, and an emergence of claims to power, based on actual and imagined hurts and previous traumas. Often a social past is idealised and one of several out-groups is identified as the reason for the current troubles. People forget how to find out social truths via relationships and first-hand experience, and may deepen their isolation via social media echo-chambers, which stand in for traditional closed family systems. Social media may be a fertile source of information devoid of context. Dangerous affect-based solutions of one kind or another that might be enacted in the real world are rehearsed online. We don't yet know if social media is more effective in producing social action than the traditional political and social pamphlets that worked so well in the lead up to the First World War for instance. In an earlier piece of research on the fate of Anglo-German communities in the UK, I found examples of the promotion of fears of invasion. In these, anyone who read the *Daily Mail* from March 1906 onwards would know which English town the 'invading German army' had 'overrun' that week (Williams, 2015, pp. 130–131). There are clearly similarities and differences between then and now, but it is only a four-generation spread in terms of time. The social conditions that make people keen to join in this ostracisation of a certain group are remarkably familiar. The politics of resentment and reactionary forms of populism are signs that the social projection of insecurities and shortcomings onto ethnic and national others have a depressingly unwavering social history. There is an established literature on this (see, for instance, Crociani-Windland and Hoggett, 2012; Richards, 2018). If these otherings cannot be converted into actual losses and known social events, then the process of breaking social links accelerates, and widespread social disintegration occurs. Typically, renewal is sought through social violence and war, rather than through politics and community-based dialogue. From pain to violence rather than from conflict to dialogue.

That social memory is a continual target of manipulation is a sign of its importance in helping us remember how things work, who to trust and what the signs are of being closer to or further away from verifiable information and helpful experience. Social memory needs to be connected to actual problems and embodied social identities. In the psychosocial sense, it is the psychic tissue of life. It is the capacity to 'pick up' what is happening and to remember what and who is trustworthy. It is part of our attachment and generational heritage.

References

Beradt, C. (1985) *The Third Reich of Dreams: The Nightmares of a Nation 1933–1939*. Translated from the German by Bruno Bettelheim. Wellingborough: Aquarian Press.

Bollas, C. (1987) *The Shadow of the Object: Psychoanalysis of the Unthought Known*. London: Free Association Books.

Bourdieu, P. (1977) *Outline of a Theory of Practice: 16 (Cambridge Studies in Social and Cultural Anthropology)*. Cambridge: Cambridge University Press.

Bourdieu, P. (1984) *Distinction*. London: Routledge.

Brunner, L.D. (2019) *Director's Report* [online]. Germany: Partners Inconfronting Collective Atrocities. Available from: http://p-cca.org/2019/03/14/directors-report-march-2019/ [Accessed 23 September 2020].

Crociani-Windland, L. and Hoggett, P. (2012) Politics and affect. *Subjectivity* [online]. 5 (2), pp. 161–179 [Accessed 20 September 2020].

Deer, C. (2008) Doxa. In: Grenfell, M. (Ed.) *Pierre Bourdieu: Key Concepts*. Stocksfield: Acumen, pp. 119–130.

Elias, N. (1978) *The Civilising Process Vol 1: The History of Manners*. New York: Urizen Books.

Figlio, K. (2017) *Remembering as Reparation: Psychoanalysis and Historical Memory*. Basingstoke: Palgrave Macmillan.

Freud, S. (1930) *Civilization and Its Discontents*. Translated by David McLintock. London: Penguin, 2014.

Frosh, S. (2019) *Those Who Come After: Postmemory, Acknowledgement and Forgiveness*. Basingstoke: Palgrave Macmillan.

Hampden-Turner, C. (1981) *Maps of the Mind*. London: Mitchell Beazley.

Lerner, L. (1992) Illusion and culture: A tribute to Winnicott. *Psychoanalytic Review* [online]. 79 (2), p. 167 [Accessed 23 September 2020].

Lewin, K. (1997) *Resolving Social Conflicts and Field Theory in Social Science*. Washington: American Psychological Association.

Livingston, K. (2010) Opportunities For mourning when grief is disenfranchised: Descendants of Nazi perpetrators in dialogue with Holocaust survivors. *Omega: Journal of Death and Dying* [online]. 61 (3), pp. 205–222 [Accessed 23 September 2020].

Manley, J. and Trustram, M. (2018) 'Such endings that are not over': The slave trade, social dreaming and affect in a museum. *Psychoanalysis, Culture & Society* [online]. 23 (1), pp. 77–96 [Accessed 22 September 2019].

Ramsay, C. (1997) The need to feed. In: Hayden, T. (Ed.) (1997) *Irish Hunger: Personal Reflections on the Legacy of the Famine.* Dublin: Wolfhound Press, pp. 137–142.

Richards, B. (2018) Exploring malignancies, narcissism and paranoia today. *Psychoanalysis, Culture and Society.* 23 (1), pp. 15–27.

Roth, P. (2005) The depressive position. In: Budd, S. and Rusbridger, R. (Eds.), *Introducing Psychoanalysis: Essential Themes and Topics.* London: Routledge, pp. 47–58.

Schore, A. (2009). Attachment trauma and the developing right brain: Origins of pathological dissociation. In: Dell, F.D. and O'Neil, J.A. (Eds.), *Dissociation and Dissociative Disorders DSM-V and Beyond.* New York, Routledge. pp. 107–143.

Sharp, C. (2016) *In the Wake: On Blackness and Being.* Durham: Duke University Press.

Shevlin, M. and McGuigan, K. (2003) The long-term psychological impact of Bloody Sunday on families of the victims as measured by the revised impact of event scale. *British Journal of Clinical Psychology* [online]. 42 (4), pp. 427–432 [Accessed 22 September 2019].

The Eye of the Storm (1970) [TV]. William Peters. American Broadcasting Company, no date.

The School That Tried to End Racism (2020) [TV]. Channel 4, 25 June.

Tucker, W.T. (1965) Max Weber's *verstehen*. *The Sociological Quarterly* [online]. 6 (2), pp. 157–165 [Accessed 22 September 2019].

Williams, N. (2015) Anglo-German displacement and diaspora in the early twentieth century: An intergenerational haunting. In: O'Loughlin, M. (Ed.) *The Ethics of Remembering and the Consequences of Forgetting: Essays on Trauma, History and Memory.* Lanham: Rowan and Littlefield, pp. 125–142.

9

Conclusion

Overall Themes: Maps in Time and Space

My aims as set out in the introduction of this book were to explore and more clearly define multigenerational memory and to find out whether this understanding made a difference both for the practice of psychotherapy and for other kinds of interventions that are psychosocially informed. I hope it is now clear that the issue of the generations and social memory have relevance to the general public perhaps more than the professions, as the big changes that are required in the current period are political and social in the broadest sense.

My own personal focus—research into my ancestry—has widened out to include the experiences and thoughts of many others via the research. I feel greatly enriched by this. The framework for the key organising maps of memory was derived from an analysis of the themes in the research data. This is important: my main arguments about the cyclical nature of social memory come from the research thematic map (Fig. 2.2). This map has proved adaptable and useful in providing a frame of reference for both psychological and social interventions (Figs. 7.1 and 8.2). The flexibility of these frameworks may of course be limited by the social and cultural background of the participants in that they are mainly European and North American, but nonetheless they have cultural breadth and depth. The point now is to try them out more. In the book, I have provided several examples from case studies to actual memories. It is now down to the reader to try them out and experiment! The maps should work as well with personal ancestry research, psychotherapy and with larger social interventions.

Another map (Fig. 2.1) involved the basic explanatory frameworks for memory available to us at this point in time. They are drawn from the social and natural sciences and intersected by longer and shorter spans of time. While a discussion of this is not the main focus of the book, I have wanted to make a map like this for some time, having had the feeling that different approaches are needed, depending on how deep in time a problem or issue was germinated. Psychoanalysis has been a method for exploring our personal and species past, but we need to use other approaches as well. The fields of epigenetics, anthropology and binocular or 'two-eyed' research stand out as approaches that help in terms of working in deeper time and with profound cultural difference.

As it may already have become apparent, I like maps! They don't suit everyone, but the spatial organisation of information can help to draw together areas that are normally thought about and experienced in their own boxes. The other map (Fig. 8.1) is about social fields and what anthropologists and psychotherapists call liminal and transitional spaces. To think about the generations and social memory properly, we also must think about spatial networks and geography. We live in time both shorter and longer terms and we live in extended and discontinuous social and geographical networks. These are most obviously intertwined when we look at the experience of migration and war. However, any community or societal conflict spreads through networks. What this map does is alert us to the presence of attachment to people and place in each network, and this in turn tells us about the grain and uniqueness of the relations of care therein. Memory spreads out in time and in space but it does so in a way that echoes the identities and capacities of the people involved.

This brings me to the more unusual ideas that have occurred to me while analysing the data in the research. While no one participant told me they had or were in possession of a 'multigenerational self', as I began to let go of the idea of a tightly bounded sense of self and thought more about the 'many in the one', the idea of a sense of self extended through time became quite plausible. It is in tune with many of the contributors' accounts in the research in that when they talked about their ancestors, it was clear that they were also talking about themselves.

I have linked the idea of being able to imagine the relationships between the generations to the presence or absence of intergenerational storytelling. I have taken this a little further to suggest if that these storytelling relationships exist, then we start to get a different kind of future that has greater emotional and practical continuities in it. The research and this book are an example of that kind of extended narrative that says something about the relationships between the generations. It is, in itself, a story.

Imagining the Generations

Imagining the generations extends the idea of intergenerational mentalising to include the social dimension and that of deeper time. This past/future focus is informed by a multigenerational perspective. By implication, the idea of the ebbing and flowing presence of a multigenerational self also suggests the possibility of an extended multigenerational society. The main mechanism for this extension of multigenerational relationships is intergenerational companionship. Intergenerational mentalising, however imperfect, is an outcome of this companionship. The relative presence or absence of this mentalising at any one time defines the degree to which any continuity exists between the generations. This in turn affects the degree to which society can be said to remember, and what kind of remembering this is. If the memory is more trauma-informed, then a haunted relationship between the generations will predominate, with all the potential for repetition that unworked traumatic memory brings. If the mentalisation is more informed by a knowledge of the loss of actual relationships, then a mourning process is more likely which in turn may lead to the emergence of new forms of relationship and creativity between the generations.

Several therapists I interviewed talked about needing to expand and change their sense of what the therapeutic was, in order to accommodate their own experiences of finding ways of pulling creative intergenerational threads together. The theme of storytelling is key here. Yet the tension between facilitating insight and joint intergenerational collaboration remained a feature, as if the expert clinical role is nearly impossible to relinquish. Sometimes these creative educational processes are talked about as clandestine activities smuggled into the everyday institution, whether that be clinical or academic. Sometimes the older generation of teachers brings about for their students something from which they themselves were never able to benefit.

Beyond the academy, in the struggle to introduce experience-based learning and autobiographical memory into research, the world of psychotherapy is referred to as 'better', in that it offers emotional containment. However, it is also spoken about as another closed system when it is blind to cultural and social difference rooted in deeper family and social history.

Some respondents felt that creativity and shutting down often alternated during their working lives. It seemed to take a lifetime to find their voices separate from their profession and family of origin, but once this had happened, 'giving back' was easier because of feeling less fearful of judgement by peers and managers.

References to the role of intergenerational relationships within the professions and in people's working lives occurred frequently because the relationships between the generations are often mediated through work and social productivity.

Furthermore, the institutions of society are more or less open to creativity in different periods. This is mirrored in people's working lives which are often the arena of creativity and shutting down for them.

When people tell stories that lead to new intergenerational relationships, a different past and new future can be imagined. This capacity to mentalise requires new relationships and arrangements, which involve some risk-taking, and professional openness. New forms of collaboration between the generations then become more possible.

Intergenerational competitiveness can distort collaboration. If one generation feels it has to kill off the other in order to have its say, then the creative contribution of both the older and younger voices is harder to hear. Staying open to one's creativity in later life can help to enable social continuity. Equally, younger generations can help to heal the hurts of their elders by offering recognition and acknowledgement that had not already been given. In this reciprocal way, the generations can help each other in ways that are often not imagined and therefore not explored.

Dangers of Haunted Relationships Between Peoples and States

Society as well as individuals can be haunted. Examples of the Irish Famine recurred in our data, the key aspect that emerged was how memory was held by subsequent generations. If it was traumatically informed, then the past might feel that it had never gone away. Different societies tended to deal with memory differently. Colonialising powers seem to have shorter memories when territorial occupation, population movement and displacement are involved.

Moods such as those from the Irish Famine haunt and trouble some of the research respondents. The unease is sometimes hard to pin down, but at other times it is very clear, yet no one in the respondents' lives is acknowledging it. This is similar to trauma that involves abuse. It is a feature of transgenerational processes that contain personal and whole-society experiences. The conditions under which lost generations find their voices in subsequent ones are at once deeply personal and potentially very political. The colonialising power has also to be 'ready to talk' rather than doubling down on tradition and privilege. Maybe as in revolution is has to be overthrown, at least in people's minds if nowhere else. The translation from an intergenerational to a transgenerational process is signalled where personal therapeutic work has been done but something else is required that is reparative. This takes the personal/cultural form of offering new forms of education that foreground the personal biography in deeper context, but it breaks off in the face of larger-scale political events that are still affected by unacknowledged histories between states and peoples. This is an area in which an understanding of multigenerational memory has a major contribution to make.

One can find the most prosaic examples of this non-acknowledgement of history in school curricula where the history of colonialism and empire is little taught. Culturally and historically short-sighted national syllabuses make a major contribution to transgenerational non-mentalising.

Hauntings are not all negative if they are explored rather than exploited. Hauntings can lead to the recovery of lost histories, identities and capacities. They can be a key to opaque aspects of personal and social identity. They could even be thought of as a method or way of working that relies both on archaeology and trance methodologies for their elaboration and embodiment. The large-group meetings, social dreaming matrixes and adapted group relation conferences as discussed in Chapter 8 are all examples of this.

Recognition is a key element in this process. This can be direct—the acknowledgement of what has happened and what was lost and the social justice elements of recognition in victim–persecutor dynamics. But importantly, finding a new group that can recognise and welcome the work or cultural contribution of a migrant group is also vital. Much positive cultural mixing performs this vital function of love and acceptance. It often leads to blending, either literally via inter-ethnic relationships, or culturally by the generation of hybrid identities.

Identities: Individuals, Generations, Groups, Epigenetics

The two-way learning and collaborating between generations can get interrupted by trauma, social dislocation and different access to social resources. Sometimes multigenerational memory is tangible and a resource for survival and flourishing; at others it is apparently almost absent.

Generations, like individuals, have identities. Some generations can be a difficult act to follow, so creative or so destructive or indeed mediocre, indifferent or staid. In the data, we can see instances of one generation 'not wanting to know' and being unwilling to share information and memories. This is often the case with memories of war; the next generation wants to understand but is blocked. Children often represent, for their parents, a ray of hope for the future. Manic qualities in one generation can lead to reparative and depressive impulses in the next. The Edwardian social reform and emancipation movements were the beginning of an attempt to counter the extroversion of the imperial Victorian era. They in turn were swamped by the trauma of world war which was arguably driven by the outdated politics of empire and industrial rivalry typical of late nineteenth-century Europe. Mania often pushes against depressive reflection and drives to something more destructive. Bollas (2018) points to the First World War as the start of the crash away from the mania of modernity, but without the accompanying capacity to understand human destructiveness it has been replaced with a gradual shallowing of culture as capitalism has attempted to recover from its crises by making the consumer sovereign. Perhaps there is an oscillation between generations that are driven by the mania of progress and those that are more depressively organised and more aware of loss.

In order to track and address these multigenerational processes in memory, I have had to redefine what memory and remembering are and what forms they can take. Intergenerational memories typically lasting no more than three generations get extended or complicated by transgenerational ones. In this study, the presence of longer memories of the identity of a group, ethnicity or nation block and trouble people. Being inescapably of a particular ethnic group, gender or class produces a long-term source of identity and conflict. The Irish diaspora and the Holocaust have loomed large in my data, but one can add the African, Afro-American and Caribbean diasporas as having profound effects on identity independent of intergenerational relationships. It is interesting that most of the transgenerational aspects of memory are, in this research, negative. In the context of the current Black Lives Matter movement, something of the transgenerational trauma of slavery may be shifting. The transgenerational, if traumatically informed, is vital to the transformation of more personal intergenerational conflicts. In this sense, attending to it can be liberating and can make it clear what any individual or group is actually up against. It is the apparent lack of positive transgenerational memory that generates the main conclusion of the book. When we are hampered by a lack of intergenerational companionship and collaboration, and if this is maintained across several generations, then the result is a lack of positive transgenerational memory. Producing positive transgenerational effects and increasing society's capacity to survive and flourish rest on relations of care and collaboration between the generations. It is interesting that many of the enduring organisations are religious, while the longest-lasting secular organisations in the West are universities, followed by banks and standing armies. The transgenerational is often tied up with the fate of empires, nations and religions yet has a quieter and less visible existence which is closer to the body and to human relations of attachment and care.

I have described multigenerational memory as being embodied. Elias (1978) and Foucault (2000) emphasise the power and control over bodies held by different states and societies. Elias (1978) identifies a way in which, over time, relations of power and discipline are internalised. By taking memory as something that can exist in an extended and distributed way and yet is deeply linked to human attachments, I have explored how human cognition and memory extends beyond the individual. The idea of extended cognition that is both spatial (geographical) and existing in time (generational) is central to this.

I have used the social psychology of Shevlin and Mcguigan (2003) and Lewin (1997) to show how traumatic memory spreads across social networks and through time. An understanding of the relationship between social fields and transitional space is important in this respect and its potential was discussed in Chapter 8.

While my arguments about the nature of civilisation as always being discontent are broadly in line with Freud's, I don't think that the Oedipal story is the main driver of intergenerational dynamics. I take the view that traumatically driven processes are more powerful than the developmental drama of the emergence of individual personality. I also think there isn't a universal template for human development or if there is, we don't yet know what it looks like. Freud's argument rests on the drives being universal, so any collective psychology must be based on their vicissitudes. The generations and their attendant memory processes need a culturally wider perspective and more inclusion of sociological, psychological and biological processes. I suspect cultural variations are too great for there to be a single human developmental process. Referring to the generations and memory in the ways, I have described them in this book gets us outside or at least to the edges of colonial and Eurocentric thinking.

An important and emerging field in genetics is beginning to explore the idea that the genetic process is also 'extended' beyond the sexually transmitted genome. The idea that many other sorts of information are epigenetically transmitted through time should caution us from looking for universals like drives in the Freudian sense.

The alternative, that enacted hurt and its repetitions runs down the generations, is a more likely source of multigenerational conflict. It is more in touch with the realities of nation, class, poverty and ethnic conflict. This does not mean there is an ideal society to return to; it just means that some generations and some societies are more resourceful and integrated than others and that this situation is always changing. One generation may wreak enormous trauma and social destruction, while another may have built a quiet and confident peace and prosperity.

Broken Social Links, Hauntings and Museums

Broken social links are key to understanding how trauma takes the form of haunting. These are particularly strong for migrants who may lose all sense of their previous identity quite quickly if they need to acculturate rapidly. Social links can be broken inside non-migrating families by war trauma where individuals choose not to talk about their experiences. One of the take-home messages of this research is that this decision not to speak produces the opposite of what is intended. A generation of children and their children are disturbed by the secret until it surfaces or is lost altogether. Unless the society itself becomes discontinuous, as it does for migrants whose nation has been destroyed or disrupted by war, then the transgenerational memory is present in some shape or form in culture and social networks. Transgenerational hauntings begin when the inscription of events in culture stops. I have become aware of some of these while researching for this book. There are many in the modern world where diasporas and genocides have become the new normal. Some go largely unrecorded (see Chapter 3).

In thinking about memory, I've also used the distinction made by post-memory theorists between communicative memory embodied through families and groups, and cultural memory encoded in symbolic systems. The break-up of symbolic systems and their replacement by the incoming dominant group or power is also part of the destruction and creation of social memories, many of which are entirely artificial or fictional.

Volkan (1998) talks about the power of chosen trauma which is often a decontextualized historical event or a false claim to a territory via an imagined bloodline or national/ethnic identity. In short, transgenerational memory is notoriously unreliable. Norman Davies (2011) comments on the changes in a number of museums in Galicia from the Soviet era to contemporary times. The Sądecki Ethnographic Park in Nowy Sącz, Poland, shows how a largely fictitious account by Soviet-era curators of the early 1960 s gave way in stages to a gradual acknowledgement of other ethnic and national voices. While the full story of the Galician diaspora is still untold after a 70-year period and two generations, the museum now has a fuller transgenerational story. It can't quite let go of a deep cultural trope that the native Rus were never Russian, or that Jews were in the majority in various towns and cities, yet it has evolved away from a formal Soviet-era definition of Polish identity. The multiplicity of a complex (both culturally and linguistically) former nation is gradually being reinstated. The museum in a way shows a similar pattern to intergenerational memory in families, the third generation being a fulcrum point for change, either with an increased curiosity for what happened or a movement further away from it.

It is these kinds of processes that link most closely to one of the most influential but hard-to-evidence theories of multigenerational trauma—the work of Abraham and Torok (1994). They say that a collective psychology comprising several generations exists in each individual. The therapeutic implication is that one must listen for the voices of one generation in the unconscious of another. There is a social and transgenerational parallel to this. In a way, the museum of Nowy Sącz portrays this process, whereby a complex, continuous and embodied memory of people, time and place was shattered by the clash of Russia and Germany in two world wars, genocide and traumatic diaspora happening in several phases. The museum in its immediate Soviet phase could be seen as a false self, presiding over a landscape of apparent recovery, but a closer glance shows many peoples missing, dead or migrated. If the museum represents a segment of transgenerational memory, it is deeply distorted. If something like this is internalised by survivors of diaspora then the resultant sense of self is very provisional. New national boundaries built on such provisional and recently constructed identities are also fragile. Perhaps the truth behind the idea of the generation-hopping phantom is that a self and a nation built on transgenerational sands is indeed unstable and prone to breaking down and acting out.

The alien cultural introject, whether personal or national, if undetected, gathers moss like a stone rolling down the generations, according both to Abraham and Torok (1994) and to Davoine and Gaudillière (2004). States with murderous histories and genocides, as with the example above, have a fragile national identity. It will take two or three generations willing to reconceptualise loss before something more solid emerges. Transgenerational haunting may take over if this doesn't happen.

Cycles of Memory

This idea of movement and stones gathering moss leads to another main explanatory framework: the idea that multigenerational memory can be thought of as cyclical. What is important is that this scaffold offers a dynamic way of describing how memory works across the generations in time and geographically. I have discussed one more psychological cycle that is mainly intergenerational, and another mainly social one that is more transgenerational. In summary, the top segment or arc in each of these maps (Figs. 7.1 and 8.2) describes the kind of memory involved in problem-solving, working with loss and potential. On a social level, this is mirrored in groups, families and institutions where society has sufficient imagination and cultural capital to solve problems. Much of this activity goes on in families but also in the world of work where generational relationships also exist and play out. I call this activity 'reconceptualising loss' and 'reaching for creativity'. In Chapter 4, I described how we reconceptualise loss across the generations in ways that are very personal and intimate as well as linked to work and intergenerational family relationships. I talk about how, for many families, creativity as much as difficulty and trauma runs in an intergenerational pattern. These experiences are always close to the body. Physical skills may be imitated; capacities to work in certain ways may be passed on. This work can involve working through trauma, diaspora and family secrets. The social level of traumatic experiences of war, famine and genocide feature here, but in each instance the fate of the memories determines what happens next. Very broadly, if the losses are personal or social and can be thought about, they can be mourned. This might involve the effects of PTSD in the parents, the belief that not speaking about trauma stops it being passed on, or the burden that children have when they carry the unrealised hopes of their parents whose lives were blighted by events. It can also be the power of family secrets and the silences they engender. The power and role of storytelling and intergenerational companionship emerges in this picture. With these resources, quite difficult intergenerational issues can be worked with and eased. All of this problem-solving has gone on for a very long time, but psychotherapy has increasingly come to play its part as well.

Some losses are too complicated to remain in the top-level arc and emanate from another level of memory where states of mind haunt or puzzling events remain unexplained. In a way, the relatively intact social fabric that reconceptualising loss works with is more fragmented in the next area—that of hauntings and unhappy interment. Here, the role of transgenerational process comes to predominate. This is partly because of the passage of time beyond the key three-/four-generation span where 'living memory' can still have an influence, and partly because of the social and cultural power of previous history.

Here, memory is less complete, less available or more distorted. These 'first-arc' memories are almost always intergenerational, in that they follow a two- to three-generation pattern. They may involve traumas and dislocations but are part of ongoing living. With hauntings, it is often the case that a more transgenerational element starts to feature. People who are from groups who have been subject to a shared trauma that has not been acknowledged or recognised find that they are blocked from psychological work. Survivors of the Holocaust and the Irish Famine were significant presences in our data, but experiences of little-known migrations and issues of social class, racism, war and national identity also abounded. To the extent that a haunting can be understood better, then loss and mourning can be experienced, and so new aspects of identity may emerge. Equally the events may be so difficult and the transgenerational issues so long-standing that a personal resolution isn't really possible. This is true in societies that are deeply conflicted. Empathy is in short supply and the willingness to witness others limited. When the transgenerational memory moves, it can be seismic. The fact that slavery has now come to the fore in the Black Lives Matter movement illustrates this.

Memories are also lost forever. Death guarantees this, as do ongoing differences between how little or how much the generations are in tune with each other. This loss is captured by the idea of availability heuristics: a way of expressing how much any society can remember about how it does things and how to respond to risk and danger. This is particularly pertinent in the age of the COVID-19 pandemic. The thesis put forward here is that the degree of connectivity between the generations and the amount of intergenerational mentalising that is available have a big impact on any society's ability to confront novel and difficult problems.

Hauntings also suggest their own methodology where the mediumistic, dream and trance states of mind may be helpful in letting these partly lost experiences come to life and speak. Hauntings also link to another feature of memory which is the sense of an expanse of experience which is so long it is unencompassable. Some of the longest memories on the planet partake of this antiquity and are imbued with a wisdom that comes from 'time out of mind'. In this book, the contributions of First Nation cultures are shown to reach into deep time and offer wisdom and problem-solving via dreams, totem animals, rituals and landscapes.

The idea of landscape ushers in the last part of the cycle of memory which is a central point between the upper and lower arcs. Here, our respondents fluently use their relationship with nature to explain how hauntings, traumas and secrets can be addressed in an open and accepting way. Given the cultural background of the participants, nature may also stand in for religion, God or spirits.

Perhaps the most interesting finding is the one that shows an acceptance of the power of a relationship with nature that is both personal and other. Nature, for many respondents, is another way of talking about the transgenerational—the much longer term outside of normal human time spans. Collaboration with this natural big other extends the sense of the self from one generational to many. The part of memory that connects with the natural world is the one that seems to most clearly offer the idea of a multigenerational self-possessing a deep past and a strong future focus. This central part of the cycle of memory also has the strongest connection with imagination and dreaming.

The Social as an Arena for Haunting and Intergenerational Moods

Christopher Bollas (2018) suggests that social moods leading to deep-level changes in attitudes can be creative or malignant. He believes that a current large-scale difficulty in mourning is starting to threaten our social contract in the West. The social unconscious is the source of the 'unthought known' and is made up of unresolved social conflicts. He suggests that the main problem that rebounds into us from the unthought known is our inability to think about our social destructiveness. This is confounded by a culture of consumption which turns people away from deeper introspection and social responsibility. The consequences of being unable to mourn social loss are clear in this research; our collective capacity to resolve problems of all kinds is going to shrink; our societies will become less complex and consequently less able to adapt to change. In terms of the current research, this worrying development is described in the ways in which intergenerational trauma interacts with transgenerational trauma, and how longer traumatic histories limit the life chances of certain groups and peoples.

The social is also an arena for hauntings. Stephen Frosh (2019) describes hauntings as both timeless and ever-present which speaks to a continuous traffic between inter- and transgenerational memory. He suggests it is in haunting that we are most challenged to think both psychologically and socially.

Attachment, Memory and Deeper Time

In the research, it seemed clear that memory and attachment are connected. The links between persons, places and memories have a haunting presence for many. People and objects form networks in our minds. Friends, parents, siblings, landscapes, tools and paintings emerge as networks of memory across the research. This suggests to me that attachment, memory and deeper time are connected. In the chapter on nature, for instance, identity is experienced as being linked to place, tools, objects and artworks. Each also has a sense of history or time which suggests one of the ways in which shorter-term intergenerational memory is informed by other longer-lived objects that may be physical or cultural. It is the confluence and combination of these that connect and characterise the difference between inter- and transgenerational mentalisation.

Similarities and Differences Between Inter- and Transgenerational Mentalisation

In counselling and psychotherapy, mentalisation has to do with a developmental process and capacity that emerges through a combination of intimacy, affect regulation and recognition. It leads to the development of a theory of mind(s), knowing the presence of the others in the self and the self in other minds. Mentalisation is always partial, incomplete and changing. It is subject to crisis and alteration which, in attachment therapy terms, is referred to as rupture–repair dynamics. Mentalisation can be interrupted by trauma. In short, new experience and learning from experience arises out of conflict and its negotiation.

This essentially one-to-one model for mentalisation also implies the way in which we internalise other experiences if there is enough 'give and take', or if relationships are experienced as having sufficient reciprocity. This then ushers in an understanding of what John Bowlby calls Unconscious Working Models (Bretherton and Munholland, 2008) and how they have been internalised. Internalisation is a key assumption concerning how therapy works. I have found some evidence that it extends to the generations partly through our identifying with other groups and organisations, but of equal importance are identifications with known and unknown ancestors. This, I think, encapsulates the essence of intergenerational mentalisation: it is rooted in rhythms of care, but it also extends outwards in space through siblings, friendship and group networks, and backwards in time via grandparents and occasionally great-grandparents.

Intergenerational mentalisation is based on attachment. This is partly informed by a relationship between bodies—the rhythm of care between one generation and the next. It is also based on stories that become memories. These stories can help to manage affects or can be containers for something stranger and haunting.

This is a watershed in memory and experience. On the one hand is experience that is available through everyday understanding or inquiry and can also be explored by psychotherapy and counselling particularly if it has conflictual or traumatic elements within it. Therapy most commonly contributes to ameliorating intergenerational problems by intervening early enough in the life cycle to change dysfunctional aspects of parenting or attending to trauma that has its origin in the current life cycle. On the other side of the watershed is transgenerational memory which may also be mediated by trauma, but which emanates from a deeper time socially. The links to this are at once tenuous and very powerful. Here, trauma may come through via internalisations from a previous generation. This is the generation-hopping phenomenon as first described by Abraham and Torok (1994). The transgenerational is also informed by other deep-time histories that have to do with group, ethnic, national and religious attachments that feed back into individual and group experience via social fields as described in Chapter 8.

Beyond this I have identified another level which is trauma-related but where in some way the trauma of one generation is carried in the body of another. The experience of famine is one example, but other traumas may also be transmittable. This loops back to the idea that transgenerational memory is embodied. How we don't yet fully know. The most likely answer lies in the idea of extended genetics or epigenetics as well as an extended self. These two may turn out to be the same thing.

A further important element in transgenerational memory is a sensibility for the long term and its history (Elias, 2000; Braudel, 2000). This is typically not trauma-informed but incorporates capacities and sensibilities which help to promote social stability and problem-solving, typically found in smaller-scale societies. This is the realm of First Nation peoples. It is also characteristic of all those who have tried to create longer-lasting social ties and networks.

Therapeutic work with transgenerational trauma rests on the therapist's awareness of her own ancestral patterns and a capacity to enquire and explore socially and politically. It can extend beyond an individual focus to a more psychosocial one where the intervention will be more group- or issue-based. It may also involve psychosocial methods that work best in group or networked situations. In this approach, the expert facilitator or therapist is replaced by people taking up more transient roles that are learned, known about and passed around in a social network. This applies a bottom-up approach to complex problems and makes it more likely that learning from local experience takes place. People in this way of working can better embody, express and explore hauntings and transgenerational issues that affect them and others around them, and do it in ways that make sense to them, whether that be by toppling the statue of a slave trader or campaigning for new settlements of old hurts, or through a more inner focus on healing hurts, confusions and hauntings where the past blocks something new from happening in the future. Examples of this drawn from my own experience are the social dreaming matrix and larger meetings informed by group relations approaches, but there are many others and no doubt more yet to be invented. The role of trance, imagination, social empathy and ritual is attendant on these transgenerational meetings.

Signs and Consequences of Inter- and Transgenerational Delayed Mourning

On a social level, the need for extended mourning is an essential element when thinking both about personal resolutions of unhappiness and in social conflict resolution. If one generation has put off the task of mourning, this has consequences. If mourning has gone unaddressed for many generations, then the consequences are more complex and harder to work with.

Collective difficulties in accessing memory also have their own effects. Accessing the kind of memory that is implicit and multisited, both in our internal worlds and in our social networks, requires sustaining an act of social imagination. Transgenerational memory is, by definition, 'dissociated' in that it does not strictly belong to any one individual. If we can hold this paradox in mind, we can move from repetition to recognising states of social anxiety and conflict. This in turn allows us to move from hauntings to contact with actual events and ancestors. To do this we have to run the personal gauntlet and the fear surrounding dissociation and loss of control. We must be clear about what is making us feel mad or depressed and where this comes from.

In this research, the theme of reconceptualising loss was almost equal in terms of importance to the theme of haunting and unhappy interment. This suggests to me that our participants were telling us that we are evenly balanced or poised between these two very different and divergent pathways of experience and memory. Maybe all societies are, but it's clear that we are at a social tipping point between loss and its acknowledgement of deeper cycles of social destruction. In reconceptualising loss, the social fabric, although strained, has remained intact enough for losses to be thought about and acknowledged.

In hauntings relating to events that affect larger numbers of people who have subsequently dispersed through migration and diaspora, it is likely that the need to grieve is complicated by a combination of trauma, social and psychological dissociation. For people haunted in this way, there can also be an accompanying experience of feeling 'hardened' which is at once a strength and an obstacle. Some of the respondents in this research said they felt their ancestors directly affected by these events were still 'present' and that a whole past stood close behind them. Others spoke about being haunted by knowing something had happened but not knowing what it was. When these sorts of experience predominate, they tell us that the work of reconceptualising loss has been replaced by the experience of haunting and unhappy interment. Whole societies can feel hardened and that can make reconciliation less likely and othering more possible. This book has pointed to just some of the histories behind these problems.

Memory as described in this book is like a changing cell boundary— more or less extensive at different times, sometimes porous to new experience, and at others tightly closed and protective.

When society is shutting down, memory is affected, becoming shorter, and our capacity to imagine and dream decreases by being pushed into private spaces, even that of sleep. In these times of social breakdown, social links are broken while other imaginary ones are invented. Chosen traumas become the news of the day; more complex social identity is minimised. In more open periods of time, the living boundaries of memory increase and the generations communicate. In the social and psychological realm, people feel they have more resources to solve problems. Imagination, nature and complexity are closer at hand.

The third generation is particularly significant in memory work. My findings suggest they pick up much of the work of reconceptualising loss or complete the process of forgetting trauma and secrets that have gone through preceding generations.

In any generation, there is a dynamic tension between the desire to remember and to forget. The processes of generational companionship that underpin the capacity to intergenerationally mentalise are a powerful integrative factor. Its opposite is the move into hauntings that takes us into the world of trauma, secrets and mystery. Haunting may be the last form that memory takes before it ceases.

By contrast, haunting leading to hearing and witnessing can open new futures. Some must hold their memories deep inside them before the conditions arise in which their voices can be heard. I have described some of the ways in which this can happen, but there are many more waiting to be voiced and discovered.

We need to find the potential in the generations to create a fuller social and psychological sense of ourselves in deep time and across social and geographical spaces that is adaptive and not colonialising. This implies letting go of the desire for power over others and power over nature and exchanging this for a trust in others and an attachment to futures longer than the ones we currently allow ourselves to imagine. In this sense, I echo Wright Mills (2000)—we suffer what we can't imagine. Applying our sociological imagination, locating it in a sensibility for deep time that brings us close to nature perhaps restores our chance of survival. It will need a complete change of mind. Like any good change of mind, it has to be total. After it, nothing is the same and new beginnings are possible (again).

Multigenerational awareness and remembering the future could be a new pathway forward. It might help us solve a few intractable problems, like finding the capacity to live creatively in a post-anthropocentric future. Given that we are part of nature and party to its processes of extended cognition (Capra and Luisi, 2014), then the generations that flow through us are perhaps a little like Gaia, alive in their emergence and passing.

References

Abraham, N. and Torok, M. (1994) *The Shell and the Kernel.* Translated from the French by Nicolas T. Rand. Chicago: University of Chicago Press.

Bollas, C. (2018) *Meaning and Melancholia: Life in the Age of Bewilderment.* Abingdon-on-Thames: Routledge.

Braudel, F. (2000) *The Mediterranean and the Mediterranean World in the Age of Philip II: Vol. 1.* London: Folio Society.

Bretherton, I. and Munholland, K.A. (2008) Internal working models in attachment relationships: Elaborating a central construct in attachment theory. In: Cassidy, J. and Shaver, P.R. (Eds.) *Handbook of Attachment: Theory, Research, and Clinical Applications.* New York: The Guilford Press, pp. 102–127.

Capra, F. and Luisi, P.L. (2014) *The Systems View of Life: A Unifying Vision.* Cambridge: Cambridge University Press.

Davies, N. (2011) *Vanished Kingdoms: The History of Half-Forgotten Europe*. London: Penguin Books.

Davoine, F. and Gaudillière, J.-M. (2004) *History Beyond Trauma*. New York: Other Press.

Elias, N. (1978) *The Civilising Process Vol. 1: The History of Manners*. New York: Urizen Books.

Elias, N. (2000) *The Civilizing Process: Sociogenetic and Psychogenetic Investigations*. 2nd ed. Oxford: Blackwell Publishers.

Foucault, M. (2000) *Discipline and Punish: The Birth of the Prison*. London: Penguin Social Sciences.

Frosh, S. (2019) *Those Who Come After: Postmemory, Acknowledgement and Forgiveness*. Basingstoke: Palgrave Macmillan.

Lewin, K. (1997) *Resolving Social Conflicts and Field Theory in Social Science*. Washington: American Psychological Association.

Shevlin, M. and McGuigan, K. (2003) The Long-term psychological impact of Bloody Sunday on families of the victims as measured by the revised impact of event scale. *British Journal of Clinical Psychology* [online]. 42 (4), pp. 427–432 [Accessed 22 September 2019].

Volkan, V. (1998) *Bloodlines: From Ethnic Pride to Ethnic Terrorism*. Boulder, CO: Westview Press.

Wright Mills, C. (2000) *The Sociological Imagination*. 40th ed. Oxford: Oxford University Press.

Index

A

Active forgetting 35, 109–111, 114, 115
Affect xii, 20–22, 24, 26, 29, 31, 34, 41–43, 49, 107, 113, 115, 129, 144, 146, 161, 166, 175, 188–190
Affect regulation 64, 128, 157, 161, 187
Ancestors viii, xi, xv–xvii, xix, xx, xxii, xxvii, 1, 2, 4, 9, 12–14, 23, 24, 30, 35–37, 47, 50, 58, 59, 65, 90, 98, 101, 102, 104, 106, 108, 110, 111, 122, 127, 128, 133, 135, 143, 145, 146, 155, 156, 160, 162, 164, 165, 167, 175, 188, 190
Ancestral patterns 189
Ancestry xv, xvi, xx, 2, 28, 30, 43, 65, 83, 91, 103, 110, 128, 138, 161, 173, 174
Attachment theory xxi, 3, 52, 64, 126, 131
Autobiographical memory 21, 93, 176
Autobiography in training therapists 129
Autopoiesis 20

B

Beyond words 126, 144
Binocular vision 53, 163
Breaking the social link xxii, 4, 61, 136, 169

C

Cell boundary 142, 191
Change of mind 192
Chosen trauma ix, 48, 91, 142, 166, 182, 191
Civilising process 151
Colonialism viii, 12, 37, 45, 46, 63, 178
Communicative memory 48, 182
Complexity 134, 164, 191
Countertransference 61
Cultural capital 157, 158, 183
Cultural memory xxii, 4, 182
Cultural transmission 18, 106
Cyclical memory 173, 183

D

Decolonialising the curriculum 166
Deinternalisation 144
Diaspora xxiv, xxv, 6, 7, 14, 17, 27, 34, 46, 83, 84, 99, 101, 106–108, 114, 121, 122, 134, 143, 145, 153, 162, 179, 182–184, 190
Disenfranchised grief 165
Distributed memory 19, 138, 143, 151, 180

E

Ecological 33, 118
Embodied memory 182
Enlightenment thinking 50
Epigenetics xxi, xxiii, 3, 5, 14, 16, 19, 42–44, 57, 64, 98, 105, 118, 155, 174, 189
Eurocentric thinking 181
Extended cognition 20, 180, 192
Extended heredity 105
Extended present moment xxvi, 8, 50

F

False self 134, 144, 183
Families vii, xii, xv, xvi, xix–xxii, 1–4, 12–16, 18, 20, 23–25, 30, 31, 34–37, 44, 47, 48, 50, 58, 59, 65, 83–87, 89, 90, 93–95, 98–102, 105–108, 110–113, 115, 122, 123, 126–128, 130, 131, 135, 153, 158, 160, 161, 164, 165, 169, 176, 181–184
First Nations xxi–xxiii, xxv, 3–5, 7, 27, 28, 47, 49, 62, 185, 189
Fragile national identities 183
Free association xvii, xxiv, 6
Friendships xix, 1, 26, 87, 130, 166, 188
Frozen histories 141

G

Gaia 192
Genealogy xix, 1, 30, 31, 43, 66, 98, 99, 102
Generational identity 53
Generation hopping 112
Generations viii, xi, xvii, xix–xxvii, 1–9, 11–14, 16, 17, 20–22, 24–29, 32–37, 41, 44, 47–53, 56, 57, 62–64, 66, 81–89, 91–95, 97–99, 101, 102, 105–108, 110, 111, 114, 115, 117, 118, 120–124, 127, 129–139, 141–146, 153, 155,

157–161, 167, 173–185, 188, 190–192
Genomic research 43
Ghosts xii, 14, 100, 102, 109, 111, 160
Grandparents 14, 86, 87, 142, 155, 188
Greater nature 120
Group Analysis 54, 55
Group Relations 55, 163, 178
Groups xvi, xxi, xxii, xxiv, 3, 4, 6, 13, 15, 17, 18, 20, 25, 26, 28–30, 33, 34, 37, 47, 48, 53–56, 60, 66, 83, 84, 86–88, 90, 91, 94, 95, 98, 99, 103, 108, 111, 115, 121, 127, 129, 133, 135, 144–146, 156–158, 160, 161, 163–165, 167–169, 178, 179, 183, 185, 186, 188, 189

H
Habitus 157, 158
Haunting xii, xvi, xxii–xxiv, 4–6, 14, 17, 18, 21, 22, 35, 37, 46, 58, 61–63, 84, 87, 97–102, 104–109, 114, 115, 129, 141–144, 153–156, 162, 163, 165, 167, 178, 181, 183–191
Healing practices 12, 47
Hearing voices 146
Hidden migrations xxiv, 6, 153
Holocaust 16, 42, 44, 65, 113, 139, 165, 179, 185

I
Identity xx, xxii, xxiv, xxvi, xxvii, 2, 4, 6, 8, 9, 15, 21, 25–27, 29–33, 36, 37, 43, 46, 52, 53, 62, 85, 90–92, 95, 99, 101, 105, 111, 118, 120, 124, 131, 154, 162, 169, 174, 178, 179, 181, 183, 185, 187
Identity wars 168
Imagined communities 26, 49, 90
Implicit memory 106
Inner world 93, 127, 160
Intergenerational companionship xvi, xxiv, 6, 89, 94, 104, 124, 125, 127, 131, 132, 175, 180, 184
Intergenerational memory xxii, xxiv, 4, 6, 12, 13, 15, 16, 22, 25, 26, 44, 48, 52, 100, 153, 167, 179, 182, 187
Intergenerational mentalisation xxiv, 6, 92, 94, 119, 128, 131, 157, 188
Internalisation 61, 64, 134, 137, 139, 157, 164, 188
Internal working models 64
Irish Famine x, 99, 104, 107, 114, 121, 154, 177, 185

M
Madness 59–61, 144
Mania 62, 179
Manic reparation 63, 93, 165
Mapping 43, 66, 133
Maps in time and space 173
Matrices xxiv, 6, 55
Melancholia xii, 58
Memorialisation x, xxv, 7, 62, 66

Migration xii, xxii–xxvi, 4–8, 13, 14, 26, 28, 30, 34–36, 46, 50, 65, 66, 81, 82, 84, 86, 89, 93, 98, 99, 122, 123, 127, 134, 143, 153, 159, 162, 163, 167, 174, 185, 190

Mourning x, xii, xvi, xxv, 7, 30–32, 58, 62, 63, 87, 132, 163, 175, 185, 186, 190

Multigenerational identity 153, 156

Multigenerational memory xxi, xxiv, 3, 6, 15, 20, 23, 24, 28–30, 33, 35, 38, 42, 55, 65, 117, 138, 139, 157, 173, 177, 178, 180, 183

Multigenerational self xxii, 4, 139, 174, 175

Multigenerational society 175

Multigenerational storytelling 125

Museums 66, 98, 151, 154, 155, 162, 181–183

N

Nature xxii, xxiii, 4, 5, 12, 21, 22, 27, 29, 32, 33, 50, 54, 56, 88, 91, 98, 112, 118–124, 132, 134, 142, 163, 173, 180, 185–187, 191, 192

Negative capability xvii

O

The Organisation in Mind 138

Organisations 25, 48, 86, 88–90, 94, 117, 132, 133, 136–138, 180, 188

P

Past-to-future xxiii, 5, 175, 176

Physical transmission xxi, 3

Populations ix, xxvi, 8, 43, 84, 156, 164, 177

Postcolonial aspects of psychotherapy 134

Post-memory xxiii, 5, 45, 47, 48, 55, 63, 182

Post-Traumatic Stress Disorder 16, 17, 44

Pre-memory 47

Professional genealogy 59

Psychoanalysis vii, viii, x, xi, 20, 53, 54, 57, 61, 65, 174

Psychodynamic xvi, xvii, 47, 145

Psychosis xvi, 59, 61, 130

Psychosocial methods 12, 49, 152, 189

Psychosocial research xvi, xxii, 4, 159, 161, 162

Psychotherapy xii, xvi, xxi, xxiv, 3, 6, 21, 23, 61, 64, 82, 86, 91, 93, 126, 134, 173, 174, 176, 184, 187, 188

R

Racism 17, 34, 37, 63, 93, 112, 139, 144, 156, 159, 164, 166, 167, 185

Reaching for creativity 31, 184

Recognition ix, xxv, 7, 17, 22, 26, 32, 35, 36, 54, 56, 65, 83, 102, 108, 124, 138, 139, 142, 145, 162, 177, 178, 187

Reconceptualising loss xxii, 4, 31, 34, 37, 82, 83, 86, 88, 97, 107, 142, 184, 190, 191

Reparation xii, 62, 63, 165
Research as an intervention xxiv, 6, 156
Researching beneath the surface 146
Reverie xxiv, 6, 128, 145
Ritual 35, 48, 133, 185, 189
Rupture-repair dynamics 131, 187

S

Secrets xi, 23, 32, 57–59, 97, 98, 103, 109, 112, 114, 129, 130, 142, 144, 168, 181, 184, 186, 191
Self-making 20
Sensibility for the long term xxv–xxvii, 7–9, 53, 132, 151, 189
Shaman 160
Shame 26, 30, 32, 58, 83, 88, 93, 97, 99, 107, 108, 110, 111, 146, 162
Shutting down xxiii, 5, 13, 32, 35, 87–90, 92–94, 176, 191
Siblings 35, 52, 64, 110, 111, 187, 188
Slavery Syndrome 139
Slave trade 16, 27, 114
Social contagion xxi, 3
Social dreaming xxiii, xxiv, 5, 6, 55, 66, 151, 152, 154, 155, 162, 163, 178, 189
Social empathy 53, 189
Social fields xxiv, 6, 17, 144, 145, 155, 156, 158, 159, 165, 166, 174, 180, 188
Social memory xvii, xxi, 3, 11, 13, 25, 44, 48, 55, 65, 142, 169, 173, 174

Social rejection 140
Social unconscious xxiii, 5, 53–55, 62, 186
Sociological imagination xvi, xxv, 7, 52, 192
Sociology xxi, xxiii, 3, 5, 42, 157
Sociology of knowledge 50, 51
Storytelling xxiv, 6, 31, 48, 53, 88, 89, 92, 126–128, 132, 133, 161, 175, 176, 184
Supervision xvi, xxiv, 6, 66, 91, 125
Symbolic systems 48, 182

T

Thematic maps 66, 173
Third generation xxii, 4, 17, 23, 35, 36, 83, 84, 87, 100, 142, 155, 182, 191
Thirdness 145
Training institute xxiv, 6, 93, 126
Trance methods 145–147, 178
Transference 60, 134
Transgenerational memory xxi, xxiii, xxiv, 3, 5, 6, 11, 13, 14, 23, 25, 27, 47, 48, 98, 101, 142, 154, 156, 158, 160, 166, 167, 179–183, 185, 187–190
Transgenerational phantom 22
Transitional phenomena xxiv, 6
Transitional space 142, 145, 157–159, 174, 180
Trauma viii–xii, xvi, xxi, xxiii, 2, 3, 5, 14, 15, 17, 18, 23–27, 30, 32, 41–49, 56, 59, 60, 63, 66, 84, 87, 90, 91, 93, 95, 97–101, 104, 105, 108, 113, 126, 128–130, 135, 139–144,

155, 156, 158, 159, 162, 177–179, 181, 182, 184–191
Two-eyed seeing 12, 47, 49, 50, 174

U
Uncanny 14, 102, 109, 144, 145, 161
Unconscious viii, xi, 14, 22, 24, 54–57, 112, 115, 134, 139, 140, 146, 157, 158, 160, 163, 182
Unconscious racism 134
Unhappy interment 14, 17, 31, 35, 113, 153, 184, 190, 191

Unthought known 62, 113, 152, 186

V
Verstehen 53, 157
Victim/persecutor dynamics 164, 178

W
War trauma xxii, 4, 22, 24, 26, 57, 61, 135, 181

Printed by Printforce, the Netherlands